ALSO BY BILL CARTER

Red Summer:
The Danger, Madness, and Exaltation
of Salmon Fishing in a Remote Alaskan Village

Fools Rush In:
A True Story of Love, War, and Redemption

BOOM, BUST, BOOM

A STORY ABOUT COPPER,
THE METAL THAT RUNS THE WORLD

BILL CARTER

SCRIBNER

New York London Toronto Sydney New Delhi

SCRIBNER
A Division of Simon & Schuster, Inc.
1230 Avenue of the Americas
New York, NY 10020

First Scribner hardcover edition October 2012

SCRIBNER and design are registered trademarks of The Gale Group, Inc.,
used under license by Simon & Schuster, Inc., the publisher of this work.

For information about special discounts for bulk purchases,
please contact Simon & Schuster Special Sales at 1-866-506-1949
or business@simonandschuster.com.

The Simon & Schuster Speakers Bureau can bring authors to your live event.
For more information or to book an event contact the Simon & Schuster Speakers
Bureau at 1-866-248-3049 or visit our website at www.simonspeakers.com.

Manufactured in the United States of America

1   3   5   7   9   10   8   6   4   2

ISBN 978-1-4391-3644-7
ISBN 978-1-4169-8722-2 (ebook)

For Leigh, Josie, and Poppy
and
John Crow

The meek shall inherit the earth, but not the mineral rights.

—J. Paul Getty

CONTENTS

BOOM, BUST, BOOM

1

Tainted Vegetables

I like my town with a little drop of poison.
—Tom Waits

Every spring I plant a garden, a small but noble pursuit. Small in the sense that there are many more important items on the daily calendars of our lives, but noble because each step of self-sustainability has a lovely feeling of beating the ever-invasive food industry at its own game.

In my line of work, I travel a lot, sometimes to places where food is measured by cups of rice a week, and water is delivered to homes by ten-year-olds who have walked five miles through desolation to get to a well. Planting a garden is a way of keeping the harsh realities of the world at bay. It seems a sane practice in a world hell-bent on destroying itself.

When home, I try to talk to the plants every day. I grew up on a farm, so speaking to budding pomegranates seems natural to me, sometimes more so than speaking to my neighbor. Peaches and apricots are good listeners, too. I go to them for comfort. I trust the plants. And the seeds, although invisible, give great solace as they incubate in the ground.

This particular spring carries special meaning for me. My wife is pregnant with our second daughter and our two-year-old is eager to take on the chores of watering and helping her dad with the daily garden duties. My plan is to create a large vegetable garden in a backyard area we have never used. It is situated between two tall trees, perfect for morning and afternoon sun but shaded during midday.

After two full weekends of digging, raking, and trips to the hardware store, I complete a drip irrigation system. My daughter and I spend a Sunday morning planting squash, tomatoes, lettuce, spring onions, jalapeños, green peppers, and several herbs, including basil, thyme, and chives. Each morning, for weeks thereafter, I wake with the sun to see how much the garden has grown overnight. In the beginning the progress is slow, but soon the vegetables burst through the thin layer of dirt and begin to morph into yellow, red, and green.

After six weeks of daily attention, I collect my first batch of spring lettuce. I coddle each leaf as I wash it in the sink. Finally I prepare a salad for dinner. My wife won't eat the lettuce or any other item from the garden. She's not a food snob, but she is careful what she eats because of the baby that grows inside her. I argue that the food is as organic as we can find. She replies that she doesn't trust the dirt.

She has a point. We live in Bisbee, Arizona, a small hamlet couched in the Mule Mountains, a mile above sea level. Bisbee is a dormant mining town, located eight miles from the Mexican border as the crow flies. The copper mine closed down more than thirty years ago, but the effects of its existence remain. Mine shafts pockmark the hillsides and sulfuric acid runoff stains the cliffs a burnt orange. Giant headframes dot the horizon, reminders of the elevators the size of houses that used to carry men a thousand feet below the surface. And then there is the open pit, a large crater on the edge of town where all the water from our torrential monsoon rains pours off the mountains into this mile-long giant bathtub.

My wife and I met in Bisbee, not long after we both moved here in 2000, mostly to get away from anything resembling suburbia. As I've passed through the decades, I realize I have a few steadfast requirements for what I call quality of life. Most important is not driving in traffic. At all. I need to walk out my front door to a good hiking trail. I also like the ability to barter, if money is short, for any vital necessity. In Bisbee, I have always been able to trade one of my books for a meal, a poker buy-in, or a bottle of wine, or all three. Money is required here, but bartering is accepted.

In Bisbee, no two houses are quite alike. In fact, they are spectacularly different, reflecting the individual owners who built them, most more than a hundred years ago. Several streets are so narrow that driving down them requires bending the mirror inward to avoid clipping it off. Gas lines run exposed up stairways, occasionally doubling as railings. Each homeowner must adapt to the nuances of his or her home, and no manual exists to help with repairs. Local plumbers and electricians have to throw their training out the window because no job in town resembles that of a modern-day house.

Bisbee is no ordinary mining town. In its heyday it was one of the largest copper towns in the United States. Phelps Dodge, then the owners of the mine and once the political and economic alpha force of Arizona that owned almost every large copper mine in the state, took more than $8 billion in copper from this place. You don't take that much from the earth without leaving a scar or two.

In 2007, Freeport-McMoRan bought the Bisbee mining operation and everything else Phelps Dodge had owned in Arizona and throughout the world for $25 billion—including mines in Africa and Chile. Freeport now owns a majority of the land to the north and south of Bisbee. They own the dormant mine. They own the twenty-seven hundred miles of mining tunnels that run beneath the town. They own some parcels of the mountains, sections of the outlying desert, and many buildings in town. Even though they don't own most of the homes, at times it feels like the only things they don't own or control are the people and the sky.

Originally based in New Orleans, Freeport began as a sulfur-mining company in 1912. In 1981 it merged with McMoRan Oil & Gas Company, the latter part of the name being a combination of the surnames of the three men who started the company: W. K. McWilliams, James Moffett, and B. M. Rankin.

Freeport-McMoRan employs 29,700 people in several countries and in 2012 ranked 135th on the Fortune 500. It has an estimated 102 billion pounds of copper, 40 million ounces of gold, and 2.5 billion pounds of molybdenum—a mineral used to strengthen steel—in reserve. The company expects to produce more than 4 billion pounds of copper per year for the next several years, making it the largest publicly traded copper-mining company in the world, second in size only to Codelco, the national copper company of Chile.

The company has always lured a collection of powerful families and individuals into its ranks, including the Whitneys—of the Whitney Museum of American Art in New York City. Rockefellers have served on the board of Freeport for several decades. Augustus Long, the director of Texaco from 1950 to 1977, was also a prominent board member along with Robert Lovett, son of R. S. Lovett, president of Union Pacific Railroad and commonly known as a "Cold War architect." Henry Kissinger has long been a board member and today holds the title director emeritus.

Currently, James Moffett is the acting chairman of the board, president, and chief executive officer of Freeport-McMoRan, whose headquarters has relocated from New Orleans to Phoenix, a result of buying Phelps Dodge. In 2010, Moffett's yearly compensation package was $47 million, including his base salary and various exercised stock options, making him the highest-paid person in Arizona, with second place going to Richard Adkerson, the cochairman of the company, who has earned $180 million since 2006, at an average of $33 million a year.

In 1988, while still based in New Orleans, Freeport gained national attention for dumping toxic water into the Mississippi. That year, Citizen Action, a national Washington-based environmental watchdog group, named Freeport the sixth-largest producer of toxic waste in the United States and the number-one water polluter. More recently, in 2008, the Political Economy Research Institute at the University of Massachusetts in Amherst listed Freeport as the country's twenty-second-worst air polluter, with a grand total of four million pounds of toxic air released in one year.

As part of the transaction with Phelps Dodge, Freeport assumed an obligation to reclaim all the polluted soil in the Bisbee neighborhoods. By 2008, Freeport began a program it calls "soil recla-mation," which means they are testing every household in Bisbee to check for contaminants in their yards. If the company finds toxins above the allowed level, it removes all the contaminated dirt from the yard and replaces it with new dirt. Then the com-pany wipes its hands and moves on to the next house.

I applied for Freeport to check our soil, which they did, but that had been months ago. A team of geologists, chemists, and environmental engineers walked the perimeter of our house, probing the soil to a depth of two feet. No one would answer any questions I had, other than to say the results would be ready in several weeks. Over the past few months it has been hard not to notice these teams of professionals driving in new gray jeeps with the word SHAW sprawled across the door. Shaw, I find out, is also a Fortune 500 company with ties to the industrial, chemical, and petrol industries and based in Baton Rouge. Among other ser-vices, it offers environmental remediation. The company prides itself on cleaning up highly toxic sites, including areas polluted by the manufacture of biological weapons. Months passed, so I assumed our soil was fine. Meanwhile, spring waits for no one, and I want to grow food. I want to teach my daughter it is pos-sible to eat from our backyard and not Safeway.

The first night I eat a salad from our yard, my wife eats some-thing else. As much as my daughter likes gardening, she doesn't like salads, or anything remotely resembling a vegetable. She opts for macaroni and cheese. The salad tastes delicious, but know-ing it came from the backyard, *our* backyard, makes it even more scrumptious. I do this daily, sometimes twice daily, for two weeks, each time feeling great pride in my efforts as a gardener.

One night I have a nagging headache, which intensifies the fol-lowing night. My stomach feels nauseous. I tell myself the head-aches and nausea are a result of a bug going around town. One night I wake up with quite a different sensation altogether. I have diarrhea and severe cramping in my stomach. Crawling to the toi-let, I throw up, again and again. At this point I am nervous, think-ing I have a serious sickness. My mind goes where so many in America go: medical insurance, which I don't have. This cycle of physical sickness and mental anguish goes on for another week. In that time I have stopped eating anything other than basic staples.

After several more days, I am able to walk, and to eat once again. I have forgotten all about the garden; I don't even care that it exists, although it still does because the drip system keeps working, thanks to the timers attached to hose spigots throughout the yard.

Feeling better, I walk to the post office and pick up my mail, eager to feel the sun on my face. Along the way, I look up and see the usual landscape, which in a state of weakness I remind myself is beautiful even as every angle makes me think of the mining days of yesteryear. There, in the side of Bucky O'Neil Mountain, exists a hole the size of a two-story building, the first entrance ever made into the famed Copper Queen mine. Like most mining camps, Bisbee was home to hundreds of individual mines, but the Copper Queen, built entirely underground, would become one of the richest copper mines of the early twentieth century.

After reading the local paper, I pick through the bills at the post office and notice a letter from Shaw.* I read the letter a few times before its meaning registers: My front yard has 564 parts per million of lead, 32 percent higher than acceptable levels. In my back-

---

* If I had to pick a single item that week in and week out reveals the most about the residents of Bisbee, it is the one-page police beat in the weekly paper. One entry catches my eye right away: "A woman requested getting a snake out of her house. It became lost in the clutter."

Another states: "An anonymous caller reported an unknown Hispanic man had left loads of marijuana at his residence in the 2100 block of S. Kentucky Lane." Is the caller still anonymous when the police know it is the actual resident of 2100 block of S. Kentucky Lane who made the call?

Here is another typical entry: "A Bisbee resident returned home and found ice cream covering her car. The back door was open and a light that had been left on, was off."

Sometimes the person who writes these entries takes a moment for a public service announcement: "Several javelina—a wild peccary—were struck and killed on Bisbee roadways this week. Be alert for living or dead javelinas on the roads."

For me, the police beat validates the notion that humor is the antidote to the predictability of everyday life.

yard, where the lettuce, peppers, and spring onions are flourishing at this very moment, the soil has arsenic levels of 79.3 parts per million, more than 100 percent higher than acceptable levels for residential soil.

How the arsenic and lead got to my yard is not a mystery, but because I can't see these poisons, I allowed myself not to believe my soil was laced with heavy metals. I knew of several large smelters, towering chimney stacks that exhaled smoke and heavy metals, which used to exist a quarter mile from my house and dominate every view in Bisbee. I've read stories from the early 1900s when newcomers visited the town for the first time at night and reported a haunting feeling of entering a landscape of hell: orange embers flying into the night from the smelters. Slag heaps, smoke, campfires, all giving the mining camp a feel of Dante's Inferno.

The copper mines in Bisbee opened in earnest around 1881 and the final one closed in 1975, twenty-five years before I set foot in town. The smelter was dismantled in 1908, more than a hundred years ago, the result of upper management not wanting to live in the same town as a poisonous smelter, and the fact that the company had stripped almost every tree from the surrounding mountains to keep the smelter burning twenty-four hours a day. It took several decades for the trees to come back. And yet to this day, the arsenic and lead levels in the topsoil remain toxic. A hundred years of wind, snow, and rain since then, a century for nature to pound the earth, bleach it, leach it, flood it, grow over it, and erode it—and still the poisons remain. It is ironic how little copper is in the soil, but it makes sense. It would have been extracted in the smelting process, leaving the arsenic and lead particles to be belched into the wind and settle on the surrounding yards.

The smelter is not the only cause of the poisoned yards, however. Bisbee is transected by two parallel gulches, separated by a ridgeline covered with homes on both sides. Many of these homes, perched on hillsides, have anywhere from ten to one hundred steps to the front door. In an effort to create level foundations for some of the more upscale homes, Phelps Dodge killed two birds with one stone by leveling the land with the mine waste, called tailing piles, which it didn't want. The company hauled "dirt" from the tailing piles, still thick with heavy metals used to extract copper from hard rock, and trucked this dirt throughout various neighborhoods in an effort to terrace the town. Thus the foundations of many Bisbee homes are actually built upon mining waste from several decades ago.

So, in fact, I didn't have a bug that was going around town. According to government guidelines, arsenic primarily enters the body through airborne dust. Ingestion of arsenic can cause irritation of stomach and intestines, nerve injury, and possibly liver damage. For several weeks I had been digging on my hands and knees, preparing the soil for a garden. Often I did this leisurely work with my young daughter. I ate the vegetables for weeks. My mind is abuzz with the realization of how little I know about the history of where I live.

I stop and I take a moment to be grateful for two things, that my pregnant wife didn't trust the dirt and that my daughter doesn't like salads. Both are fine. But I am not.

All this heavy metal in my soil might be easier to forget if I hadn't heard rumors for the past several months that Freeport-McMoRan will reopen the mine, which would effectively alter the economic, cultural, and geological landscape of this town. This makes me realize I have a lot to learn about how mining companies affect towns in close proximity to their operations.

One afternoon, as we stand on the back porch, my wife and I talk about the long term. We are wondering if raising our kids in this town is a good idea. And even if the mine does not reopen in the next few years, there is no guarantee that it won't open in five or ten years. Either way, it feels like a ticking clock hanging over our lives, and I'm afraid the sound will only get louder as time passes.

I stare out at my arsenic-laced garden, glistening in the afternoon sun. So much work lost to a phantom toxin I can't see, taste, or smell. Suddenly I begin asking myself a series of questions, first and foremost, what would be the effect of a modern-day mine on the surrounding community and land? Bisbee's mining operation was relatively small by today's standards. The pit looks like a fishing hole compared to the ocean-sized pits of today's mines. A modern-day mine would be larger, use far more land, and create much more waste. Even though we own a house here and are deeply entrenched in the local life, would I still want to live in Bisbee if the mine reopens?

It's a question my wife and I have asked each other before, but never with any sense of urgency. Now we feel that as parents we must find an answer, and soon. Still, when we bring it up, neither one of us has an answer, as if we are playing a game of chicken, seeing who will be the first to declare we will walk away from our friends, our community, our garden, and our home.

2

Bisbee, Arizona

Bisbee is 100 miles, and 100 years from Tucson.
—Local saying

Located eight miles north of the Mexican border and a hundred miles southeast of Tucson, Bisbee is precariously saddled between two canyons in the Mule Mountains. Rising above the desert floor like rolling camel humps, the Mules are what geologists call sky islands—small mountain ranges, unconnected to other ranges that dot the map of southeastern Arizona. Here snow falls every winter and junipers grow in abundance on the mountaintops. Standing on one of those mountains I can see deep into Mexico in one direction, a clear line of high riparian desert unblemished by the touch of man. Looking east I see the Chiricahua Mountains, which stand above the rest at ten thousand feet. This range is home to ocelots, the summer tanager, and the occasional roving jaguar from Mexico. These mountains also gave their name to the tribe of Geronimo's Apaches, the Chiricahua Apaches.

As for Bisbee copper, there are various stories of how it was found then developed. Different players got involved as the copper kept coming. But there is one man who has all the historical credit for both finding the Copper Queen mine and for losing it.

George Warren had a large mustache and wore suspenders. Warren had been a prospector and a drunk. It was the 1870s in the Southwest, a time of wishful thinking and thieving. The scars of the Civil War were fresh and people were in the mood for new land, new riches, and new scenery. Stories of gold and silver traveled back and forth along the pioneer trails that crisscrossed the American frontier.

It was in this setting that Mr. Warren found himself sitting on a stool in Tombstone, Arizona, one afternoon in 1878. Drunk and most likely talking about what was going to happen when he struck it rich, Warren was engaged in conversation with Jack Dunn, an army soldier on his way back from the Mule Mountains, where he had spent several days tracking Apache warriors near a spring that the Apaches liked to frequent on their journeys back and forth from the Chiricahua Mountains to raiding strikes in Tubac and Tombstone. Dunn and his party didn't find any Apaches, but they did find evidence of copper and lead and subsequently made a claim.

From that chance meeting, Dunn grubstaked Warren—a prospecting term that means in exchange for working the claim, Dunn paid for all costs and gave a percentage of his findings to Warren. Warren wasted little time getting himself to the Mule Mountains, where he set up camp and began digging. He found copper almost immediately. Others quickly followed, and soon there was a makeshift mining settlement with saloons built out of tree branches and stagecoach canvas. Women followed, knowing a miner's buck was the easiest in the territory.

Then one day in 1879, after long hours prospecting for copper, Warren made a bet that both he and his heirs would forever regret. He bet his one-ninth share of the Copper Queen mine that he could outrun a man on horseback to a distance of fifty yards, plant a stake, and return the same fifty yards, ahead of man and horse. He lost. Two years after losing his share of the Copper Queen mine, he was declared insane by a Cochise County judge. Soon after, he traveled to Mexico for a while but then made his way back to Bisbee, where he died in 1892, a pauper and town drunk. By the time of his death, the Copper Queen was at full production and his earnings would have been $20 million, in 1892.

Either as a historical consolation, or out of respect for what he did by finding the Copper Queen, Warren was put on the state seal. And in Bisbee, the area of the town built for the executives was named after him.

At first Bisbee was like any other mining camp, which is to say it was not built to last. Officially, it became a town in 1880, named after Judge Dewitt Bisbee, from San Francisco, one of the financial backers of the original Copper Queen mine, which would become the largest copper mine in the district. Over the next ten years, Bisbee filled with transient miners, poor European immigrants, army deserters, and homesteaders, who quickly constructed the town just as countless other silver and gold camps in the area were thrown up seemingly overnight. This explains why, in the older part of Bisbee, which locals refer to as Old Bisbee, no two houses look alike and are mostly old mining shacks that, like their owners, have survived through the years out of pure stubbornness. The miners built homes on their days off and then imported their families to this new place high up in the Mule Mountains. After twenty years of mining, the town became known as Queen of the Copper Camps, and it was clear the town was going to be here awhile. By the late 1890s, it was the biggest city between St. Louis and San Francisco, with three opera houses, a trolley line, and banks full of cash. Then a world war happened, and then another, all of which only increased the wealth of the mine. Eventually the architecture began to reflect a people able to invest in their community: churches, schools, and three-story brick commercial buildings selling the finest clothes and products. The fact that these buildings still stand is a testament to Bisbee's past prosperity. Many of the copper camps that sprung up around the same time are long gone, dismantled by the wind and violent floods that hit Arizona every summer.

The miners who worked the camp were largely veterans of America's twentieth-century wars—World Wars I and II, Korea, and Vietnam. As Bisbee became a town that wouldn't go away, the vets returned from the wars and got jobs. It became a blue-collar life in a mountain paradise on the border of Mexico.

Most people, tourists and locals alike, arrive in Bisbee by driving south from Tucson, a route that makes the driver climb up Banning Canyon for several miles before reaching the longest tunnel in Arizona. On the other side of the tunnel is Bisbee, which at first sight looks like a mismatch of houses hugging the canyon walls of both Tombstone and Zacatecas Canyons, like scorpion babies clinging to their mother's belly. And when it rains, the town hugs a bit tighter to those canyon walls, for everything here has a way of tilting toward the pit.

My first visit to Bisbee was in 1996. I was living in Tucson and rode my motorcycle down on a winter day. It snowed that night and I was stuck for three days before I could get back to Tucson. Content with being stuck in what seemed like a town from the nineteenth century, I walked streets curled around the hillsides with no particular plan in mind. I walked up and down stairs and peeked into homes that had no architectural resemblance to the neighbors on either side. And the mine, covered in snow, seemed like a dormant hole, something that would be taken care of at a later day by some federal agency—a cleanup project. I thought I could enjoy living in Bisbee and was curious who actually lived there.

When the mine closed in 1975, the miners left town in such a hurry that homes could be bought for less than $1,000. With Vietnam over, Bisbee now attracted a steady flow of counterculture types wanting to be as far away from the Man as possible. Suffice it to say there is also a minority of the population that subsists off the government in the form of a Section 8 check, or more commonly known around town as the "crazy check."

On slow days, Bisbee is one of those towns that feel as if the only people who occupy it are the merchants who make a living off the steady trickle of tourists. What I didn't know then, and would take years to discover, is the wide range of people who live here: ranchers, hippies, drunks, retired miners, bird freaks, web designers, authors, and defense contractors working at nearby Fort Huachuca, one of the army's bases for satellite intelligence and drone technology. We have the small-town drug dealers peddling meth and pot at the local bars, and because of our proximity to the border, we have a steady supply of mules looking for a quick buck by carrying pot across the border. Scattered throughout Bisbee are also New Agers, crystal worshippers, million-aire investors, retired car company executives, celebrity comics, famous photographers, sculptors, painters, and day laborers, half of whom seem to have an art studio attached to their own house. And let's not forget the man standing vigil at various street corners for the last decade with a sign that reads NEED WORK. I HATE LIARS SO DON'T TALK TO ME.

One of the more interesting types that live in Bisbee are the rock hounds who migrate to Bisbee with hopes of finding easy money beneath a few layers of dirt. Almost clannish, these men generally stick together in small groups, afraid their "secrets" may be found out. They scramble over the tailing piles in the dark of night with flashlights hidden under coats, hoping to avoid the night watchman. They are not looking for veins of gold or copper, which would be too much to ask. They will settle for a piece of turquoise or anything resembling a shining gem. In my experience, these men are not after honest work. Instead, they are looking for an easy buck and end up spending their entire time working for the hardest dollar ever made. They are more desperate than the street-corner panhandler. Picking up cans on the side of the road would be more lucrative than anything they find.

As time goes by they recede further into a maze of paranoia and delusion, confident the next big thing is waiting for them, tomorrow. I know one resident who spent years digging a dangerously deep hole in his backyard, often enticing young miner wannabes to dig his hole for him, usually in exchange for a hit off his bong. Later, when I see some of these rock hounds in the bar they are covered in dirt, bragging about how hard their day was, when in reality it was spent high as a kite talking to a fellow rock hound about striking it rich one day. Meanwhile, I can always rely on them to turn to me and ask, "Buy me a beer today? I will return the favor one day in spades."

In the past decade I have been to parties in one-room miner shacks, abandoned mine shafts, a rock house built into the side of a mountain, and mansions that resemble the old-money estates of Boston and Philadelphia, both cities from which the original elite of Bisbee emigrated and built the large homes sitting on a part of town called the Vista. Of course the homes aren't worth as much as they should be, because a hundred-foot-tall pile of decaying waste from the mine abuts their backyards.

Here is a story told by longtime residents of Bisbee. One Saturday in the 1950s, a man stepped out of a whorehouse on Brewery Gulch, one of the two main streets in town. It was late July and the yearly monsoon had been beating down for days. The torrential rain was falling sideways, but he had to get back to the mine. He took his first step onto the street and the water hit him like a wall of cement. As he washed down Brewery Gulch, some people reached out, but no one could get a grip on him. There was not a chance of stopping him as he tumbled down the street with tons of rocks and boulders pouring off the mountain. Down by the Stock Exchange Bar, he tried to grab something, anything, but the current was too strong. Who knows if he had time to see the large hole that disappears under the highway? They found him the next day, dead, hundreds of feet down in the mine.

Today a large steel grate covers the hole under the road. It prevents teenage skateboarders and wandering drunks from getting swept into the pit by flash floods.

Every small town possesses certain intangibles that manage to unite its people. In the case of Bisbee, it is the aforementioned crater on the southern edge of town simply known as the Pit. It sits at the edge of town like a cancerous tumor that no one wants to talk about. Measuring half a mile wide, almost one mile long, and 950 feet deep, the hole was once an open-pit mine, where miners found gold, lead, zinc, turquoise, uranium, and silver. But the big money was always copper. By the time Phelps Dodge turned off the machines in 1975, the Pit had produced more than $8 billion in copper.

There is no graceful interval in the landscape between what locals call Old Bisbee—the historical downtown district—and this large man-made crater, which looms a half mile from my house like a giant sinkhole. To the casual tourists, the Pit takes them by surprise. As they drive toward Mexico, the earth suddenly falls away, nine hundred feet off the side of the highway.

To live in Bisbee one must accept the Pit as part of one's life. It defines each resident's sense of geography and creeps into the town's daily language. If a local gives directions to a tourist anywhere east or south of town, his first words invariably contain the words, "Once you drive past the Pit . . ." If I drive to the only supermarket in town, I pass the Pit. If I go to the hardware store, I pass the Pit. If I go to the vet, the ballpark, Mexico, the breakfast café, the cemetery, any of the town's schools, or to the dump, I pass this massive hole in the ground. In a single day, I may pass by the Pit half a dozen times. And yet, shockingly, in only a matter of months of living in Bisbee, the Pit does not exist as a large hole, only as a blank canvas upon which our eyes paint sky and mountains. Soon this enormous scar in the earth becomes the same as the tree at the end of the block, or a traffic light, or an old barn everyone uses as a local landmark.

Halfway around the Pit, on Highway 80, exists a turnout with a single monument that states the proper name of the crater: Lavender Pit, named after Harrison Lavender, who served as the vice president and general manager of Phelps Dodge in 1950. While the majority of Bisbee mines had been underground, open-pit mining had also been used in Bisbee beginning in 1917, but the operation was small by comparison to what Lavender Pit would eventually become.

By the mine's closure in 1975, miners had dug a total of twenty-seven hundred miles of underground tunnels in an area of three square miles, and to a depth of three thousand feet. Aboveground, in Lavender Pit, 86 million tons of ore were extracted from the earth, and from this ore 600,000 tons of copper were produced, meaning the copper yield averaged 0.7 percent per ton of dirt, a relatively high yield. There was a lot of dirt, some 256 million tons of waste, most of which still exists in and around Bisbee. In the Warren district, which is on the other side of the pit from Old Bisbee, where I live, sits dump pile number 9, a hundred-foot-tall mound of pulverized rock that bleeds red and sits up next to people's backyards. Many people think that pile is just dirt from the earth, when really part of it *is* Sacramento Hill, which once rose out of the Mule Mountain chain like a singular island, with a bold red hue, a geological signature to early prospectors that a special mineralization lay underground.

At the turnout, tourists stop to take photos of the dormant open-pit mine. But like all the tourists before them, they can never fully capture the enormous size of this hole in the earth. They go home and see some red rock with hints of orange and brown in their photo. The rest of the picture is mostly shadow as the hole swallows up the sun.

But the tourists do come, from all corners of the globe. Some come for the weather, and some come to see an old mining town that still exists. Almost all of them take the mine tour, a two-hour trip inside the old underground Copper Queen. I took the mine tour, which begins by straddling a small-gauge train and traveling a thousand feet into the mountain. The ride is pitch-black, and once the train stops inside the mountain, two retired miners lead the tour up wooden staircases into an old stope hole—a large cavern miners created by using dynamite and then cleared using jackhammers to chip away at the rock ore containing copper.

I asked the two elderly miners, who both worked underground in Bisbee until the closure, about miners carrying out valuable minerals in their lunch boxes, minerals such as malachite, azurite, and an extremely rare form of turquoise known as Bisbee Blue.

One of the men smiled and looked around the room, as if checking if anyone else was listening.

"I won't deny it. If it was there, we took it," he said. "And why not?"

I thought of how theft always plays a part of the mining process. In diamond mines throughout the world, workers have to be searched after every shift. Today, in almost all mines, regardless of the mineral, workers are monitored for even the smallest infraction. But copper mines rarely see any theft of actual copper because the quality of ore is so low that a single miner would have to steal several tons of ore to make even $100. For reasons having to do with economy of scale, Bisbee Blue held no interest to the executives of Phelps Dodge, but on the open market this turquoise was an extremely valuable commodity.

"You always knew when someone was taking something home.

The arm holding the lunch pail was swinging with a lot of weight. But most of the shift bosses for the company were in on it. They all took a piece of the action."

Back then miners would travel to Tucson on their day off and sell the Bisbee Blue to a gemologist for use in jewelry. Today, Bisbee Blue remains one of the rarest and most expensive forms of turquoise in existence. Other than a few merchants in the Southwest, retired miners are the sole remaining source of the mineral.

Oddly enough, there are educational benefits to driving by an open-pit mine every day. It allows me to enjoy a geological journey through Earth's crust. For the few minutes it takes to round the pit, the car glides through a narrow stretch of Highway 80, effectively trapping me inside a cross section of what used to be a mountain. The eerily strange but rich mix of reds, purples, oranges, browns, grays, and pinks doesn't exist on the surface. Out the driver's side window remain the claw marks of the machinery that tore into the mountain, still visible as long striations running up and down the jagged rock. In the canyons that retreat from the side of the road, a deep rust color grows bolder as each year passes—a sure sign of sulfuric acid runoff, one of the single most damaging results of copper mining. The mix of exotic colors, which create a beautiful canvas, can suspend for a moment the reality that one is driving through a mountain that isn't there anymore.

Outside the passenger's side window runs a chain-link fence a mile long that hugs the highway. The narrow sidewalk turned burnt red long ago, again from the erosion of copper and acidic runoff. In fact, almost any natural or man-made object in the vicinity of the pit has a particular hue of red.

The shoulder ends at the fence, and beyond it shadows stretch down to where the sun can't reach unless directly overhead. At the bottom is a large pool of crimson red liquid, a toxic cocktail still evolving. As the years pass, and the seasons change from one to the next, the water below often resembles a vat of melted crayons, their shapes slowly blending and creating new swirls of red, green, or purple.

Far off in the distance stands a tall triangle of rusting steel with various cables hanging down. This headframe indicates that there is a deep mine shaft directly under its apex. Seven such large shafts dot the Bisbee landscape, each one having acted as an elevator that lowered workers into the dark to work the mines. Not long ago, the company wanted to dismantle these large apparatuses and sell the metal for scrap. The town petitioned the company to leave them in place, something the locals in charge of the campaign called "preserving Bisbee's mining tradition."

Before reaching the end of the pit, you can catch a glimpse of the roads descending along its walls. The walls of the pit are actually a series of man-made "benches," a term to describe the vertical levels of the hole. The benches, which occur every fifty feet, would be used as roads for earth-moving machinery and dump trucks. Once the miners reached another fifty feet of extraction, they would create another bench, offset from the last one in order to limit rock slides. The benches eventually drop to the bottom of the pit and illustrate how miners dug their way into the earth one decade after another. If you can get past the vast scale of this large geological scar, you can see small black openings just above the benches. This is where heavy machinery digging the open pit sliced into one of thousands of old underground mines, another reminder that this land was already being heavily mined for seventy-five years before the shovels started digging away everything in sight.

So day in and day out, year after year, I drive around and around the pit, usually adrift in other thoughts, regarding the hole to my immediate right as just another large boundary my car has to get around, a permanent shadow that my lizard brain has allowed me to ignore for so many years. That is until someone from out of town visits us and I drive in the direction of Mexico, waxing on about border issues, and they screech from the passenger seat, "What the hell is that?"

Then I am reminded that Bisbee is not ordinary. Most people don't live in a town sitting atop thousands of miles of tunnels. Nor do they have five million tons of copper worth tens of billions of dollars just beneath their front yards, waiting to be mined.

*   *   *

Months after my arsenic-induced illness, I stand at my front window and stare into the clear bright night looking for answers. Snow fell last night and the water lines are still frozen. The garden lies fallow. My family has relocated to another house in town where Freeport has paid to put us, so its employees can empty the yard of all the dirt down to a two-foot depth. I am here to check on the pipes and adjust the furnace.

The plan is for Freeport to replace the yard with new fill and cap it off with topsoil. The problem is not the new dirt. I want that. With my wife nine months pregnant, we are expecting our second daughter any day now. I am just not convinced I want to keep living here, regardless of how much landscaping is done to our yard.

I am lost in a rush of thoughts of what Bisbee would look like if the mine did reopen. Dozens of trucks the size of houses driving up and down the road. Dirt and dust pollution creating a constant haze of brown over the town. Whistles and loud beeping noises of vehicles backing up echoing through the canyons. Constant dynamite blasting as miners dig an expansion of the existing pit. Just ask the senior citizens. For thirty years, the people of Bisbee stopped their lives at 3:25 p.m. each day, to wait for the daily blasting. School buses stopped on the side of the roads, waiting for the blasting to end. All activities in town were organized around this daily act of destruction.

An elderly woman who had moved to Bisbee in the 1950s told me, "Every day I took all my photos off the walls five minutes before 3:30. I waited for the blasting and then put the photos back on the wall."

And then there would be the influx of new labor. Miners tend to be transient souls, men and women who move from town to town chasing the paycheck, which is generally higher than that paid for most other jobs in the area. Some bring their families; others leave their families behind and send the money home. The bars get packed with overworked men, never a good thing.

I must tell you of a ranch where I once lived outside Tucson, on the backside of Mount Lemmon, near the town of Oracle. I was paying $200 a month to squat in a cabin on the famous Bill Cody ranch. Old Bill had been a circus man, taking his cowboy show from city to city, continent to continent, but he was also a miner. Even though he blasted his share of holes on this mountain, he never struck it rich.

The mornings were hot an hour before sunrise, and I would stand on the porch and welcome the scorching sun, staring into the vast nothing of the Galiuro Mountains. The only thing between the mountains and me was a large smelter that rose out of the San Pedro river basin like two giant chimneys reaching for the sky. Down below, out of sight, was San Manuel, a company town, built in the 1950s. The copper ran deep there in an underground mine. The miners of San Manuel, when asked about the mine, say the "ore just poured out."

At night I would drive down to the local watering hole: four walls, a broken door, a concrete floor, and a bar with stools. The place was packed every night with miners, mostly of Mexican American heritage. Because I wasn't a miner, I couldn't get a conversation started.

The one time I did, the guy asked, "You ever go across the border and get a brown girl and a room for thirty dollars?"

I told him I hadn't done that.

"You a fag or something?"

He wanted to fight. He picked up his bottle and said something about bleeding me. I had no idea what he was talking about, but I knew I was in trouble. I backed out, keeping my eyes low and my back to the door.

Today in Bisbee my wife and I can walk into almost any store in town and know someone. The peace and quiet of the nights are broken up only by the chorus of birds in the early morning. If five hundred new faces were to show up, with their eyes and hearts locked on making as much money as fast as they can, I'm not sure this would remain the case.

Still, there is something to be said that we humans, given enough time and repetition, can adapt to living almost anywhere. How else does one explain people living near old uranium mines, or a few miles from a nuclear plant? The answer is simple. We subconsciously choose to make terrible decisions. Our brains shut out the very things that quite possibly threaten our lives. We block it out.

Or we move?

The first employee of Phelps Dodge, and then later Freeport, that I ever knew personally was Tom Weiskopf, whom I met playing a game of pool in the Bisbee Grand Hotel. I liked him immediately. He has a gentle smile. He usually wears blue jeans and long-sleeve shirts. His laugh is contagious and he never says anything he doesn't mean. When I met him, he was the site manager of the Bisbee mine. Phelps Dodge was still the king of Arizona copper and no one had tested my yard for heavy metals. Back then there was very little talk of the mine ever being reopened. Then one day Freeport-McMoRan bought out Phelps Dodge. Months later a fleet of small trucks with Freeport logos on the side began cruising our roads. Not long after, Shaw started testing our soils. A few months later, Tom took a new job for Freeport and transferred to the Tenke mine in the DRC, the Democratic Republic of Congo.

Before he left, we talked about the mine over a few drinks.

"If it opens, the town will be a boomtown. It will be hopping and fun," he tells me with his soft-spoken positive way of speaking. I disagree, but he insists that boomtowns are fun. He tells me there is lots of money floating around and people are happy to have extra cash. I tell him I think the town will suffer from a change of culture.

He laughs and tells me I'm overthinking it.

"Hey," he says in a friendly way, "we need copper, and if this place has enough to justify opening up the mine, then I'm all for it. In the meantime, I want to work like hell to fix all the damage that was done before."

Tom's a geologist with an expertise in environmental reclamation, which was his main job in Bisbee for several years. He is most proud of the native grass growing on the man-made hillside behind the cemetery, which used to be a waste dump. The reconstruction happened under his watch and so far it doesn't look native, but in a few decades and with some heavy rains I'm sure it will blend into the natural topography.

When thinking of living in a town where a mining company once wielded a great deal of power, and may once again, it is worth mentioning what happened in Bisbee in 1917.

On the eve of World War I, most of the mines in Arizona owned by Phelps Dodge went on strike. Organized labor wanted enhanced safety procedures and an increase in wage. The miners knew that the war in Europe was making the company a lot of money, and they wanted a piece of the pie.

As the strikes multiplied, Bisbee followed. Soon after, the Republican governor of Arizona, Thomas Campbell, sent an urgent cable to the White House in hopes of getting federal troops to intervene on behalf of Phelps Dodge. In the cable, Campbell describes the conflict as a "pro-German" and "anti-American" problem, playing upon the fact that the labor pool in Bisbee was mostly ethnically European. With the country verging closer and closer to entering the European war, the company, hoping to break the strike and get the mines reopened, used an old tactic, one that feels eerily familiar in today's political arena: It created a false fear for its own economic gain.

The White House declined to help, and so on July 12, 1917, Phelps Dodge, using the local sheriffs, merchant class, and various other vigilante groups that didn't like organized labor, rounded up twelve hundred men before sunrise. This sort of operation takes planning and cooperation from multiple parties. The sheriff, Harry Wheeler, had the direct blessing of Walter Douglas, son of the infamous James Douglas, who founded the Bisbee and Morenci mines and was the acting president of Phelps Dodge. Together they hired the largest posse ever assembled in U.S. history, almost two thousand men, to round up the striking miners.

That morning they confronted the twelve hundred miners. Not all the men rounded up even worked for the mine, but in the confusion it didn't matter. They were seen as "sympathizers." The vigilantes marched their captives down to the Warren baseball park, which must have taken a few hours. Meanwhile the sheriff asked for, and received, the blessing of the El Paso and South-western railroads to supply a train to act as a rolling jail. The miners and the "sympathizers" were loaded onto cattle cars and railroaded sixteen hours through the desert to Hermanas, New Mexico. From there they were sent to Columbus, New Mexico, where they stayed almost three months living off army rations as the courts tried to figure out their fate. Before being dropped off in the middle of the New Mexico borderlands, they were warned never to return to Bisbee.

The deportation reshaped Bisbee's labor pool but didn't stop the sheriff and Phelps Dodge from imposing vigilante law. For several months the sheriff posted armed guards on all entries and exits to Bisbee and Douglas. People were given passports, made by the sheriff and the Citizens' Protective League, a vigilante group founded by Phelps Dodge. Finally the federal government did step in and arrested two dozen Phelps Dodge executives and the sheriff for kidnapping.

Not one went to jail or paid a fine. And Bisbee was never quite the same after that. Walter Douglas remained the president of Phelps Dodge and didn't flinch from this event. He was also the president of the American Mining Congress, where he promised to break every union in every mine. After the deportations of Bisbee, he didn't hide behind a wall of lawyers and public relations people, as is the norm today. He walked the halls of Phoenix and Washington, D.C., full of bluster. For him, the rationale was easy. He ran the most powerful mining company in the West, damn it, and he was going to run it his way. He seemed to dare anyone to tell him differently.

When I ponder how much power Phelps Dodge had in Arizona, acting as it pleased, knowing that the state and federal governments would not dare act against them, I am filled with contempt for corporate belligerence. At the same time I am reminded of a singular economic fact: With war raging, the nation and the world needed copper. For everything. Almost a hundred years later things haven't changed in this respect. Copper is big business, and more important, it is a crucial resource to run a modern world, in war or peace.

Today the copper mines in Arizona account for almost 60 percent of the entire copper production of the United States. In 2009 there were eleven copper mines producing upward of 750,000 metric tons of refined copper every year, which added several billion dollars to the state's economy and contributed to more than fifty thousand jobs, either directly related to mining or indirectly related to the industry through sales, government, and various businesses. Ten of those mines are in southern Arizona, within two hundred miles of Bisbee. The biggest mine is Morenci, the smallest Miami, which will likely soon lose that position with pending plans to mine directly under the town.

Although copper is king in this state, when I ask people to name a few things they think of when they hear the word "Arizona" the common answers are the Grand Canyon, the O.K. Corral in Tombstone, the Minutemen, guns, long stretches of arid desert on the I-10 corridor, conservative politicians, and border problems. Some talk about the beauty of the White Mountains or Flagstaff, but lucky for us, not often. Those secrets remain somewhat safe. What I never hear is copper or mining, which is strange because there are more than thirty-five thousand active mining claims on Arizona's public lands. There are also an estimated twenty-seven thousand abandoned mines, ranging from small exploration pits to deep shafts filled with groundwater. And there are over ten thousand mines, prospects, quarries, and processing mills and plants, extracting gold, silver, copper, uranium, clay, gypsum, turquoise, salt, marble, stones, and sand.

I try to remember why I moved to a state so linked to mining. After all, I would never move to West Virginia, which in my mind is geographically beautiful, but also nothing more than a coal colony full of mining companies racing to clip off the top of every mountain in the state. So why did I move here? Or more accurately, why didn't Arizona's mining history deter me? The only answer I can think of is that unlike West Virginia, mining is not the first thing I thought about when I thought of Arizona. In fact, I never thought of mining in Arizona at all until I moved to Bisbee, and even then it was more of a fascination with the past, not a knowledge of anything happening near me, or in the town where I live.

Now I am wondering if I can even sell a house in a mining town that may reopen the mine. A dozen workers have been in the yard for two weeks. One of the workers has been a miner for twenty years and tells me he really likes our house and that reclaiming yards is better than driving a crane inside an open pit. He has been away from Bisbee for decades, working in operational mines, but couldn't pass up the chance to come back. "It is a special place, not a normal mining town." He does metal sculpting in the evenings and on weekends and has had family working in the mining business for sixty years. I don't ask him any questions; he just wants to share with me.

The poisons in my soil have stirred something inside me, both as a parent and a resident. I have become a student again. During the day I scour the library for old books on Bisbee. I devour charts, documents, anything to understand the correlation between the mine and my backyard. I feel like I have been blindsided. When debating whether to live in Bisbee, I kept reminding myself that it always was a mining town. But then I convince myself that was a long time ago, and today it is not. Of course I know that is not true, but I want it to be. I was more focused on the new and vibrant community that thrives here. I live in a quiet neighborhood with interesting and eccentric neighbors. And it's the only liberal town in Cochise County, one of the most conservative counties in Arizona. This is the place where the Minutemen gather to have playdates with one another, sitting in their foldout chairs along the border, playing sheriff. This is where politicians come from Washington to talk tough about the border, of keeping America safe. They don't actually come to Bisbee, but they circle it in helicopters and then drive to the ranch areas, feeding on the rage that simmers in the rural areas of Cochise County. One day they built a taller fence, hired more agents, and made it is impossible to drive north without going through border patrol checkpoints with dogs. Yet nothing stops the flow of humans going north.

For years I have walked the mountains and taken note of the deer and javelinas, and tried to differentiate between bobcat and mountain lion scat. And counted the dozens of wildcat mines along the trail, black mouths with tailings drooling down the hill.

I think of the souls who walk the Mule Mountains at night, the ones who scratched the holes in these mountains, hoping to make small fortunes. Some did, most did not. Most died early.

In my house I filter my water, because why would I trust the water where a mine was in use for a hundred years? And now I feel like a fool. In all this time I never really thought how else the mine could still affect my life.

Some of the town's merchants are excited about the possibility of the mine reopening. It would mean a small boom in the economy, infusing a steady stream of income. Many of the hotel owners are happy at the prospect, except for the ones who arrived in the hippie migration in the late 1970s. A few of those old hippie types keep telling me to not believe the report on toxins in my backyard. They say, "It's all lies. This is just a way for them to test the soil on all our land. For gold and copper. If they find it, they won't buy our homes; they will tunnel under the town and take the ore."

I ponder the rumor that the company is looking for more copper in our yards. Most likely this is an overblown paranoid delusion of those holding tight to their way of life. I think of our second daughter, who will be born in a matter of weeks. I think of living here for two decades, raising a family. I try to convince myself that they won't open the mine. The majority of the town wouldn't want it, and besides, the only remaining copper is of poor quality that will cost too much to extract. But what do I know, really? Not enough.

The snow, as it does everywhere, blankets the town with a measure of calm. I don't know the answers to all these questions, but I do know I have to learn more about my town, about copper, and about how mining companies operate. The following pages are the result of exploring the world of copper over a three-year period.

The journey begins in earnest by reading Exhibit A of my homeowner title. In this document I see, for the first time, that my plot of land sits on a mining claim called AL HASSON in an area of town called Quality Hill. It also states very clearly that:

Said Owner owns surface only to a depth of 40 feet immediately below the surface of that part of AL HASSON PATENTED MIN- ING CLAIM, in Warren Mining District being shown on Mineral Survey No. 1387 on file in the Bureau of Land Management, as granted by Patent recorded in Book 14 of Deeds of Mines, page 415, records of Cochise County, Arizona.

J. Paul Getty died in 1976, a year after the Bisbee mines closed, but I can hear him whispering in my ear in a smooth, hushed voice, with the faintest hint of entitlement. He is saying, "You may own your house, but someone else owns everything under- neath it."

3

The Beginnings

A land whose stones are iron and out of whose hills
you will dig copper.
                                    —Deuteronomy 8:9

I am on my knees trying to reach a lever to my water heater, which
is located in my kitchen, yet one more building code violation
in my home. I called the plumber hours ago, but he couldn't be
bothered to answer my call, not unusual in Bisbee. Many here
work just enough to get through the month, and anything else is
a distraction from the art of living. I would not be surprised if he
is a sculptor or painter or bird expert in real life, and a plumber
on the side.

Our house consists of two bedrooms, separated by a bathroom.
There are also a kitchen, living room, and dining room, all divided
from the bedrooms by a long thin corridor that spans the length
of the house. This space has walk-in closets with small doors, all
typical for a Bisbee house built in 1900. These were the first pre-
fabricated houses, also known as the Kit Homes. Kit houses were
a cheap and simple way for miners to build a house without actually investing much time and money in the structure. The homes
were ordered from a catalog and delivered by train from Michigan. Off-loaded near Bisbee Junction, a few miles from town and
on the border of Mexico, they were transported to the home sites
in sections: walls, roof, trim, and so on. A team would assemble

the whole thing in less than a month. They used no insulation and most of the pipes ran along the outside of the house, exposed to the bitter cold. By today's standards, these homes are quaint but woefully outdated.

When we bought our house, we ripped out all of the interior walls and stripped out the old thick black cord wiring from the 1930s. We put in insulation, covered it with Sheetrock, and painted. In doing this we added hundreds of pounds of copper in the wiring and new appliances. Not that I thought of this at the time.

I turn on the lever and the leaks begin immediately. Struggling, I tighten the flexible copper pipes leading from the water pipe in the wall to the top of the water heater. A few more turns and the leaking stops. Simple, really. My cell phone rings and I ignore it. I need more light to adjust the gas valve, so I turn on a flashlight. What do all these acts have in common? Copper. Later I get in my car, and as I near the post office I brake to avoid hitting a dog. In the afternoon a friend at the café shows me something on his computer. Copper—in the phone, the car brakes, and the computer. More? I will fly ten times this year. I will rent ten cars. Planes, computers, water heaters, cell phones, cars—they all require copper to function.

To avoid copper on any given day would take nothing short of a monastic effort. Think of a solitary man secluded in a forest meadow with no tent or backpack, both manufactured by machines with enormous copper in them. No one living in an urban setting would pass this test. Then again, even the guy camping for two days in the wilderness is likely to be using copper. Does he have a GPS device? That has copper. Does he have a small cooking stove? That has copper inside the elements. Does he still have his cell phone, for emergencies? Loaded with copper. Did he drive to his remote location to get away from everything? Sure he did, and his car has forty pounds of copper in it. More if the car is a Prius, since the electric aspect of the vehicle requires more copper.

Copper has proven itself the perfect metal. In metallurgy, the scientific study of metals, copper is known as the eternal metal for a simple reason. It does not decay or rust. Easy to recycle, almost 80 percent of all copper ever extracted from the earth is still in use in some way or another. Copper is also malleable, allowing for expansion and contraction under great tension and heat. It softens when rubbed and hardens when hammered. Such flexibility allows metalworkers and plumbers to work copper into any particular shape without ever losing its chemical integrity.

Here is a sobering thought: Every man-made thing we use aboveground was once underground. Everything. Concrete. Steel. Nails. Glass. Tin. Plastic, which is made from oil. Aluminum. Even wood. All trees started as a seed in the ground. As for copper, it can be found in certain places where deposits of minerals were pushed up from Earth's core tens of millions of years ago. Most of the copper deposits in Arizona, and the entire Southwest, date back to a geological event that happened some fifty-eight million years ago. No one knows why, but a surge of heat and minerals pushed up through fractures in Earth's crust. There they sat for millions of years, cooling and shifting shape and composition. Some of these deposits became what we know as gold, silver, and copper. Bisbee's copper is unique. Here the copper deposit dates back more than two hundred million years. Geologists like to talk in terms of millions of years and seismic events, but no one knows the hidden mysteries of Earth, or why the copper mined from Bisbee during its peak was of the highest quality ever found in North America, outside of Michigan.

For the greater part of human history, getting copper from the ground involved people picking up the red metal and beating it with a rock or hammer to separate the metal from the rock. Mining got more serious around five thousand years ago, with a steady supply of slave labor in place to beat the metal out of the rocks on a large scale. Remember the Romans roaming Europe and northern Africa looking for gladiators, women, and wine? They were also looking for metal, specifically tin and copper. All those quarries that exist in biblical tales and in movies about Spartacus and gladiators are mostly copper or tin mines. Carthage, in modern-day Tunisia and the namesake of the famous battles with Rome, was home of a large copper mine, the very reason the Romans wanted to conquer it. Rio Tinto in Spain has been an active copper mine for almost four thousand years. As the name suggests, the creeks near the mine run copper red and always have. Today Rio Tinto is also the name of one of the largest copper-mining companies in the world, which bought the famed Rio Tinto mine from Spain in the late 1800s.

The story of copper predates written history. It predates the events in the Bible by eight thousand years, if not more. In fact, the Bible has twenty-seven references to copper, most of which depict God encouraging his people to live a better life in the pursuit of the ore. Reading some of these passages today, I wonder if the men who wrote the Bible were making the case that God was a proponent of mining. Using the book strictly as a source of historical record, the Bible is decidedly late to the game when it comes to explaining how human civilization had been using copper.

Long before King David and King Solomon created a small copper economy in 800 BC (the mines are thought to be located in Khirbat en-Nahas, or the "ruins of copper," in modern-day Jordan), the Egyptians, the Greeks, and the Romans all throughout Anatolia and the Balkans had mined copper. In Asia, there is archaeological evidence of copper being melted and hammered in Thailand, China, and Japan as far back as 2500 BC. The Chinese, like the Swedes three thousand years later, used the metal for making coins. In South America, the Incas mined for copper beginning around 2000 BC. And in the Americas, Native Indians in the Michigan region were using copper as early as 6000 BC.

Since the Middle East is the point of origin for several major religions, and many mythologies, it makes sense that copper's oldest known artifact—thought to be a comb—was found in northern Iraq, dating back to 8000 BC. This was the land of the Sumerians and Chaldeans living in ancient Mesopotamia. They are credited as the first people to use high-temperature fire to smelt copper out of ore. The Sumerians traveled up and down the Euphrates River to trade copper throughout the Fertile Crescent. It is no surprise, then, that *Urudu,* the Sumerian word for the Euphrates, literally translates as "copper river."

* * *

Copper has many uses in our lives, even for our health. Not many know this, that copper is in our blood, and without it the body dies. Too much of it and we also die. For most, balancing the correct amount of copper happens without ever thinking about it in a lifetime. As a trace element, copper helps the body absorb iron, helps protect and regulate the nervous and glandular systems, and assists the development of muscle and bone. Too much copper and we can experience headaches, fatigue, psychosis, and cirrhosis. It can induce nausea, damage the kidneys, and cause hair loss, mostly in women. We don't have to put in much effort to get the correct amount of copper since it is found as a natural substance in common foods such as sunflower seeds, walnuts, almonds, mushrooms, shrimp, and most types of beans. Our chemical sensitivity to copper has even led some people to argue that copper is the true reason behind war and violence. They explain that violence is a direct result of an imbalance in copper that goes undetected in entire societies, allowing for a sort of collective madness.

For several millennia, copper has been known to have medicinal benefits, and over the last five thousand years, cultures have used copper to cure everything from insanity to hangovers. In sub-Saharan Africa, coppersmiths were thought of as shamans, due to their knowledge of the earth and their ability to extract minerals from rock. The Romans and Egyptians also used copper for such household items as drinking cups, platters, and plates. These may seem minor applications of a metal we now use in most of our advanced technology, but three thousand years ago using copper as a water vessel counted as a major scientific breakthrough. Copper has natural antimicrobial properties. Water carried in copper cisterns did not develop slime. The quality was better. Not that these ancient civilizations knew the exact scientific properties of copper, but they did know that people who drank from copper goblets didn't get as sick as those who sipped from wooden ones. What is it about copper that is unique to inhibiting disease? The metal releases ions that penetrate the cell walls of microbes, which in turn disrupts their ability to reproduce, i.e., spread as an infection.

This realization that copper acts as a potent pesticide and fungicide has been known for thousands of years, with perhaps the most revolutionary use as the lining of wooden ships. By the time Christopher Columbus was sailing to the New World, hundreds of ships had already been lost at sea due to wood rot, mostly caused by Teredo worms, which are actually clams but look like long worms. The female lays the eggs onto the wood shell of the boat, and from birth the small clams bore into the ship's hull, using the wood for food. To prevent rot, the ships' hulls were lined with a copper sheathing. Columbus had copper attached to the bottom of his boat, which is lucky for him because the warm waters of the Caribbean, where he began his slave-trading days, have the highest volume of Teredo worms in the world. Still, the use of copper as standard protocol to protect boats did not become common until the mid-1770s, when England's Royal Navy was at war with the French and soon to be at war with the American colonies. The British needed their armada to withstand being in the water for an extended time without having to dry-dock for repairs. The answer was copper.

This prophylactic property of copper has far-reaching implications. Today, some hospitals are beginning to revisit using antimicrobial copper as a form of instant sterilization in an attempt to curtail the highly contagious Methicillin-resistant *Staphylococcus aureus*, also known as MRSA, a staph infection that kills up to twenty thousand people per year, most of whom obtained the infection from a hospital. In 2005, the Centers for Disease Control released a report that stated more people die in the United States from this infection than from AIDS. Some hospitals are looking for any way to stop MRSA from spreading from patient to patient. One answer is changing their building codes to make all doorknobs and bedrails from copper, which immediately kills germs upon contact.

I find it comforting that ancient civilizations held this knowledge. If this move toward copper catches on—and there is no reason to think it won't—perhaps all commercial kitchens will use copper as the main surface, instantly killing any traces of E. coli. One company has already figured out a way to use copper in fabrics, such as socks and pillowcases, where microbes linger. Remember the Chilean miners who were stuck underground in a gold and copper mine in the summer of 2010? To stave off infections, they were sent socks lined with copper to kill any fungus.

Historically, those civilizations that had access to copper made it the metal of choice. The Egyptians built their pyramids using copper tools. They had copper aqueducts dating back four thousand years that still work today. They also used the mineral copper for makeup, usually blue and green found in malachite and azurite, both minerals that contain copper. Luckily for the Egyptians, they found copper nearby on the Sinai Peninsula, making it the largest copper-mining region in the ancient world. They took their copper supply seriously and assigned one of their gods to protect the source: Hathor, the Egyptian goddess of the sky, music, dance, and art was the patron saint of Sinai. She was also called the Lady of Malachite.

Soon copper became a valuable export, and it wasn't long until it made its way to Asia Minor in exchange for cedar trees from Lebanon. Then copper was discovered on Cyprus around 2600 BC, and a new industrial center was born. "Cyprus" comes from the Latin word *cuprum*, which means "metal of Cyprus." Cyprus quickly became the new supplier for the Egyptian, Greek, and eventually Roman empires, making it the most important source of copper in the Bronze Age. The Skouriotissa mine on Cyprus has been active for almost four thousand years, with occasional work stoppages due to war. With today's prices sometimes skyrocketing to more than $9,000 per ton, the mine is once again up and running.

As Egypt fell and Rome grew, copper became an even more valuable resource, a mineral that any empire needed to control to maintain its grasp on power. It is believed that at the height of its empire, Rome produced almost twenty thousand tons of copper annually. Because the Romans had figured out how to melt copper with tin to make brass and with iron to make bronze, copper meant weapons. Copper was the metal of armies and empires.

After repeated invasions by the barbarian army in the fifth

century, Romans began to feel the crumbling edge of their vast empire. In a calculated move to preserve what they still had, they abandoned all lands west of the Danube River, a voluntary retreat to save modern-day Italy. The result of leaving all that territory behind was a political, economic, and military vacuum that would eventually be replaced by a system of feudal lords, also known as the Dark Ages. This continued for almost four hundred years, until Charlemagne became emperor of Rome and decided to unite the lands now known as France, Germany, and the Czech Republic. There were known mines in these regions, most dormant for hundreds of years, and once a central government was in place, people began venturing off the lands of the lords. They needed minerals and weapons if they had any hope to survive.

For the next one thousand years or so, mining changed little—accomplished by hand with men and beasts of burden, copper, gold, and silver could be processed only on a small scale. The arrival of the Industrial Revolution would change that.

In the early years of the American colonies, copper's role was mostly limited to household items, tablewares, and musical instruments. But as America grew, so did its use for copper. When Americans built a maritime fleet to carry cargo all over the world, those ship's bellies were lined with copper. The first well-known coppersmith in America was Paul Revere. He made a living putting copper sheathing on the bottom of boats and making large copper roofs. His business was so successful it didn't take long for the demand to overwhelm his talent and his sources of copper. A new supply of copper was found in Michigan soon after the end of the American Revolution. This discovery of rich native copper—sitting in plain sight, not unlike a placer mine—created America's first true copper barons. The largest copper nugget ever found was in the Keweenaw Peninsula in 1857, weighing in at 420 tons. But Michigan played out long before the big transformation that would forever change civilization and create the economic forces that allowed American industrialists to finance large copper mines in Chile, Arizona, and Mexico.

This new age for copper began in a laboratory on December 31, 1879, in Menlo Park, New Jersey, when Thomas Edison turned on the first incandescent lightbulb, declaring, "We will make electricity so cheap that only the rich will burn candles."

Once electricity came along, thousands of miles of copper wire were needed to plug America, and the rest of the world, into this new invention. By 1880, the telephone began to spread as a means of communication, exponentially increasing the need for copper. By 1900, large-scale mines were necessary to keep up with demand. Eventually copper became such an important part of modern society that Wall Street began to call the mineral "Dr. Copper," implying that the stock market invariably followed the ups and downs of the price of copper. When copper is up, the economy must be expanding, as industry uses more copper to build buildings, cars, and infrastructure. And when the price of copper takes a dive, it means the industries that drive economic growth are slowing down.

Demand for copper in the twentieth century followed the growth and contraction of the largest economies around the world. War also boosted copper production. As the mines became larger, ever-greater economies of scale came into play. Small mines began to disappear, being swallowed by larger operations. What may have been a successful underground operation now became a large open-pit mine. Instead of mining 1 percent copper ore for a twenty-year window, now a mining company could produce 0.05 percent copper for forty years.

In most countries, the central government collects a royalty on any mineral extracted from its soil. In the United States, the government collects exactly zero dollars in royalty for leasing out public land to hard-rock mining at the bargain rate of $5 an acre. Ever since Ulysses S. Grant signed the 1872 General Mining Law, not much has changed in how mining companies go about their business on land that is considered public domain, the majority of which is located west of the Mississippi. The Mining Law, similar to the Homestead Act, was originally meant to encourage capital and labor to move west to populate and profit off new land that the government had taken from Native Americans. Giving away the mineral rights seemed like a way to get prospectors and mining equity out west, for the robber barons and their political allies in Washington knew that if gold or other minerals were found, miners would help bring the railroad, and ultimately the expansion of the United States, into what was thought of as savage country.

Although the world has changed by leaps and bounds, very little has changed in the law. Once a mining company files a claim with the local county clerk, and, if needed, with the Bureau of Land Management, it is granted the right to explore for and extract minerals from that tract of land. The cost of filing the original claim varies from state to state (in Arizona it is $200), but in general the claim owner must spend at least $100 a year working the land. And what is the price to pursue these hard-rock mining claims that extract millions, if not billions, of dollars' worth of minerals from this land that is owned by the U.S. government? Still $5 an acre. Currently all oil and gas-mining claims on public lands pay between 8 percent and 12 percent royalty. Coal pays a royalty as well. Hard-rock mining, such as gold, uranium, and copper, pay zero royalty. Hard-rock mining companies have earned a profit of billions of dollars in 140 years and paid the U.S. government, and the states they are located in, zero for extracting minerals off public land. Or, to put it another way, they have paid the U.S. taxpayer zero.

In descending order, these are the largest publicly traded mining companies in the world: BHP Billiton from Australia; Vale from Brazil; Rio Tinto and Anglo American from the United Kingdom; Freeport-McMoRan from the United States; Southern Copper from Peru; Teck Resources from Canada; and Grupo Mexico. Of these, Freeport is the largest copper miner.

When arguing to keep the 1872 law in place, these and other mining companies and their lobbyists use the rationale that they pay wages, taxes on revenue, and a great deal on infrastructure and various other expenditures. All these statements are true, but they have nothing to do with paying a fair share for riches extracted from our land. There are many arguments for and against hard-rock mining, all of which offer up complicated issues—economics, pollution, and local issues are just a few—but what is not complicated is no longer allowing hard-rock mining companies to continue profiting essentially for free on our public land.

Maybe the worst aspect of this archaic law is that federal agencies are unable to stop a mine from being built. Yes, there is a permitting process and various obligatory environmental impact studies, but if the mining company meets even the lowest standards of those processes, the agencies can't deny the mine from going forward, even if it is obviously against the best interest of the surrounding citizens. And to add insult to injury, all this holds true whether the mining company is domestic or foreign.

For example, halfway between Bisbee and Tucson stand the Santa Rita Mountains, a little-used region of high desert that has been home to ranchers for the last century. Although the region, known as the Helvetia mining district, was first mined in the late 1800s, it shut down as an active mining district in 1951. Since then, several large companies have been exploring the land for signs of a large deposit. In 1963, Anaconda Mining bought the property and officially identified a major deposit of copper. Once Anaconda dissolved as a company, the American Smelting and Refining Company (ASARCO) bought the land in 1988 with plans to develop it. But then ASARCO, facing bankruptcy, sold it in 2004. Augusta, a Canadian company, bought the land in 2005 and after further analysis planned to develop an open-pit mine for a twenty-year operation beginning in 2013. The mine plan calls for an open pit with a diameter of more than a mile, and twenty-nine hundred feet deep. The mine will produce 234 million pounds of copper per year for twenty years. Those who oppose—homeowners, ranchers, bed-and-breakfast outfits, environmental groups—and those who are for it—the chamber of commerce and mining lobbyists—have been having a very public fight for several years.

Because large parts of the mine and the waste dump will be on U.S. forest land, the U.S. Forest Service is in charge of assessing the mine. The final draft of the environmental report released by the USFS on June 1, 2011, states it would favor approval of the mine. The report also states that "the proposed action [the mine] would result in the direct loss of conversion of 6,225 acres of habitat and indirectly impact up to 90,780 acres that may have the potential to impact animal behavior. . . . Because of the magnitude, intensity, length and round-the-clock timing of the project, all special status plants and animals that occur in the area are expected to be impacted."

The report discusses several ways the mine may adversely affect the immediate area. The Forest Service predicts that groundwater supplies may diminish on both sides of the Santa Rita Mountains and that the mining operations would more than triple emissions of large airborne particles and more than double emissions of fine particles. They estimate the nearby Saguaro National Park would have noticeable impaired visibility for thirty-four days of the year.

In a rare display of federal agencies sparring over the decision, in March 2012 the EPA gave the Forest Service their lowest rating on the environmental draft report, something they have done only four times since 1989. The Forest Service has been formally asked to revise the environmental report, stating that the document contains "inadequate information."

It is expected that even with revisions, the Forest Service's final report will come out in 2012. Attached to the report will be various environmental conditions that Rosemont Copper must legally agree to in order to open the mine, but in the end the Forest Service cannot legally stop the mine from going forward; it can only set various benchmarks to which the mine must adhere. The 1872 law forbids them from stopping a legitimate mining operation. In fact, Forest Service officials have repeatedly emphasized this restriction when speaking to opponents of the mine. As Heidi Schewel, Coronado National Forest spokesperson, said emphatically, "According to law, regulation, and policy, the mine will be allowed. What we're doing is considering a number of alternatives to determine the method by which to operate the mine."

As for Augusta, the mining company has spent millions in advertising: The operation will be safe, it will have little environmental impact, it will use solar power for parts of the operation, and the company will build an earthen wall to block the view of the mine from the scenic highway. What Augusta does not mention is that the mine will suck the water table dry and leave a pile of waste and destruction in its wake. So far no one has figured out how to refill an open mine pit without spending another twenty years doing so.

When the 1872 law was written, the internal combustion engine had not been invented. No one understood how large hard-rock mining operations would become or how much damage these mines would create. The antiquated law lacks teeth to enforce penalties for environmental damage and thus has left poisonous mines and watersheds scattered throughout the West. In 2000, the EPA reported that hard-rock mining, which does not include oil, gas, or coal, released 3.4 billion pounds of toxins—that's 47 percent of the total released that year by all U.S. industries. By 2007, toxic emissions were down, but hard-rock mining was still the number-one polluter. In July 2009, an EPA report stated that "the agency examined its 2007 Toxic Release Inventory, and this data revealed that the metal mining industry (gold ore mining, lead ore and zinc ore mining, and copper ore and nickel ore mining) releases enormous quantities of toxic chemicals, at nearly 1.15 billion pounds or approximately 28 percent of the total releases by U.S. industry."

The report goes on to say, "Hardrock mining facilities also generate an enormous volume of waste, which may increase the risk of releases of hazardous substances. Annually, hardrock mining facilities generate between one to two billion tons of mine waste. This waste can take a variety of forms, including mine water, waste rock, overburden, tailings, slag, and flue dust, and can contain significant quantities of hazardous substances. Hardrock mining facilities reported large releases of many hazardous substances, including ammonia, benzene, chlorine, hydrogen cyanide, hydrogen fluoride, toluene, and xylene, as well as heavy metals and their compounds (e.g., antimony, arsenic, cadmium, chromium, cobalt, copper, lead, manganese, mercury, nickel, selenium, vanadium and zinc)."

To both increase royalty rates and hold mining companies more responsible for their toxic pollution, various members of Congress have tried to amend the old law. In 2007, Representative Nick Rahall, a Democrat from West Virginia, introduced H.R. 2262, the Hardrock Mining and Reclamation Act, which would have levied a royalty rate between 4 percent and 8 percent and made mining companies more fiscally liable for accidents and mine cleanups. The bill had sixty-two cosponsors but never became law. Since then representatives such as Senator Mark Udall from Colorado have tried to amend the law but failed. In addition to the powerful mining lobbyists keeping constant pressure on Congress not to alter the law, there is the consistent lack of support by the Democratic majority leader of the Senate, Harry Reid. In the current cycle of Congress, it is he who ultimately controls the agenda of the Senate. As the son of a miner and an elected official of a state that relies heavily on mining for jobs, he has never supported changing the law. When elected, President Obama promised to address the inadequacies in the law. He instructed Secretary of the Interior Ken Salazar to get the 1872 mining law updated, but so far that hasn't happened.

By 2012, there were 156 hard-rock mining Superfund sites throughout the United States, which will cost between $7 billion and $24 billion to clean up. Many of these sites were owned by bankrupt companies, which thus escape any legal enforcement to clean up their mines. Today mining companies are legally obligated to secure a cleanup bond before mining, but the point is that this antiquated law still encourages extremely wealthy companies to take for free and be responsible for nothing when they leave.

The mining companies point out, accurately, that their operations are difficult, are slow to pay off, and require enormous investments. There is a saying in the mining world: "It used to be one poor man digs a hole and gets rich. Today a rich company digs a hole and goes broke." History is riddled with stories of the solo prospector finding a gold nugget the size of a baseball and striking it rich overnight. That no longer happens. Now, large multinational companies, often merged together in partnerships, spend on average more than $1 billion to open any copper mine in the world. That figure can rise rapidly if the location is difficult to access or if the host country has political and military obstacles. To open the Tenke mine in the Democratic Republic of Congo, Freeport has spent almost $3 billion and counting.

For the environmental movement, the issue of highly pollutant hard-rock mining is becoming more complicated. No industry creates more toxins in the United States than hard-rock mining. No large-scale copper mine has ever *not* had an adverse effect on the surrounding groundwater. This industry takes its time finding the ore and developing it, and then once companies begin to dig, they don't stop until the copper is either gone or no longer profitable to mine. When they begin to strip the earth, the result is terrifying. Utter destruction of what was there is the only possible outcome. This has made hard-rock mining, especially of copper and gold, an easy target for the environmental movement. But today's economic and political shift toward renewable energy creates a strange dilemma for the environmentalists. Wind and solar energy require massive amounts of copper, which means more open-pit mines. Renewable energy requires less coal and oil but more electrical conduits for turning wind and solar into electricity. On a wind farm in Sweetwater, Texas, one hundred miles of copper wire are required to run sixty-one turbines. The energy is more efficient, far less pollutant than coal or oil, but it uses far more copper. The circle of energy and pollution continues.

I am at odds over all this information. Copper is invaluable to our lives or, more accurately, to our lifestyles. I try to construct a theory of how a moral person should live in these circumstances, knowing that consumerism drives wars and environmental tragedies. Thinking about copper is not easy. Mining is a necessity of modern civilization. That much is simple. Without it, we would have to agree, collectively, to give up all our modern appliances and almost all forms of electricity. There would be no Internet without copper because there would be no satellites, electric cables, or computers. One thing is certain about technological and civil evolution. It has a very difficult time going backward. We would be a civilization of walking beings and, as in the Dark Ages, isolated within our small communities. We would not be unlike the pioneers who traveled west, the very ones who found these mines in Arizona and the rest of the western United States. They ventured on horseback and in wagon trains, and pumped water from springs. Could I do that in order to morally justify arguing against any and all copper mining? Perhaps. Maybe for a little while (I lived like that for a few years when I was younger). But can we, as a society? No. We would tear one another to shreds. We would regress and suffer and die.

It's hard not to realize that I am a hypocrite, for I don't want the mine to reopen in my town, but I do desire all the benefits that come from the copper mined in other people's towns. I want to cook in copper pots and pans. I want to type on my computer. I want my phone to work. I just don't want them to get the copper needed for all this from the mine down the street from my house.

As we go about our days picking up kids from school, going to work, making a cup of coffee, and planning the next mortgage payment, there is little time to dwell on the staggering number of products directly using copper. In 2012, more than one billion personal computers were in use around the globe, and by 2015 there will be more than two billion. The average amount of copper in a personal computer is one and a half pounds. Tablets and iPads account for another hundred million products. Every cell phone has sixteen grams of copper, and by the end of 2012, there will be nearly two billion cell phones, with that number expected to grow another half a billion in the next five years. Cars? Beijing adds fifteen hundred cars to its roads every single day, and in 2011 there were a billion cars in use, with almost sixty million more produced every year. All these products, which grease the wheels of our modern society, use copper. In fact, they cannot exist without it.

Like it or not, the expanding growth of civilization requires the mining of ore, whether zinc, copper, cobalt, iron, or dozens of other metals and minerals. This begs the question that fuels debate anywhere someone is trying to build a mine. If we don't like large open-pit mining, how are we going to get the basic minerals we need?

4

Company Town

The greater the power, the more dangerous the abuse.
—Edmund Burke, 1771

Every day I pass the mining museum in the center of town. Housed in the old Phelps Dodge mining offices, the museum was the first in the Southwest to become an affiliate of the Smithsonian, which states on its website that "the Bisbee museum exhibitions bring to life the history of Bisbee and how copper from this small town shaped a city and a nation." All this history is fascinating and a large draw for tourists, but it does not do much to help me understand what it would be like to live in an active mining town. For that I need to get out of Bisbee.

I decide to drive north three hours to Morenci, named after Morenci, Michigan, home to the largest producing copper mine in North America. Located in the remote eastern part of Arizona in Greenlee County, a county literally created so that Phelps Dodge, the original owners of the mine, could control all aspects of anything that could impact their mine, Morenci has been in operation since the late 1870s. Open-pit mining began there in 1937, and the mine has been one of the world's top producers ever since. Morenci mines more than eight hundred thousand tons of rock per day, and in 2011, produced five hundred million pounds of pure copper. It supplies 25 percent of all the copper produced in the United States, and during peak production it employs up to

47

four thousand miners who work in constant rotating twelve-hour shifts, which keeps the mine open 365 days a year. With unknown millions of tons of copper still in the earth, the mine will be active for a few more decades, if not longer.

Morenci is not really a town, not in any traditional meaning of the word. In normal towns, there are mayors who kiss babies as they angle for votes. In most towns, every business owner has to think about advertising, property taxes, and payroll. And in most towns, city council meetings are the setting for both back-stabbing drama and genuine concern for the community. Not so in Morenci. There is no mayor or city council. All the property in this town is owned by one entity: Freeport-McMoRan, the same company that bought Phelps Dodge and owns the mine in Bisbee. The bartender, the guy in the bowling alley who cleans the lanes, the garbage collector, and the cashier at the pizza parlor all collect their weekly paychecks from Freeport. There are a few private businesses that lease property from Freeport and run private enterprises, such as the Chinese fast-food café, the tuxedo shop, and the supermarket Bashas', a chain also in Bagdad, the only other company town in Arizona, and which is also owned by Freeport.

Other than having full control of its employees, one of the main reasons to own the town is being able to move it if the mine needs to be expanded. Morenci, the town proper, has been moved twice in the last seventy-five years, both times to accommodate an expanding open pit. And both times there were no protests, no community-organized petitions asking the city or the state to stop physically moving people's homes. Everyone just packed their bags, loaded up their trucks, and helped the company move buildings or destroy them. And then those same residents went to work the next day and began blowing up the earth where their homes used to stand. The mine is the purpose of the town. Its continual growth supercedes any other priority.

By sundown I am drinking draft beer with a young miner named Scott in the bar at the Morenci Motel, which is also owned by Freeport. The room looks like something out of an Elks lodge. The television is permanently fixed on a channel called Speed.

Scott is twenty-three and what is known as a fuser, which means he spends his days laying pipe in the leaching fields that begin a few miles from this bar. The leaching fields are the first geographical aberration a person sees when approaching Morenci from the south. They first come into view as a vast yellow stretch of flattened land. It takes several minutes of driving sixty miles an hour straight at these fields to realize they are, in fact, man-made mountains of pulverized rock standing side by side with the natural mountains around them. In the Morenci mining district there are several large fields, some of which span five hundred acres, and altogether the fields cover seven thousand acres.

Working the fields is a tough and lonely job. Scott has been employed at the mine since he was eighteen. He keeps telling me he wants to be different from his father, who labored in the mine his whole life.

"It pays well," he says, putting down his drink and sinking the four ball in the side pocket. We are gambling on the game, our second, but not much. The room is full of young faces, buying pitcher after pitcher of Bud Light. Half of them look like college graduate geologists—young men with full beards, bright eyes, and Patagonia sweatshirts—and the other half look like kids from blue-collar families—Carhartt clothes, thick boots, thin in the face. They are all in groups. No one is alone, except me. When people ask who I am, I tell them I am just traveling through, which makes them smile and then turn away. They know I am lying; no one passes through Morenci and stops to spend the night in the company motel. Everyone in this motel is either a contract worker or direct employee of the mining company. Tourists drive in for the day, take a mine tour, and then keep driving to a place where the air doesn't smell like pulverized rock and leaching chemicals.

"Everyone in here works at the mine," says Scott, who proceeds to sink three more balls. I ask if he wants to stay in Morenci.

"I put in an application with the Border Patrol. My brother works there. He says it pays great, and that I can sit in a truck and play video games." He sinks the eight ball, corner pocket. Now I owe him another $10.

Scott tells me he went to high school here and that everyone's parents either work or have worked at the mines. No one else lives here. And he says, "Everyone wants to get out, but it's not easy."

Scott and his friends leave abruptly, probably because they realize I am asking too many questions. I suspect they just wanted to kick my ass in pool and fleece me for a quick $20 and a pitcher of beer. Looking around for new faces, I begin a conversation with a young happy-looking Apache couple who also work at the mine.

"What else is there?" the young woman asks rhetorically. "'Cause even if you work as a schoolteacher here, you are working for the mine."

They tell me they rent a house from the mining company. The terms are clear: If they are fired or laid off, they are expected to move out of the house within thirty days. This arrangement is the same for every person who lives in Morenci, Arizona, one of America's last true company towns.

By their very nature, company towns are designed to fulfill basic social necessities while maximizing profits. They are thus both hypercapitalistic and socialist at the same time. The companies maintain dictatorship authority over the towns and the residents but provide for certain needs so that their workers stay happy and, much more important to the company, productive. The free market is not at play in places like Morenci. Housing is hugely subsidized to the point that rent for a three-bedroom home is $250 or less, more than affordable on an average miner's paycheck, which ranges from $45,000 to $80,000 a year. Supervisors and contract workers are paid even more. When a person is laid off or fired, the electricians, cleaners, and plumbers—all on the company payroll—come in and revamp the place for the new worker and his or her family.

Company towns used to be more common throughout Arizona, places such as San Manuel and Kearny. The arrangement made perfect sense. The laborers, many of them first-generation immigrants, had little money or resources to cover the expense of the day-to-day grind of life. Company towns took care of this.

By building all the houses, and owning them, the company could rent to workers cheap. And a miner's credit was good as long as he or she was still working.

Phelps Dodge started both Morenci and Bisbee in the early 1880s, but technically Bisbee was never a company town. In both places, Phelps Dodge was the largest employer, but in Bisbee the majority of the miners who worked in the shafts owned their own property. Also, in Bisbee private enterprise thrived. The towns had other differences as well. As the decades passed, Bisbee and Morenci both grew in size and productivity, but they were never alike in pay for the workers. In Morenci the labor pool was predominantly Mexican, most very skilled, who migrated from mines in northern Sonora, only four hours to the south. Yet even though Bisbee is several miles from the Mexican border, the miners there were almost exclusively of European heritage—many came from Wales, Ireland, Italy, and Serbia. The Mexicans were not allowed to mine underground in Bisbee, which was considered a white man's camp. Although they all belonged to the same union, the Industrial Workers of the World, also known as the Wobblies, Bisbee workers were called "miners" and in Morenci they were called "laborers," which had nothing to do with the work they did. They all did essentially the same jobs but were of different ethnic backgrounds. Because of this distinction, the Bisbee miners were paid on average three times more than the Morenci laborers.

Because mining towns never sleep, the best way to experience one is at night, when the rest of the world is neatly tucked away in bed. It is a chance to peek at the nocturnal portrait of man digging a continuous hole into the earth. I leave the motel and drive north up Highway 191, a treacherous stretch of road that curves northward to the White Mountains. The road used to be named State Highway 666, a distinction that ended in 2003 when New Mexico and Arizona officials decided to change the name in order to address some local concerns that the road was cursed, due to so many accidents. The authorities also stated they wanted to reduce theft of the road signs.

The mine headquarters is to the left, and to the right runs a train track from here to Lordsburg, New Mexico. The line was built by Phelps Dodge to deliver chemicals—mostly sulfuric acid—needed for extracting copper from rock.

Up ahead a conveyor belt crosses the highway 150 feet above the road. Hundreds of tons of rock travel from the mine down the belt and dump out of the sky into a pile of earth next to the highway. I scan for faces working the machines but see only bright lights.

Crossing under the conveyor belt, I speed up. I can't help but have the feeling that I have driven upon a crime scene and that somebody is getting away with something here. Like they are stealing everything in sight under the veil of night and doing it in a hurry before we all wake up and shut it down.

Abruptly the road climbs uphill. Heading farther north, the mountains rise steeply in front of me. After a few miles of driving through an eerie quiet, I realize I am not driving around the mine but *through* it. When driving around the open pit in Bisbee I also cruise along a stretch of highway that cuts through the mine, but the scale here in Morenci makes the pit in Bisbee feel like a back-yard pond. Out of the darkness I come to a section of road where activity abounds on both sides. Trucks pass under me, through tunnels the size of airplane hangars, as they bring piles of earth from the far edges of the open pit to the conveyor belts, leaching piles, and crushing plants, which operate twenty-four hours a day. Every day.

For eight miles the road travels through and above the mine before I actually exit the mining district, which covers nearly sixty thousand acres, or ninety square miles. Morenci has five open-pit mines, three of which are in use today. Wanting a static look at this operation, I stop at a designated turnout and peer down to see a string of large lights illuminating the mine. The innards of the earth are laid out in various colors of pink, yellow, purple, and gray, with a permanent dust that hovers inside the pit, which is approximately two thousand feet deep. As the miners disembowel the earth day in and day out, it is worth remembering that this action has been going on for almost seventy years, continuously. Generations of miners have come and gone here. It is likely that some of the men and women in the pit tonight are the grandsons and granddaughters of the men who clipped off the top of the original mountain that once stood here.

Near the bottom of the pit the workhorses of this operation are busy: large mechanized rotating shovels, called electric rope shovels because they are powered by electric cords as thick as a telephone pole. These machines can pick up seventy cubic yards, or about a hundred tons, of ore in a single scoop. This is how the process works: During the day a crew places charges into drill holes and sets off an explosion, which loosens the ground. After the explosion, the shovels are brought into place to begin loading up the dirt into dump trucks the size of houses. These trucks, measuring twenty-three feet high, fifty feet long, with twenty-four-foot-wide boxes, are one of the technological marvels of hard-rock mining. Depending on the model, they have between two-thousand- and thirty-five-hundred-horsepower engines that allow them to carry between 50 and 240 tons per trip. The most expensive ones, the Caterpillar 797 model, cost upward of $5.5 million and are so large they are built on the mining property by a team of mechanics who take three weeks to assemble the truck. Empty, these giants weigh two hundred tons. Full, they can weigh in at almost six hundred. They carry one thousand gallons of fuel and burn around forty gallons per hour. The tires alone measure thirteen feet tall and cost more than $40,000 each.

With more than seventy of these earthmovers, the Morenci mine has one of the largest fleets of mining trucks in the world. On a good day, nearly a million tons of raw ore are processed in Morenci. Most of that will be what is referred to as "waste," dirt that has no valuable minerals. Crews recycle this dirt back into the pit, essentially backfilling the hole while other crews continue to expand in other directions.

Everywhere I look, trucks are driving up and down a road as wide as a six-lane highway, either full ones delivering ore or empty ones driving back to get more. I wonder what it is like to drive a two-hundred-ton truck for a night shift in a mine. What mental games would I create to stay awake and to keep away thoughts questioning my occupation? I know from my trips to other mines that there is a building somewhere on the property full of men sipping coffee and tracking each movement of these trucks and the people who drive them. The Morenci mine was one of the first in the world to use GPS technology and computer-controlled dispatching in the haul trucks and shovels. The company frequently updates the algorithms created for these trucks using data collected by real-time positioning software. They monitor the speed of the truck, the gas mileage, and the amount of time it takes the driver to take a bathroom break. They monitor noise, pollution, vibration, and the tire pressure. Nothing is unchecked. It is all about safety and time management, not spying. The ones driving the trucks know that how they perform in their twelve hours behind the wheel will be reflected in their weekly checks.

In most mines throughout the United States, miners are evaluated several times a year for bonuses and raises, and their safety records are one of the most, if not the most, important components of their ability to climb the economic ladder. And crashing a truck usually results in a deadly outcome. In 2009 in Ray, Arizona—150 miles to the northwest—two men in a pickup truck were called to inspect one of these trucks. They drove to the truck yard and waited. Meanwhile, a miner just beginning his shift started up his truck and drove over the smaller pickup, killing one man and injuring the other.

Having seen enough of this mine for the night, I drive back to the motel. As I lie in bed with the air conditioner on, my thoughts drift to my life at home, where my wife is busy with two children under the age of three. When I am home, we share in the daily duties of changing diapers, cleaning up messes, and calming the crying and screaming, all while trying to figure out how to make a living. I find some blissful relief being able to lie in this bed, alone, with the possibility of sleeping through the night. All day long my mind has been consumed with thoughts of Morenci, the mine, and mining. When I am home, I can barely remember the topic of mining, and I live in a town with a man-made mining crater in the *middle* of it. Life is just too busy to look up: kids, paying the bills, sleep deprivation. My friends and I rarely speak of the mine. Until

I got sick from the dirt in my yard I never thought of the mine as anything but a novelty, a unique component of living in a Wild West town. Now, staring at the water-stained ceiling of this crumbling room, I realize my version of Bisbee is too perfect to be real. At the same time I have a sinking feeling that any place we decide to live in this world will harbor its own particular type of poison.

In the morning, I join the mine tour, hoping to see copper mining up close. I am the youngest person by far on the bus, which is filled with retirees in T-shirts, baseball caps, white socks, and white tennis shoes. The wives wear visors and tinted sunglasses. The men all have cell phones attached to their pleated tan shorts. The tour guide, a retired miner, singles me out and says, "There aren't any jobs in Morenci right now."

At the time I have no idea what he means, but later I find out that many young men take the mine tour prior to filling out applications for work. He thinks I am scouting the place for a potential job. I wonder if I could ever work here as a miner. Maybe driving the big trucks, or in the machine shop? Or maybe fusing pipes? I have worked as a commercial fisherman, so the hard work does not scare me. But the idea of constantly digging the same hole day in and day out does.

The two-hour mine tour takes us through the entire process of extracting copper from the earth. It is a seemingly simple process yet one that has been modified continuously for almost eight thousand years. And although copper mining is straightforward in theory—find a rock with copper, pound it into pieces, burn out the commingling metals in the rock, and pick out the copper— nothing is trouble-free when dealing with almost a million tons of rock per day. Moving earth is the easy part. It is all the minerals and metals embedded in the rocks with the copper that make hard-rock copper mining both expensive to operate and an environmental hazard.

There are very few "veins" of copper mined today. Since pure copper nuggets are rare, most copper is found in trace amounts, called porphyry copper, low-grade copper attached to various minerals, such as cuprite, azurite, chalcopyrite, malachite, and turquoise. Once taken from the earth, the metal undergoes one of two extraction processes that remove the minerals, leaving only the copper behind.

If the copper has not been exposed to air or water, it is called a sulfide mineral. Common minerals associated with sulfuric copper are chalcopyrite, chalcocite, and bornite. In Morenci, chalcopyrite, also known as yellow copper due to its golden color, is the dominant primary copper sulfide. Sulfide ore bodies, which are much more common in the world, cause the greatest pollution risk because when the ore is exposed to air and water, it instantly begins to dissolve, thus creating "acid rock drainage," in other words a hemorrhaging of acidic water. Once the oxidization begins, toxic metals trapped in the ore are released, sending metals such as lead, arsenic, and cadmium leaching into the surrounding area. The eventual contamination to surrounding groundwater is not a matter of *if* but *when.*

If the copper has been oxidized, it means at some point over the last several hundred million years it was exposed to air and water. Oxidized copper is usually associated with azurite, malachite, chrysocolla, and turquoise. In Morenci, the predominant oxide copper mineral is chrysocolla.

Exposing the actual minerals that contain the copper is often the most expensive phase of mining. To get to the copper, a certain amount of overburden must be taken away. This can be thought of as a cap, a piece of Earth's crust that has to be dug through; the larger the cap, the more expensive the mine and the greater the destruction. Furthermore, since most mines in the world today are sulfuric ore bodies, the moment the digging begins, the acid rock drainage also begins. Basically we are digging up elements in the earth that have never been exposed so quickly to air and water.

When considering whether to begin a mine, the cost-benefit analysis is based on several factors, one of them being the thickness of the cap. Even though it is estimated that there is enough copper within a mile of Earth's surface to supply the world's needs for a million years, getting to the copper is the challenge.

One of the ways hard-rock mining has increased its efficiency and profitability is during the smelting process. The traditional method of extracting copper from ore is smelting, whereby once the ore is crushed by whatever means necessary, the minerals are burned out, leaving behind the metal. This has been the more popular method for several thousand years. Smelting also results in an impure molten metal copper, which must go through an electrolytic purification process to extract the copper from the iron oxide, which cannot be burned out. The remaining iron becomes slag, a by-product often used in sandblasting to remove paint from ships' hulls, bridges, and other surfaces. Long believed to be relatively harmless, this practice of using copper slag has gone on for decades, but that may change soon. In March 2012, the Occupational Safety and Health Administration (OSHA) released a report stating copper slag contains trace amounts of the highly toxic beryllium, arsenic, and various other contaminants. Even though many sand-blasting companies use safety gear, including air-fed respirators, inhaling even the smallest amounts of beryllium, a naturally occurring metal in rocks, can cause chronic beryllium disease, which causes scarring of the lung tissue and can lead to shortness of breath, fatigue, and eventually heart problems.

Traditional smelting is highly polluting, with large smelter stacks belching out toxic metals, a practice still common throughout the world, with the dominant players being Japan and China. Due to regulations and a growing resistance to having smelter stacks near communities, smelters have become uncommon in North America. Also as mining technology advances, smelting is a costly choice, mostly because in large open-pit operations the rock must be pulverized so completely that it is like talcum powder before the copper can be extracted, which uses vast amounts of costly energy.

Morenci uses a different method, which relies entirely on leaching, or putting the rocks out in a large pile and covering them with a sulfuric acid solution to melt the copper away from the ore body, speeding up what would happen naturally if the ore were exposed to rain and air for long periods of time. Sitting on top of the leaching fields is an elaborate sprinkler system that constantly wets down the pulverized rock with a mixture of sulfuric acid and water. Once detached from the host rock, the copper seeps to the bottom of the pile, which has a catchment system to funnel the copper-laden solution from the leaching field to a company pond. From there the solution is transferred to an electrolytic tank, where it undergoes electroextraction, also known as electrowinning. In this process, a current is passed from an anode through the copper solution, allowing pure copper ions to migrate away from the solution toward cathodes placed in the tank. The resulting copper, now in the hardened metal form of a cathode, gets dried and stacked in bundles, finally becoming copper ready for the market.

Because dry smelting extracts copper into a liquid solution, it allows mines all over the world to get more copper from lower-grade ores, some of which have been sitting in large fields near shut-down mines for decades. It is also a self-contained operation. The sulfuric acid runs through pipes over the ore body, and then when separated from the copper it is recaptured to be recycled over and over again.

In theory, the leaching process at Morenci mitigates sulfuric acid runoff, which usually occurs when mines expose minerals to the air and water and leave them in large piles to decay without any control over the discharge.

Of course this invention, or any invention, cannot prevent all human error, or explain how 168,000 gallons of sulfuric acid were dumped from the Morenci mine into the Chase Creek riverbed on October 30, 2008. The narrative offered by Freeport is that the company acted quickly on this potential environmental disaster and built a few earthen dams to stop the flow. What the company doesn't talk about is how the liquid, after being stopped behind the dams, likely seeped into the groundwater. In Utah, there is a seventy-square-mile sulfuric acid plume extending underground outward from the Kennecott mine toward surrounding communities. Known as the world's largest man-made excavation, Kennecott is also one of the world's largest groundwater contamination sites. The damage was mostly done during a twenty-seven-year process, between 1964 and 1990, when millions of gallons of sulfuric acid leaked day after day into the surrounding groundwater. There are extremely costly solutions to mitigate this problem, such as water-processing plants, but in truth no one has come up with a solution to sulfuric acid poisoning groundwater other than using an alternative source of water.

Evidence of what can happen when highly acidic copper ore is released into the natural world is perhaps understood best by looking at China's track record. In the summer of 2010, the Zijin Mining Group spilled 2.4 million gallons of acidic copper from the Zijinshan mine into the Ting River, killing enough fish to feed seventy thousand people for a year. The *Guardian* reported that residents in nearby villages have long gone without a local source of water and know to keep their bodies out of the Ting due to the swelling and itching caused by exposure to the water. That large environmental disasters happen repeatedly every year somewhere in the world is no surprise, but it does make me wonder at what point the damage caused by extracting minerals will alter how we justify the many conveniences of our modern lives.

A small footnote: Freeport ended up paying a $150,000 fine for the 168,000 gallons it spilled in Morenci. It made page ten of the Tucson newspaper. For a multinational company like Freeport, this is just the cost of doing business.

Like most of the mining towns in Arizona, Morenci is remote. The only nearby town is Clifton, which has been here as long as Morenci. Some historians say Geronimo was born approximately where the town of Clifton now stands, only a few miles down the road. This would make sense. A peaceful setting, Clifton sits in a canyon surrounded by high cliffs at the confluence of the Blue and San Francisco Rivers, tucked between the Gila and Peloncillo mountain ranges. Before white men arrived, it would have had plenty of game and a constant source of water, perhaps the reason the Spanish conquistador Coronado journeyed through modern-day Clifton on his quest for the lost city of gold. Eventually the trade route meant that bartering could be counted upon. I imagine Geronimo trekking up and down the mountains as a young boy, curious about the wave of desperate immigrants moving west like a herd of lost buffalo. He could never have guessed these outsiders would arrive, find the red metal that his people used for ornamentation, and build an empire that would eventually kill them.

Clifton has always been a blue-collar community, the majority of whom are of Mexican heritage. And even though for almost a hundred years nearly everyone in Clifton has had someone in the family drawing a check from the mine, the residents have never welcomed the company's invitations to control their world. Like in Old Bisbee, miners built Clifton, and the houses reflect the individuals who built them. Today Freeport owns everything forty feet beneath Clifton and can mine to Earth's core, but up on top Clifton remains a town of fiercely independent and proud people whose main goal in life is to remain separate from Morenci.

These two communities are divided religiously, ethnically, and socially, but also by history—by an event that happened after the sun went down on October 1, 1904.

On that date, a train entered Clifton carrying forty orphans, age two to six, who had made the seven-day trip to Morenci from New York City. They had traveled across the country to be placed with their new families, all of whom had been carefully chosen through months of correspondence between the New York Foundling Hospital—a Catholic institution—and the Sacred Heart Church in Morenci. On board were three nuns of the Sisters of Charity charged with looking after the children's welfare.

As described in Linda Gordon's comprehensive and fascinating book *The Great Arizona Orphan Abduction,* the orphans disembarked into the hands of their designated adopted families, which happened to be almost entirely Catholic Mexican families living in Clifton. It didn't take long before the white people in Morenci and Clifton realized that all the new children were Caucasian, mostly of Irish decent, and they were rushing straight into the open arms of Mexican families who had filed all the legal adoption papers. Charles Mills, the Phelps Dodge mine manager, was called. Riding with the sheriff and deputy of the county, Mills became judge and jury as they rounded up an armed posse and went door to door, took the children from their appointed Mexican families, and gave them to white families. In their minds they were doing the right thing. They were doing the *white* thing. In all, nineteen boys and girls changed hands that night. When a mob of white men and women almost attacked the nuns, the mine manager stepped in—after he took a child himself as a gift for a friend of his—and allowed the nuns to take the remaining twenty-one children back to New York.

Eventually, a prominent Catholic attorney in Tucson named Eugene Ives filed charges on behalf of the Foundling Hospital of New York against those who entered the homes of the Mexican families and forcibly took the children.

The racial question was only part of the tension in Morenci and Clifton. Religion also played a key role. The orphans and their adoptive parents were Catholic. The majority of the Anglos in the two towns and Phelps Dodge management were Protestant. As the legal battle began to take shape, it was clear that the prominent Catholics of Arizona were willing to fight against the newly arrived but much more powerful Protestants.

Ives did not file kidnapping charges on behalf of the children. He knew that no court or jury in the Arizona territory of 1904 would convict white people of "rescuing" orphaned white children from Mexican homes. Mexican families were not even legal citizens, let alone legitimate plaintiffs. Instead, the charge was on the basis of habeas corpus: that the children's civil rights had been violated when armed posses entered their guardians' homes and took them elsewhere. The charges did not address the Mexican families' civil rights being violated, or that armed men illegally entered their homes. That was never an issue in the eyes of the court. It was strictly a question of the children's civil rights.

Gordon describes the scene of the courtroom in Phoenix. No Mexican was present. No Mexican was called as a witness. This was an Anglo matter to be settled by Anglos. The Arizona courts sided with the vigilante Anglos, and eventually the case was taken to the U.S. Supreme Court on appeal. There, in 1906, the case was dismissed on the basis that children had no personal freedom rights to violate. They had a right only to care and custody, and because the children were Caucasians living with undocumented Mexicans, their kidnapping was seen as legal and just.

In Clifton, copper was first found in Chase Creek, which runs through the heart of the old part of town. The locals like to say that when it rained hard, Chase Creek would literally run green, a result of the native copper bleeding off the rocks during rainstorms. Today the copper is of such poor quality that it takes a hundred tons of earth to yield half a ton of copper.

Sitting in the mining museum on Chase Creek is Don Lunt. Though retired now, he's a company man. He loves Phelps Dodge, always has. He misses the company and doesn't know anyone with Freeport, or what he calls "the new outfit." He lives in Clifton but spent his entire working life up the road in Morenci. He worked in the mine for forty-five years, first as a boiler room operator and finally as a supervisor.

He walks me around the room, showing me old photographs and talking about the mine in the old days. He tells me his wife's grandparents came to Morenci in the late 1880s from Italy, to work in the mine. Her parents were born here, and she was born here. Everyone worked in the mine.

"I love this mine, still do," he says, showing me a photo of some 1920s women dressed in their finest attire, ready for a social outing in Clifton.

I ask about the differences between Clifton and Morenci.

"Well, Morenci is owned by the company, and Clifton isn't. And the company didn't let Mexicans shower with us or pay them as much. But World War II changed all that. How can a man fight next to you and then come home and not get paid the same, answer me that?"

I ask about the famous strike in 1983 that shut down the mine for two years. In the end, Bruce Babbitt, then governor of Arizona, called in the National Guard and crushed the striking workers, not only ending the strike in Morenci but also effectively ending all union power in Arizona mining. While many powerful companies had been fighting labor since the turn of the twentieth century, many economists single out this strike as the beginning of corporations using strikebreaking as a way to change their business model for the long haul. The idea was to not give in, under any circumstance. It was seen as a major precedent for future labor negotiations across the country, none of which favored labor.

"When it started, I watched quietly to see what was going to happen. But eventually I crossed the line and went to work. I mean, at some point you have to make a decision and I decided to work. I had a family. And there are still people in this town today that won't speak to me because I crossed the lines twenty-five years ago, but the hell with that," says Don. "Every man has to decide for himself."

The events that transpired during the 1983 strike in Morenci still ripple throughout the town, and the state of Arizona. Barbara Kingsolver's book *Holding the Line* is a detailed account of the strike and the social and economic fallout that followed. She describes how what a person, or person in his family, did—cross the line or not—would come to define anyone who was born and raised in these two towns. Even today many families don't speak to one another based on how they acted in the strike almost thirty years ago. Many of the retired workers were in the union but were fired during the strike and reapplied to the mine without union status, thus being able to play both sides of the story. Today, as a result of the Morenci copper strike, the mine is a non-union operation.

I drive out of town ten miles and then turn around and approach the mine from the south, taking the same route I drove last night when I arrived in Morenci. The road dips to the banks of the San Francisco River, and as I near Clifton large heaps of black slag hang over the riverbank like a frozen waterfall of steel. These huge banks of iron ore are artifacts from those early miners. Visually they are out of place, and it is hard not to keep staring at the black cliffs, mostly because it looks like they are going to fall into the river at any time. But they won't. Slag is hard as rock.

Up on the hillside, in Morenci, stands a cluster of newer, blue-roofed homes, each the same. Every yard is dirt surrounded by a low chain-link fence. Some are empty, with the gas and electric lines dangling on the side of the house, waiting for an occupant to move in. Because Morenci is a company town, these homes are not rented to the general public. They are either occupied or empty depending on the level of production at the mine. In 2008, when copper prices plummeted, Freeport abruptly stopped paying the subcontractors who were building the homes, and many not completed were left abandoned. The miners who had been hired and planned to live in those houses were laid off, some before they ever set foot in Morenci. As of 2012, copper prices are up and the mine is once again near full production, and workers and their families are moving back in.

Driving up the mountain, I cruise some of the older Morenci neighborhoods. I pass hundreds of houses, all with a similar efficient design. Most are two-bedroom wood homes with faded white paint. For larger families, there are three-bedroom units. No house stands alone, each physically attached to the next by a garage, which has one parking space for each house. Built by the company, each block reflects a sense of collective submission. The only signs of individualism are the types of pickup trucks the occupants buy, or the number of ATVs that sit in the driveway.

On the way home I pass several tractor-trailers carrying stacks of cathodes—99.9 percent pure copper sheets that Morenci produces every day of the year. They weigh between one hundred and three hundred fifty pounds, are one-quarter to three-quarters of an inch thick, and are one square meter in size. They are bundled in sizes ranging from four thousand pounds to sixty-five hundred pounds and are a legally tradable unit on the international metal exchanges.

Most mines ship the cathodes to mills or foundries where they are melted and cast into wire rods, billets, cakes, or ingots, with each category having a different shape and dimension, allowing metal fabricators to buy the one that best fits their needs. Wire rods are coils of half-inch rod used to make copper wire of all gauges. Billets are eight-inch-diameter logs shaped to specification for anything ranging from copper piping to tubes to an artist's installation. Cake is a slab of pure copper that can be rolled into a sheet or plate and is used as copper backing in appliances, cars, and large roof installations, or to make bed rails for hospitals. An ingot is a brick of pure copper that is alloyed with another metal, usually zinc, which when mixed with copper makes brass.

"We have three wire rod plants," says Eric Kinneberg, director of external communications for Freeport-McMoRan. "One in El Paso, one in Miami, [Arizona], and one in Norwich, Connecticut."

I ask if cathodes are the only way the copper leaves the mine.

"No, we also ship copper concentrate, to our smelter in Miami, which then produces cathodes to ship to one of our rod plants."

The concentrate is a copper liquid that contains other metals that could not be extracted in the electrowinning process at Morenci and thus have to be burned out by using the traditional smelting methods.

Freeport also operates a factory in Elizabeth, New Jersey, where it manufactures specialty copper products such as trolley wire, tin-coated wire, and various custom orders. Besides being the world's largest manufacturer of cast copper rods, Freeport sells copper sulfate pentahydrate, which is used in animal feed as well as herbicides and fungicides.

While I am pondering all this information, my truck breaks down outside Douglas, Arizona. In what I think is a strange coincidence, the man who picks me up in the tow truck is a mine worker who has been laid off from Morenci.

"I drove a dump truck. They gave me thirty days to leave," he says, driving me back to Bisbee. "They said I could stay and have really cheap rent, and go to work at the Safford mine," referring to another Freeport mine fifty miles from Morenci. "I didn't want to commute from Morenci to Safford, so I moved back to Douglas."

I quickly realize the fact that my driver is a miner is not a coincidence, but a statistical reality. Southern Arizona has ten large copper mines. Employees or ex-employees are bound to be more common than, say, bankers. I ask about Morenci, telling him the place feels like a depressed camp.

"Its an old boys' network," he says. "Always has been, even when Phelps Dodge ran it. Freeport is better in terms of safety and bonuses, but Phelps Dodge didn't fire people so easily. Freeport fires real quick. And the drug problems in that camp are out of control. Meth and coke, mostly."

We lumber past the lime mine, just outside Bisbee. "I worked there for three years," he says, nodding at the distant front-loaders clawing away at a mountain of lime. "A good job, but I left that job to go to Morenci and then I got laid off. Now I'm driving a tow truck, and the pay sucks."

Drugs and mining go hand in hand and always have. In the late 1800s, almost every mining camp in the western United States had a satellite Chinatown, where the opium dens could be found. The combined money and hard work attracted both the demand and eventually the supply of drugs. There are no longer any opium dens on the outskirts of town. Instead, meth dealers drive up to Circle K and exchange a twenty with the guy going to play a cheap round of golf on his day off after working five night shifts at the mine.

"Once," continues my driver, "I walk into the shift room, and there are drug dogs lined up at the entryway. No one knew that was going to happen. The dogs went over all our belongings, even the clothes we were wearing. Some guys were taken off to the side. Never saw them again. Fired."

The day is lovely. The window is down and I smell the distinct aroma of creosote rising from the desert after a recent rain. Thirty years ago I doubt anyone smelled this. The drive from Douglas to Bisbee is twenty-two miles and used to be choked with pollution. Phelps Dodge built Douglas, named after James Douglas, the president of Phelps Dodge and the man most responsible for establishing large-scale copper mining in Arizona in 1912, specifically for the sole purpose of erecting a smelter away from Bisbee.

For decades, Douglas, along with Cananea and Nacozari, both in Mexico, were known as the "Gray Triangle," a reference to the three-thousand-plus tons of sulfur dioxide being poured daily into the atmosphere from these three smelter operations. In 1985, independent studies by the Environmental Defense Fund and supported by the Environmental Protection Agency found the smelters in the Gray Triangle to be responsible for large amounts of acid rain falling on the Rockies. At the time, the smelter in Douglas was the country's single largest source of sulfur dioxide, a distinction usually reserved for coal-burning electric plants. Douglas produced, on average, 950 tons of the poison every day until the smelter was decommissioned in the late 1980s and taken down in 1991.

The ex-miner and current tow truck driver drops me off in front of the Copper Queen Hotel in downtown Bisbee, which is also the longest continuously operating full-service hotel in Arizona. When I ask if he thinks he will ever work in a mine again, he says, "Hell, yes. Open it up and I will be there. Love the shifts, the days off, the money. Just fucking hate the boredom of it all."

I wave good-bye to the driver and take my place at the end of the Copper Queen bar, where I begin a conversation with a hydrologist doing contract work for the mine. This, too, may seem coincidental, but these contractors are everywhere in town. They rent our houses, eat at the diners, and have their mail forwarded for a few months while they drill holes in the hills around Bisbee.

The bartender asks if I would like another. I tell her I would. The hobo musician behind me stomps on the floor with his Depression-era boots while his fingers strum a banjo. He sings about drifting from town to town seeking a love he can't find. Of course, that is the key to everything.

I ask the man, who is a water expert, if he thinks the mine will reopen.

"Well, there is plenty of copper there, but some of it is ripe for open-pit and some of it would be better suited for underground work. Either way there is a lot of water down there."

He tells me that the twenty-seven hundred miles of tunnels have been filling with water for almost thirty-five years, ever since the pumps were turned off. When I ask about the sulfuric acid plume that has been draining from the tailing pile in the direction of our town's aquifer, he shrugs his shoulders and says, "Maybe another fifty years before it gets there. Really hard to stop that one."

I take a gulp and do the math. One way or another I'll be worm food by then, but my kids won't be.

"If you pump a million gallons a day for five years straight, it would clear the mines. But you would have to build a hundred-million-dollar water plant to get rid of the poisons in that water before it hit the aquifer."

The hydrologist tells me he will stay a few more days, then collect his paycheck and move on to another mine in another town.

Before I say good night I have to ask him why he likes this line of work when it can be depressing to find out such bad news about these places all the time.

He says, with very little emotion, "They pay great."

A week later I walk into the Burger King in San Jose, a satellite community built around a mining site that was eventually annexed into the city boundaries of Bisbee. Sitting at two tables near the soda fountain are six men, all over the age of seventy. For the past decade, these men, and several others who are not present today, have been gathering at 9:00 a.m. to share coffee and yell at one another; they are all partially deaf.

I sit with Ben, Bud, and Jim, who among them have more than eighty years in the mines, almost all of it underground, in Bisbee. Since their retirements, they have been coming to Burger King for coffee.

"It's not healthy to go to bed hungry," says Bud, as he explains why he went to work underground. He tells me he came from Paris, Texas, in 1950 to work in the mine after serving two years in the Pacific theater in World War II.

"Back then they were paying almost twelve dollars a day. I was making half that in Texas. So I got here and went to work."

I ask if they liked their employer, Phelps Dodge. They all smirk, and look at one another in a way that suggests they still feel obligated not to speak ill of the hand that fed them and their families for a generation.

"Listen," says Jim, "here is the truth. They never gave anything to us that we didn't have to fight for."

"I sure as hell wouldn't work in the mines today. I wouldn't," says Bud. "They don't have any unions to back them up."

"We had to strike for nine months in 1967 just to get our pensions to the level they are now." Jim laughs slightly, in disgust.

"I collect two pensions," adds Ben, who grew up in Benson, an hour from Bisbee. "One from the county and one from Phelps Dodge, and I worked for Phelps Dodge much longer than I did for the county and the county gives me a bigger pension. That is all you need to know about Phelps Dodge."

Jim worked underground for twenty-eight years, right up until the day the mine closed in 1975. After that, the company transferred him to Morenci, where he worked another eight years.

I ask all of them if they liked living in Bisbee during the life of the mine. Did they enjoy raising their kids here?

Almost in unison they say, "It was fantastic. Best little town you could imagine."

"And Morenci?" I ask Jim.

"Morenci is a hellhole. An absolute dump," he says.

I remind myself that company towns were not built to coddle workers. They were not built to be nice. They were built to make the workers more efficient and to increase profit by owning everything the miners would spend their money on. It was a self-contained economic, social, and political system. Many people, even after they have "escaped" the company town, stay connected through a short economic rope, a slave to the consistent paycheck. They become contractors or part-time workers for the mine.

I have spent many hours talking to people who remember living in Bisbee when the mine was open. To them it was always a PD—Phelps Dodge—town. They look back on their childhoods, and adult lives, with great nostalgia, even with a reverence for the mine and those who did the work. They have a glow in their eyes and a small rise in their voice as they talk about how PD built this school, paid for Fourth of July fireworks, or sponsored the five thousand eggs for the annual Easter egg hunt down at the baseball park, one of the oldest in the country. I can't help but wonder if these feelings of nostalgia mask the manipulations of PD and the fact that the families were trapped in a spiral of economic dependence, a kind of corporate Stockholm syndrome.

In the end, the workers actually think the company, which deftly plays the kidnapper role by trapping a person for a life of work, is looking out for their best interests. They think the town is theirs and that the company has their back. That usually lasts until the company fires them.

Today, most workers can choose not to live in mining communities full-time, but they also can't seem to walk away. I know the money is better than any other job in the area, but I am convinced there is something else dragging them back. No one speaks of it in these terms, but for many it is all they know. They don't know another way to function, and like recidivists who find their way back to the safe confines of prison, they can never actually be free.

5

Cananea

The miners lost because they had only the constitution. The other side had bayonets. In the end, bayonets always win.

—Mother Jones

Up to this point, my travels have taught me about the relationships between mining companies and miners. So far the pattern reveals money and power playing key parts in a frayed marriage between labor and management. But to really get to the bottom of things I need to get out of the country. But not far, only thirty miles south of town. I've heard of this place. Now it's time to see it.

Cananea is home to the largest copper mine in Mexico as well as the birthplace of the 1910 Mexican Revolution. The city of thirty-five thousand is not on any tourist maps, and even though it is not so far from my house, few people from Bisbee have ever been to Cananea. I have a hard time finding people who have even heard of the place. There is a good reason for this. As with most mining towns throughout the world, there are very few reasons to visit.

Of the three roads in and out of town, one leads over a treacherous mountain pass to Hermosillo, a death trap of a road. The road north heads to the border town of Naco, a sleepy village eight miles from Bisbee where locals go for an occasional lunch or some cheap pharmaceuticals. The third road heads south out of Cananea and is steeped in a history of blood and adventure.

The hardest to find, it's actually a horse trail that in time became a two-lane road that crisscrosses the Sonora River several times. This is the famed route of Father Kino, the wandering Jesuit, and the original conquistadors as they made their way north, into what was known as Northern Mexico. Today this rarely traveled road is a favorite of the modern conquistadors, the drug smugglers and human traffickers.

The first mention of Cananea in the history books is in the writings of the ubiquitous Kino, who covers the ground from Sonora, Mexico, to Northern California as he rides his donkey in search of new souls. Even though he mentions a place called Cananea, there was no town to speak of, only a smattering of ranches along the Río Sonora. In 1750, fifty years before Kino marched his way across the American West, a group of Jesuit priests had already found gold and copper in Cananea, but like all miners of that time they discarded the copper and kept the gold, which was more valuable by weight and thus easier to move on the backs of mule trains.

Copper and gold tend to run in geological clusters, and it makes sense that there are vast copper deposits to the north and south of Bisbee. Still, it wasn't until the late 1800s that Cananea took the shape of a mining camp, specifically an American mining camp. In 1896, a man by the name of William Cornell Greene created the Greene Consolidated Copper Company to begin mining for copper in Cobre Grande—the Great Copper Mine. It was later sold to the Anaconda mining company. By 1899, the mine was producing seventy million pounds of copper a year, making it one of the world's great sources of copper. In 1971, the mine was nationalized by the Mexican government and sold for pennies on the dollar to another company, Grupo Mexico. Since 1994, a businessman by the name of Germán Larrea Mota-Velasco has been the chairman and president of Grupo Mexico. Mota-Velasco and his family control 50 percent of the company and as of 2011 his personal fortune was estimated to be north of $16 billion, making him the third-richest man in Mexico. Naturally, he wants to fire all the union workers at Cananea and hire contract workers for less pay and reduced benefits.

I arrive in Cananea in late May with the temperature hover-ing near 103 degrees. I am with Alexandra Boneo, originally from Agua Prieta, Mexico. I know her from Bisbee, although it turns out I don't know her that well. On the drive south I ask why she has volunteered to translate for me, and she tells me her father, now dead, was a miner from Cananea and had a secret second family there. She has arranged for her half sister to be our introduction to the miners. I ask if she has a good relationship with her half sister.

"We have never met," Alex says with a giggle as we enter the town.

Cananea, which originates in the Apache language, means horse meat. The Apaches, who considered the horse to be a culinary delicacy, were believed to ride their horses to death and then eat them. Today, the only horses in sight are a few paper-thin specimens on the outskirts of town. In another direction, cattle roam a barren field. Dogs, lots of dogs, scamper down side streets and cower at the sight of humans. As in most of southern Arizona and Sonora there are not many Apaches left, though you can see their Asian features in the occasional face of a local, long ago passed along through marriage, rape, or both.

My wife and I used to travel through northern Sonora two or three times a year, headed to hot springs, beaches, or mountain retreats. Almost every time we passed right by Cananea on our way to the Río Sonora valley. Today I travel to Mexico only if I have to. And I make it a point *not* to have to.

Like many towns within an hour of the border, Cananea has a history of violence related to the drug cartels. On May 16, 2007, fifty heavily armed men traveled in a caravan of dark-colored Suburbans from Caborca—a notorious smuggler's town deep in Sonora—up the scenic Río Sonora valley and into Cananea. Upon arrival, the caravan quickly kidnapped four policemen from the small city and executed them. They killed another on their way out of town and took a businessman hostage. By the time the Mexican army arrived, with helicopters and hundreds of troops, the gunmen were headed back down the Río Sonora valley seeking refuge in the Sierra Madre Mountains. By the end of the bloody battle, fifteen hit men and five officers were killed.

Today, I hope, will not be so dramatic.

Alex's half sister has instructed us to meet near the disco on the edge of town. She says to look for the sign. She will be waiting under it in a red truck. After some delay, we find the sister, and her boyfriend, sitting in a brown truck under a sign stripped of all its lettering, in front of a building that looks abandoned, another victim of the boom/bust cycles of a mine.

The sister and Alex look nothing alike. She is much paler than Alex. Her only true connection to the mine, other than her father's history, is her boyfriend, who used to work there until the recent strike. The boyfriend is quiet and seemingly preoccupied. All he keeps saying is that the strike is terrible and that the labor union is unbreakable.

After an awkward family reunion, the sister and her boyfriend take us to the mine.

Downtown Cananea resembles many mining towns that have gone bust. We pass the post office, the jail, and finally the union office, where dozens of idle men eyeball each and every car that passes. Tension here runs high. Many here assume any new face in town works either for Grupo Mexico or the government, both always searching for ways to erode the resolve of the striking miners. Not long after the strike began in 2007, the government accused Napoleon Gomez, the secretary general of the 250,000-member union of Mining, Metallurgical, Steel and Allied Workers of Mexico, also known as Los Mineros, of embezzling $55 million. With the help of unions from the United States and Canada, he fled to Vancouver, where he lives today in exile. Even though Swiss auditors and Mexican courts have exonerated Gomez of any criminal acts, he remains a refugee. To further tighten the noose around the striking miners, the government of Mexico has frozen nearly $20 million of the union's assets.

The road to the mine begins just beyond the union office, where it dips to the lowest point in town. Directly below are the headwaters of the Sonora River, which runs south to the Sierra Madre Mountains. Every summer, when the monsoons hit, the locals say this spot floods for weeks on end.

We go uphill. I can tell a mine exists even before I see it. Out the window are all the telltale signs of a mining operation: rusting buildings, abandoned offices, broken tractors, slag heaps, and just in case I wasn't sure, a small creek that runs red and yellow, a sure sign of acid rock drainage, also called acid mine drainage. The day is hot, but still I find it slightly unusual that there are no people in sight, only the occasional dog crossing the street.

We weave around three barricades, piles of rocks situated in such a way as to slow, not stop, oncoming vehicles. At the gates of the mine sit dozens of men in chairs hugging whatever shade they can find. Nearby is a tent with a large black-and-red flag, the symbol of Los Mineros union. In the parking lot, where weeds grow freely, half a dozen men play soccer.

The gates to the mine stand ten feet tall with three-inch-thick bars of solid steel. A large mining truck sits inside the gate, like a mighty centaur guarding the portal to Middle Earth. I try to imagine the scene at these gates one year ago. The black burn marks on the side of the truck are evidence of the battle that raged when the state police attacked the striking miners in order to open the gates.

The impasse began in 2007, when the workers demanded safer working conditions and better wages. The striking miners have been standing here ever since, staring into a dead mine, like guardians of a temple long forgotten by the gods.

In the first battle, five hundred men in police uniforms took on more than a thousand men in Levi's, pointy boots, and cowboy hats. Gunfire erupted and police helicopters began dropping tear gas bombs. When the police charged the gate, the miners didn't bend. The line held. Injuries were sustained and there were rumors that five men went missing. Instead of breaking the resolve of the union, the battle emboldened the miners' resolve. They haven't left their post since then and have no plans on giving up the strike.

I approach the group of men gathered under a tent preparing lunch. One man tells me he is a crane operator but hasn't worked in two years. I ask how they support themselves.

"It is difficult these days. We had some savings, but that is long gone. Other unions in Mexico give a small percentage of their pay to support us. Some unions in America send money. Otherwise we rely on small jobs we can do in town, or friends," says one man whom everyone calls El Loco.

A man named Rafael takes me to the water tower, to get an eagle's-eye view of the town and mine.

Rafael remembers a better time, when the Americans ran the place and paid for the electricity and gas in all the miners' houses. And they each received a healthy stipend toward paying the water bill. He remembers the barbeques with his family and friends, all of whom either worked at the mine or had retired from there. There were down payments on new cars, trips to Arizona for vacations, and bikes for the kids. He longs for the days of Anaconda, the mining company once owned by the powerful Rockefeller family. Back then, the social contract between the company and the town was honored. People like Rafael felt respected. But since the mine was nationalized and sold to Grupo Mexico, Rafael says miners are just one more piece of machinery in the system, expendable.

The hot wind whips dust in our faces until we hide behind the large steel tank. Toward the horizon, in the direction of the Sonora River, is a vast field of what looks like a salt flat. Rising from it is a white dust that reaches up to the sky in long strands resembling a desert rainstorm. This is silica, a dust particle that is a known killer, especially of copper miners. Rafael tells me of those who have died, usually after retirement, in Cananea. Across the globe an unknown number of miners die every year from the superfine particles that lodge in the lungs. After many years, the silica causes a host of problems, the most fatal being silicosis, which survivors often describe as breathing fiberglass. At a certain stage the disease is incurable, like black lung or asbestos poisoning. In the end, the miner sucks oxygen through a tube until the lungs give up. Occasionally there is a class-action lawsuit against various mining companies, but they rarely gain traction. Instead a few dollars are paid to the surviving members of the family, and if the mining town is still the single largest employer within a hundred miles, it is a good bet the son of the deceased man has already been working at the mine for a few years.

Meanwhile, a steady thirty-mile-per-hour wind blows acres of silica directly toward Bisbee and has been for decades. I've heard a few conversations about this pollution but, like my backyard toxins, never saw it. Only now, staring down at the gigantic field of white dust headed toward my house, do I realize that my wife and daughters, my friends and their kids, are potentially breathing this silica every time the wind blows north.

Rafael and I go back to the gate and seek some shade under the tent, which now holds almost thirty people. Most of the men, sitting and watching one another, slowly shift from one foot to the other. Two of them are cooking around a large metal surface that resembles a wagon wheel. Today's main dish is chorizo, a traditional sausage dish being boiled with a mixture of jalapeños, onions, and minced pork. One man heats up tortillas, while a few more prepare paper plates and small Styrofoam cups of juice. They move their hands from their front pockets to their back pockets and back again. Other than the flies buzzing the air, there is very little sound. There is no noise of work, or play, just a constant wind, blowing toward Norte America. As the meal nears completion, more men gather, some offering up their opinions on how much spice to add. Because I am considered a guest, they insist I take the first plate.

The spice is far beyond my level of comfort, but the food is tasty. A few men laugh at the tears gathering at the corners of my eyes and hand me a juice. I ask if they eat this way every day.

"Every day, for almost two years. We cannot afford to eat individually anymore. Cheaper this way," says El Loco. He used to drive one of the large cranes that scoop up the ore and put it in the back of the large mining trucks.

"I miss my job. I miss my town being the way it is supposed to be," he says. "But we cannot work in these conditions."

A few of the men show me pictures from inside the mine, showing dirt and silica piled knee-high in the crushing mill. "Before we went on strike, it was so dusty I couldn't see a few feet in front of me. That is not right. No one can work like that," he says.

In any safe and well-run mine, large vacuum cleaners are in constant operation, sucking the particles up and out of the buildings where miners work. No mine in the United States would be allowed to operate if those vacuums were not functioning. According to the miners in Cananea, the vacuums that protect the miners' lungs have been broken since 1999, and the company refused to replace them.

"Our families have mined here for a hundred years. We are not afraid of hard work, but we also know what is and what is not a safe workplace. This mine is unsafe. And we know that."

At the same time that Grupo Mexico has ignored basic safety codes, it has also been busy manipulating the government and courts to fire these workers so that it can rehire contract workers, sans benefits, and get back to digging for copper.

The men show me more pictures from inside the mine working areas. All of them show machines that look broken, beyond repair. Still, these men are certain they will win this battle and one day get back to work.

One reason they believe this is ingrained through generations of living here. Cananea is more of a mining town than any other I have ever visited. Bisbee was a mining town that went broke and reinvented itself as part hippie hangout, part artist colony, and part tourist destination. Morenci is a company-owned mining town, but it feels like a gulag. There is no joy in Morenci, only the steady rhythm of work: a ticking clock, sounds of dynamite, and a population that talks only of getting laid off or getting out.

But in Cananea, the mine has long been a source of pride, not just local but also regional and national. In the past, the mine directly or indirectly employed 80 percent of the town. Very few families don't have at least one member working in the mine. And even though many know someone who has died of silica poisoning or been unfairly treated by the employer, the relationship has endured through strikes and shutdowns.

In fact, the mine holds a unique place in Mexican history. In 1906, a strike halted production. William Cornell Greene, the American miner who started the mine in the late 1890s, called in the Arizona Rangers to act as the private police force of the mining company. By the time the strike was over, twenty-three miners had died at the hands of the rangers. In 1910, revolution erupted throughout Mexico, and as the fighting raged it was the 1906 labor strike in Cananea that became the battle cry of intellectuals, peasants, and workers alike.

As the current strike enters its second year, families have been torn apart, with some openly wanting to cross the line and get back to work. It reminds me of discussions I had in Morenci about the two-year strike that began in 1983. In some aspects the town never recovered, and many think it never will.

As we eat, one man asks me what I think about the current strike. He asks if I think they are right or wrong to hold out.

"I think," I start, but then stop, suddenly aware that thirty sets of eyes are watching me. Their faces hardened by the sun, wind, and work. All of these men's fathers and uncles worked this mine, even most of their grandfathers. They have seen owners come and go. They have seen the price of copper skyrocket and then bust. They have raised their families by working every shift in a copper mine that holds enough reserves to mine another hundred years.

"I think the workingman has a hard time against large, rich companies. And I think that is true all over the world," I say.

The men erupt in cheers and slap me on the back, welcoming me into their fraternity. They force me to eat more food. They offer me beer, but I refuse. The heat is unbearable and I have to drive back through the border station.

I ask the men, If the mine reopens, will they allow other workers to take their place?

"Never," one man shouts above all the others. "Our heels are in the soil of Cananea, as we are," he says. "We are at the center of the world for labor. We cannot give in."

I look down the mountain and see a town hanging on by a thread.

"When we win we will have a three-day fiesta on a farm outside town, near the river. We will eat a cow and drink beer. You will be our guest of honor," one man says. We slap hands and laugh deep from the belly, and for the next hour they tell stories of how they are proud miners who will never give up.

Before leaving, we drive out to the golf course, built years ago by the mining company. There is a gated community nearby and rumor has it the CEO of Grupo Mexico has a house here. The boyfriend of Alex's half sister tells the guard he knows someone who lives in one of the houses. Naturally, we are told to turn around by the gate security. I am not that disappointed. And anyway, the chance of any executive spending the night in Cananea seems very remote, unless he wants his windows to be broken.

Later, as Alex and I drive back toward the border, I think of the strike and how it will be resolved. It will not end in the workers' favor. The days of labor winning these battles are long gone.

I know they will end up being fired, kicked out, and left behind as the mining company pays the new workers less, forgoes any health insurance, and doubles its profits. I know this because that is how big business works in the world today. Labor lost the upper hand a long time ago, and today the upper hand is with the mining executives, the shareholders, and the politicians they influence.

I can't help but think that victory for these miners, even at this storied mine, is a faint dream buried in the collective memory of pride, history, and hard work. Those memories, mixed with the illusion that Mexican courts will rule in their favor, will one day come to an abrupt end.

And whatever happens, one thing is for sure. The digging will continue long into the next century, with or without them.

A little over a year after my visit, at 10:00 p.m. on June 6, 2010, two thousand Mexican Federal Police and Sonora State Police invade the mine once again. They fire tear gas and beat the miners away from the gates. The melee is brief. By June 2011, the Mexican Workers Confederation, an old union in Mexico but a new one in Cananea, makes a deal with Grupo Mexico. About nine hundred new workers are hired, with fewer benefits and lower wages.

As a final reminder that Cananea no longer belongs to Los Mineros, the company changes the name of the mine from Cananea mine to Buenavista del Cobre. As of 2012, it is at full production and profits are more than double expectations. The company produced two hundred thousand tons of copper in 2011, and by 2015 it hopes to increase that number to almost three hundred thousand tons annually.

6

Copper, Inc.

> Mining is the art of exploiting mineral deposits at a profit. An unprofitable mine is fit only for the sepulchre of a dead mule.
> —T. A. Rickard, *The Romance of Mining* (1905)

In the end we were displaced for two weeks while Freeport extracted and then replaced the soil in our yard. Where they took the contaminated dirt remains a mystery. Every time I ask someone in Shaw or Freeport about where the toxic dirt goes, their answer is simply that it was "disposed of properly." Upon our return to the house, remediation work has begun on several more houses on our street. The noise is mind-bending. Bobcat tractors and dump trucks, with their reverse beeping noises, disorient us to the point of temporary insanity. Meanwhile, the constant arrival and departure of rotating crews make the small streets difficult to navigate. It is in this environment that my wife wakes me at three in the morning. We drive two hours to the hospital in Tucson to bring our second daughter into this world.

Now half a year has gone by and summer is in full swing. I have no plans for planting another vegetable garden, but the flowers are blooming. The peach tree is ripe with fruit.

My wife and I buy an outdoor slide for our two daughters. Attached to the slide are a climbing wall and stairs. We plunk it down in the front yard and realize that in order to contain the

81

kids in this area, I need to build a fence. I buy two four-foot sections of fence and three four-by-four pieces of pressurized wood for the poles, which I sink into a concrete base. Once finished, I look with pride at the yard, ready to let the kids run around. That is, until my friend Noah Suby comes over to inspect my work. He points to the pressurized wood posts, the kind found in lumberyards throughout the country.

"Got to primer those," he says.

"Why?"

"They are poison. Especially for kids." He is a general contractor, so I take his word for it.

"What is the toxin?"

"To make it waterproof they dip it in liquid copper."

I shake my head, amazed once again at being so surrounded by a metal that is not always easy to spot and that exists in large quantities deep in the ground beneath my feet.

Up until 2004, all pressurized wood used to build docks, decks, and children's play sets contained the chemical wood preservative CCA, or chromated copper arsenate, which contains chromium, copper, and arsenic. This type of treated wood has been in use since the early 1940s and has been highly successful in slowing decay of wood that comes in touch with dirt, termites, or water. The entire reason that pressurized wood works so well against corrosion is the same reason that hospitals are thinking of using copper doorknobs to kill off germs. Copper acts as a natural inhibitor of decay. But the problem is that chromated copper arsenate also gives people cancer.

In 2003, the U.S. government released a report that stated children who play on pressure-treated wooden play sets face an increased risk of getting lung or bladder cancer late in life. Furthermore, the Consumer Product Safety Commission recommended that "if parents want to do something right now, make the kids wash their hands, and don't let kids eat on the wood, because we know that reduces risk."

In reaction to their own studies, the EPA banned all use of CCA from residential use in 2004 (except permanent structural wood foundations), but it is still heavily used for industrial projects:

guardrails, light poles, bridges, structural timber for houses, siding, and a few agricultural products, such as oyster farms, which have so much of their infrastructure built underwater.

So the wood I have planted in my children's play area does not have arsenic, but it does contain high amounts of a type of copper concentrate manufactured in Morenci for use in treated wood.

The EPA has declared the new treated wood safe for consumers. It has given it its stamp of approval, for now. But do I trust these products to be safe when my one-year-old is licking her ice cream off the wood? Not a chance in hell.

That afternoon I apply two coats of primer to the wood, then three coats of paint.

Once again by delving into the world of copper I now can't stop thinking of all the ways the metal finds its way into my life, as well as into the lives of hundreds of millions of people all around the globe. How many people are going to build a deck this summer using pressurized wood? Or an extension to their homes, using pressurized wood anywhere they believe water may come in contact with their house? The number is uncountable but staggeringly high.

At times it feels like copper keeps pouring into our lives. The mine remains dormant on the edge of town, but at the same time living here is beginning to feel like a risk I don't want to burden my children with.

Like so many in Bisbee, I want to know if the mine is going to reopen. But getting a straight answer from the mining company is not easy.

Having a candid conversation with any mining company employees can be difficult. Even after living in Bisbee for more than a decade, I rarely meet the skeleton crew who work at the mine, and if I do they are usually subcontracted geologists or maybe someone in maintenance. They are always pleasant enough, but these folks are just trying to make ends meet. These are the workers, not the executives, and are rarely trusted with any information other than the day's marching orders. The employees of Freeport-McMoRan who cleaned up my yard don't make the decisions, and they certainly don't carry the blame for what happened in the past. And when I ask any of them if the mine will reopen, they answer, "I don't know. They'll tell me when they'll tell me."

Who will tell them? And who are *they*? Most large corporate decisions are made by committee, then delivered by a corporate messenger who never reveals the details of the decision. The "they" have become the nebulous caricatures we imagine when thinking of boardrooms full of people in power suits making billion-dollar decisions.

I have spent considerable time wondering why it is so difficult to understand the who and why of copper companies. Part of the reason is due to the way corporations protect themselves generally. But copper companies are different. Most of us can't comprehend the scale of wealth they create and the length of time they have been creating that wealth. And the great lengths they go to to protect this wealth. The people on the inside know the details, but they do not want people in general to understand what the companies have done—both to the earth and to enrich the people who own the companies. Oddly enough, I came to understand how they think quite unexpectedly. I read the obituary of a woman who died on May 24, 2011. On that quiet Tuesday morning, a gilded era came to a close.

Huguette Clark was the daughter of the most powerful copper baron America ever knew, William Andrews Clark. For twenty years this elderly woman living alone in a room at Beth Israel Medical Center in New York City went largely unnoticed. Other than her lawyer and accountant, no one from her family or circle of friends was allowed to visit her in her dying years. Her death was a nonevent: She was 104 and it was expected. All that was known of her was that she was kind, was particular about her antiques, and hadn't visited either of her palatial estates—one in Connecticut and one in Santa Barbara—for almost fifty years. Not many knew that she had once lived in the single-largest-ever private home in New York City, a 121-room mansion on Fifth Avenue, built by her father. When she died, her estate was estimated at around $500 million, which includes three large apartments and countless pieces of art not seen for almost seven decades. The mansion in Santa Barbara was alone worth roughly $100 million.

Maybe her reclusive nature came from growing up so wealthy. She was born in Paris into lavish wealth, her father considered the second-richest man in the United States, after John D. Rockefeller. William Clark made a fortune owning several copper mines. Then he built electrical companies to power them and grocery stores to feed the people who worked in them. And he built railroad lines to his mines, wherever they were. That's how he founded Las Vegas, when he put down a railroad station in the desert to service his Los Angeles and Salt Lake railroad lines. Clark County, Nevada, is named after him; Clarkdale, Arizona, as well. Like his contemporary William Randolph Hearst, Clark also controlled the narrative of his wealth and life by owning the newspapers and politicians in the regions where he did business. He owned many mines, including Jerome, Arizona, but was mostly known for dominating the copper business in Anaconda, a deposit so lucrative it has been called "the richest mountain ever found." With the Anaconda mine, located just outside of Butte, Montana, Clark built an empire, and when he needed to flex more power over everything that happened in Montana, he bought the state legislators, who voted him into the U.S. Senate. He didn't fool anyone, of course, and he didn't care. As a result of bribing his way into Congress, the Seventeenth Amendment was passed, which changed the elections of senators to a result of popular votes, as opposed to being chosen by state legislators.

Clark was feared by many and hated by most. Mark Twain, who spent many years traveling the mining camps in the West, had this to say about him: "He is as rotten a human being as can be found anywhere under the flag; he is a shame to the American nation. . . . To my mind he is the most disgusting creature that the republic has produced since [Boss] Tweed's time."

Before the end of the nineteenth century, people like William Clark ran the copper industry, along with several other prominent American families. They were public figures. There was no corporate veil, just big personalities and good lawyers. Mining bigwigs were the power brokers of their time and used their capital to build everything from elaborate estates to cities, schools, and art museums.

By the beginning of World War I, the Guggenheim brothers—the seven sons of Meyer Guggenheim, who emigrated from Switzerland in 1847—owned a number of copper mines in the United States, Mexico, and South America. Even though all seven brothers were partners, it was Daniel, the second-oldest son, who led the Guggenheims into a series of relationships that made the family a dominant player in the copper industry. Beginning in the late 1890s, the brothers began to develop deep ties to Wall Street bankers and gain the inside track to people such as J. P. Morgan, who would invest in their ventures time and again.

Through their company ASARCO, the American Smelting and Refining Company, they created a highly lucrative operation. In 1903, the brothers and Morgan joined forces to open the Kennecott copper mine in McCarthy, Alaska, at a price of $20 million. They built a two-hundred-mile-long train track into the unforgiving interior. The first ore train reached Cordova in 1911 and continued moving the copper until it closed in 1938. More than $200 million in copper was extracted from the mine, which at the time made it one of the most profitable ever. The Guggenheims didn't stop there. They became the main investors in the Kennecott mine in Bingham, Utah, which has been in operation for more than a hundred years and is the largest physical mine on Earth.

Clark was the most powerful man in copper, but the Guggenheims were the metal's ruling family. Joining them were the Rockefellers, who at one time owned the copper mine in Cananea, fewer than fifty miles from Bisbee, and many others. George Hearst, father of William Randolph Hearst, made a fortune investing in various gold and copper mines all throughout the West and eventually in Peru. Morgan and Rockefeller were also part owners in dozens of mines and railroads all over the western frontier. For decades these families controlled the copper mines in the United States, Mexico, and many parts of the world. For the most part, these families no longer run the copper business, though I suspect their heirs may collect some healthy dividend checks.

These famous families didn't seek out the spotlight during their reign over the copper market, but they also did not shy away from who they were and what they were up to. Nowadays copper company executives prefer not to be known publicly. Instead, they are well insulated from the public, and other than the occasional interview and shareholder meeting they are rarely heard from. There is one exception, however, and perhaps he proves why these executives continue to remain in the shadows.

Robert Friedland, the CEO of Ivanhoe Energy and Ivanhoe Mines, both based in Singapore and Canada, has had a long career in mining and has earned a reputation as someone unafraid to speak his mind. Also known as "Toxic Bob" or "The Ugly Canadian," Friedland once served as the CEO of Galactic Resources, which between 1984 and 1991 was responsible for thousands of gallons of heavy metals, acid, and cyanide seeping from a gold mine in Summitville, Colorado, into the Alamosa River. It still ranks as the worst cyanide disaster in U.S. history. Although heavy metals and sulfuric acid runoff had been poisoning the river for a long period of time, the cyanide solution from the mine helped further kill off all aquatic life in the Alamosa. In 1992, the mining company went bankrupt and all cleanup efforts stopped. Friedland had already quit by that time. In 1994, the mine became a Superfund site and the United States sued Friedland for liability. In 2001, after ten years of negotiations, Friedland agreed to pay $27.5 million for the cleanup, which is now estimated will cost $200 million and will be paid for largely by the citizens of Colorado and U.S. taxpayers.

For most, being responsible for this sort of environmental disaster might cause one to take pause, or even change professions. But when Friedland quit as CEO of his own company in Colorado, he helped set up another operation in Guyana, where he built the Omai gold mine using the exact lining methods he had used in Colorado. In 1995, the tailing dam burst, sending 120 million gallons of mud cased with cyanide into the Omai and Essequibo Rivers. In 2006, a Guyana Supreme Court dismissed a $2 billion class-action lawsuit against the owners of the mine from twenty-three thousand persons residing on the rivers. Apparently the court agreed with a Guyana Commission of

Inquiry that found there was no criminal liability on behalf of the mine.

Although Friedland was born in Chicago, he currently holds U.S. and Canadian citizenship and officially resides in Singapore. He is worth in the neighborhood of $3 billion and consistently makes the annual *Forbes* list of wealthiest people. Seen by many as a modern-day wildcatter, he didn't start off that way. At Bowdoin College in Maine, he protested the Vietnam War until he was expelled, after he was found with $100,000 worth of LSD. After two years in federal prison, he went to Reed College in Oregon. There he met Steve Jobs, the future visionary of Apple Computers, and they became good friends.

Eventually the two parted ways, but perhaps Steve Jobs characterized Friedland best when he told his biographer Walter Isaacson, "Robert always portrayed himself as a spiritual person, but he crossed the line from being charismatic to being a con man."

For Toxic Bob, Earth is his playground. And mines are his personal sandpits. What happens when he poisons the playground? About the cyanide disaster in Colorado, he had this to say in 1996: "It is open to question whether any form of disaster, with a capital *D*, occurred." He seems also to have a noninterference policy when it comes to host nations. If a dictator wants to enslave people, or kill his own, Bob is not going to interfere or ask any embarrassing questions.

In 1994 he began a partnership with the brutal military dictatorship in Myanmar. Together with the State Peace and Development Council they started the Monywa copper mine, which has proved to be very profitable, with a reported production cost of 27¢ per pound. Universally, the price hovers around $1.30 a pound. This low cost at the Monywa mine is most likely due to a large workforce made up of slave labor, which some critics believe includes children. Myanmar has no enforceable environmental laws, which means the waters downstream from the mine run a bright blue from the copper and the people who live there complain of burning skin. As of 2007, Friedland's Ivanhoe Mines supposedly cut all direct ties to the mine, placing the entire operation into a blind trust. Then in June 2010 the China North

Industries Corporation, a formerly U.S.-banned Chinese weapons manufacturer, acquired production rights to mine the Monywa deposit. And in 2011 Ivanhoe Mines released a statement that the blind trust had paid the company $103 million. Why they were paid that amount and what prompted the payment remains a mystery, since Ivanhoe Mines insists they have no involvement with the mine or the people who run the trust.

Beginning in 2005, Friedland turned his full attention to the Oyu Tolgoi gold and copper deposit in Mongolia, which conveniently sits fifty miles from the Chinese border, the largest importer of copper in the world. Mongolia is the size of Europe but with only 2.5 million people. Few have traveled there and even fewer have stayed and prospered. But Friedland has found what the industry calls a "world-class deposit," large enough to challenge the Grasberg mine in Indonesia and the Tenke mine in the DRC for the world's largest copper reserve. By the way, Oyu Tolgoi is Mongolian for "turquoise hill," but Friedlander calls it the "treasure chest."

One of the things that make the Oyu Tolgoi copper and gold mine so appealing is its proximity to China. Already the Mongolian government, which owns a minority share of the mine and is soon expected to make almost 30 percent of its GDP from mining profits, is building an electrical grid from the mine site to China, where it will get the resources to run the mine. Also, a railroad will be built as the mine readies for production. When fully operational in 2018, it is expected to produce upward of 450,000 tons a year, or 3 percent of world production.

Friedland has expressed his excitement for the mining potential in Mongolia with great candor. He famously told a group of investors in Florida in 2005, "The nice thing about [Mongolia] is that there are no people around. The land is flat, there's no tropical jungle, there's no NGOs [nongovernmental organizations], and we're only seventy kilometers from the Chinese border. It does not snow there. You've got lots of room for waste dumps without disrupting the populations."

In some strange way I find his bluntness refreshing. Friedland is a rare breed in the mining business—brash and bold and makes statements that most mining executives will never say. Still, I doubt anyone on the street would recognize his face, or his name. The same is true for James Moffett, the chairman of Freeport-McMoRan's board and effectively the boss. If he came to Bisbee one day, no one other than Freeport employees would know. He could sit at the Bisbee Grand bar and order a beer, watch a basketball game, and never be noticed. Someone in town keeps putting up posters in public places saying things like GET FREEPORT OUT OF INDONESIA, referring to the infamous Grasberg mine, which will be discussed in later chapters. The person behind these flyers could be sitting right next to Moffett and not know him. Likewise, the people in town with conspiracy theories and fears about the opening of the mine here in Bisbee might even buy the guy a round. He would seem like just another tourist in town for the mine tour and a bite to eat. No one would know he runs the company that for years hired Indonesian military to act as Freeport's private security at the company's Grasberg mine. And no one would think the man to their left made almost $47 million in 2010.

My point is that although Moffett wields tremendous power in deciding the future of Bisbee, for most he is not the face of the company. Mining companies have evolved from being corporations run by powerful men and families into modern enigmas. When asked *who* is a mining company, the majority of people answer the question by offering up images of barbwire adorned with NO TRESPASSING signs, a stock market ticker symbol, or maybe a two-story dump truck crawling along a desolate road parallel to a lone stretch of highway.

Here is a strange thought, one I only recently fully realized. I live in a town where mining personnel, whether directly employed or contractors of the mining company, constantly drive up and down the main road in pickups with the Freeport-McMoRan logo on the side, and I don't know any of them. At least I don't think I do.

Whenever I think of the culture of mining executives, I remember a brief interview I had with a geologist who had lived and worked for the mining companies in Bisbee for twenty years.

Believing we might have mutual friends, I mentioned the names of a few people in town—café owners, merchants, people he might have met.

"I don't know anyone here," he said casually, as if that were normal.

I asked how that was possible after living here twenty years.

"We also own a house in Tucson and my wife likes going there on the weekends. I work all week and then we leave Friday night. I work here, I don't live here."

When I think of it, every mining town I have visited has this unspoken code of emotional distance. No one will admit it, but I'm certain part of the training and perhaps an actual requirement for getting a job with a mining company is agreeing not to interact with the locals.

This one candid admission by this geologist in Bisbee explains the distance I encounter when speaking to miners, geologists, and supervisors in mining towns. I imagine that many of these geologists went to college to study dinosaurs and dreamed of becoming Indiana Jones. They may have even bonded with others in their field over their fierce resistance to working for mining companies. How long did it take to realize they just needed a job and that mining companies are always hiring? Some probably took the jobs, still nostalgic for their college dreams, and told themselves they would join the company in order to ensure that someone was looking after Earth properly. Eventually they collect their paycheck and put their kids through high school and college. For twenty years they punch the clock. There is no shame in that. In fact, there is an honor in that, in providing for their families. What is strange is never getting to know a single person in the town where they work.

I could be wrong, but this behavior typifies a person who either deems the locals unworthy of investing in or doesn't want to get to know them in case one day he has to be the one who begins tearing up their town.

7

The Ring

Economies are supposed to serve human ends, not the
other way round. We forget at our peril that markets
make a good servant, a bad master and a worse religion.
—Amory Lovins, CEO, Rocky Mountain Institute

Extracting copper from the ground and then shaping it into
a product used by consumers around the world never stops.
Someone is digging up the metal every ticking second of every
day, 365 days a year. Someone else is buying or selling copper
every hour of the day. This steady cycle of supply and demand
ultimately drives the decision by mining companies to expand
or contract their operations. Those residents of Bisbee who are
focused solely on potential issues of water contamination, air pollution, and other detrimental effects that an active mine would
have on the town, and who believe they can influence any decision Freeport makes about reopening the mine, have lost sight of
the global mechanisms that drive the buying and selling of copper. No amount of protest or letters to the town newspaper will
have any impact on Freeport's decision. Although Freeport may
be the town's biggest benefactor, the relationship between Freeport and the town is not an economic one but a political necessity. It is reasonable to assume that if Freeport decides to open
the mine, the company would like to keep that relationship civil
and healthy, but if it turns sour and combative, the mine will still

93

go forward. Ultimately what matters to the company is gaining a cost-effective supply of copper to sell to a global market. A market that is in need of more and more copper.

I made a trip to New York City, and while there I decided that to better understand this global market I should visit a financial trader. I was introduced to a fellow I will call Mike, who prefers his identity be masked. Mike trades metals for a major financial institution. New York is a cornerstone in the world copper market because it is the home of COMEX, the Commodity Exchange division of the NYMEX, the New York Mercantile Exchange.

Mike sits in an office on Fifth Avenue. All around him are several dozen men who look eerily like he does, all talking into headsets and staring at the several computer monitors in front of them. I am here to see if I can learn more about the larger mechanics of the copper market and what role financial markets may play in the decision to reopen the mine in Bisbee.

"Copper is dead. Fucking useless," announces Mike as his eyes rove the multiple computer screens reading instantaneous information on the various markets he is following.

"If it's dead, then why is there all this talk of a shortage of copper and an excess of demand?" I ask, thinking this disparity is the fundamental reason Freeport-McMoRan would ever reopen the Bisbee mine.

"The only thing that matters to copper or anything else is one thing: China," he yells at me. He is referring to the fact that China uses almost 40 percent of the world's copper to build the infrastructure of its expanding economy. "If China expands, then copper and everything else rises in price," he says.

"Dr. Copper is now Dr. China. Yes, copper used to be the metal that led the markets. Whatever it did, everything followed. But not anymore. China. China. China. They run the world and we are just the bitches," Mike yells at the computer screens.

He has a point.

China has announced plans to spend approximately $1 trillion by 2020 on infrastructure projects—transport, energy, water, and telecommunications, all of which need massive amounts of copper. Part of this money, and the supply of copper, will be spent creating the largest megacity on Earth, in the Pearl River Delta area, by merging nine existing cities into one. The area is largely a manufacturing zone and includes the industrial centers of Shenzhen and Guangzhou. By uniting the nine existing cities into one large city, the Chinese government estimates the population will near forty-two million and cover an area larger than Wales. To mesh the cities together, the government will build twenty-nine new rail lines, covering thirty-one hundred miles, using copious amounts of copper.

Add to this a population that continues to migrate from rural communities to sprawling urban landscapes, and begins demanding cars, computers, and phones. Currently there are 1.3 billion people in China, and in the next ten years China expects a hundred million of its rural residents to move to the cities. The governments, both local and national, and housing speculators have been building ten to twenty new cities each year, with a large majority of them nearly empty and waiting for the great flood of people. I can't even guess at the amount of copper hiding in the walls of all those buildings, but it is a staggering amount.

As Mike scans the computer screens, I ask if he is buying or selling at the moment.

"Both. Always. That is the name of the game." He rarely diverts his eyes from the screens. "We are hedging or speculating, depending on the commodity. Really everyone is just trying to figure out what is happening a few moments *before* it happens and then sell long or short. And make a few bucks by the end of the day."

I find it strange that he can't stop yelling, but then I notice no one within ten feet even flinches when Mike raises his voice. They are all too busy yelling into their own headsets to care, or to hear what Mike is screaming at me.

The moniker Dr. Copper is still used by media pundits and economists to explain how copper's behavior in the world's financial markets can predict how the general economy will behave. But for some, like Mike, the nickname lost credibility in 2008 when the housing markets crashed, followed by the banks, and finally by a large majority of industry. The copper market did not predict the crash. In fact, it followed the crash instead of preceding it. Perhaps, however, this was an anomaly, because for the past fifty years the copper market accurately foreshadowed each recession or upswing in the market. The reason the copper market has been so reliable in predicting the economic health of our country is that copper is used in all vital sectors of our economy.

On a more macro scale, if the economies of several large countries are booming at the same time, then copper would be selling fast, which will most likely result in a near-term shortage of copper, thus raising the price and reflecting a growing world economy.

In the latest economic meltdown beginning in late 2007, the price of copper gave the markets no warning, most likely attributable to the fact that the housing market was flourishing right up until the bubble broke. When the market crashed, new home construction was still a busy market. When it all failed, the copper market was upside down and had no time to react.

I ask Mike about all this.

"People saw a bubble coming, but I am not sure anyone knew how drastic it would be," he says, calming down a bit.

"Where is the brain of the copper market?"

"There is no real center anymore," he says. "It's tradable everywhere. But two places have the most effect on the daily price: London and China, with London being the old boys' network. Those fuckers really know how to rig the game. Whatever they say the price will be, it will be, and no one other than them can do anything about it."

As he speaks, his eyes continue to dart back and forth along the computer screens, reading various graphs and numbers that rise and fall by the second. He picks up the phone and barks a few lines at someone. He quickly hangs up, and now his conversation drifts into a rant about how President Obama is ruining the country and that everything happening in America is his fault, perhaps a result of Mike's pension disappearing in the 2008 crash.

"Hey"—he gestures toward me, realizing I am losing interest in his ranting—"in the old days, the copper companies threw huge parties at the big hotels here in the city. They were famous for all kinds of over-the-top personalities and insane late-night drink sessions." He chuckles, as he stares at nothing in particular, perhaps lost in a memory of strippers and expensive scotch. "But there hasn't been that sort of party for more than a decade."

He takes little notice as I stand up and thank him for his time. In the elevator, I am reminded of a study done by the University of St. Gallen in Switzerland showing that stock market traders' behavior is as reckless and manipulative as that of certified psychopaths. But Mike is right about China and London. Other than the COMEX, the London Metal Exchange, known as the LME, and the Shanghai Exchange exert the most influence in shaping the daily, weekly, and monthly markets for copper.

The trade in metals consists of precious metals—gold, platinum, palladium—iron and steel, and nonferrous metals, a term that refers to metals that do not contain iron—such as aluminum, copper, zinc, and titanium. The LME is the world's center for nonferrous metals and has been for almost 130 years. In 2011, $11.6 trillion was traded on the LME, accounting for 95 percent of the global exchange of nonprecious metals. Thus, while copper is bought and sold continuously in trading centers all over the world, and China behaves as an economic magnet for the metal, the LME is the kingmaker of the copper market.

No one knows for certain when exactly the international trade in metals began in earnest, but intercontinental trade in Europe was most likely born when Rome invaded England in AD 43. Besides gaining access to the large amounts of tin and copper in Cornwall and Wales to satisfy the need for bronze, Roman-occupied Britain began a steady trade with Spain and France, exchanging copper for pottery, olive oil, fish, and glass.

It would take almost another fifteen hundred years before London created in 1571 its own trade market, the Royal Exchange, during the reign of Queen Elizabeth I. Then sometime in the early nineteenth century, a group of traders and financiers who dealt exclusively in metal exchange met in the Jerusalem Café at 1 Cowper's Court, in Cornhill, London. The Jerusalem Café was a hub of ship captains and merchants who did their business in the far reaches of the British Empire, including China, India, and Australia. Inside the café were files from places like Canton, Hong Kong, Macao, Calcutta, and Sydney. Shipping reports and trade transactions from South Africa to Singapore lined the rooms. Tired of the crowded space at the Royal Exchange, the metal traders decided to make their meetings at the café permanent, doing business over tea, coffee, and whiskey.

The ground rules had yet to be determined when a gentleman stood up and announced he had metal to sell, most likely tin (Britain produced almost half the world's tin at that time). No one paid attention to his announcement. Struggling to be heard over the crowd, he decided to draw a ring in the sawdust floor and yell out, "Change," a word that would come to signify that those wishing to engage in a trade need to gather around the sawdust circle and make their bids.

As a result of this rather informal gesture, the "ring" was born. The Jerusalem Café still exists, serving locals and tourists alike, but by 1877, the traders had left the café and began what is known as the London Metal Exchange. Since reopening in 1952 after World War II, the LME has evolved into the dominant force for the nonferrous metal market, with approximately $46 billion traded each day in copper, aluminum, lead, zinc, nickel, and tin. Each morning, all over the world, the principal players in the copper industry wake up to check the LME trading prices as a barometer of the supply and demand of copper.

The ring, no longer a circle drawn in sawdust, has been institutionalized. Today it is six yards in diameter with traders sitting on red couches in fixed positions around the circle. There are twelve members of what the LME calls category 1, or ring dealing. All business must pass through one of these members. No one else is allowed inside the boundaries of the ring. Historically, the members represent financial institutions or metal-trading companies. As of September 2011 the members were Amalgamated Metal Trading Limited, Barclays Capital, ED & F Man Commodity Advisers Limited, Metdist Trading Ltd., MF Global UK Limited, Natixis Commodity Markets Limited, Newedge Group (the UK branch), Société Générale, Sucden Financial Limited, MAREX

Financial, Triland Metals Ltd., and the most recent member, J.P. Morgan Securities.

Category 2 members are "associate broker clearing members" and have all the privileges of category 1 members except they may not trade in the ring. Members of this category include Goldman Sachs, Citigroup Global Markets Limited, Morgan Stanley, and Toyota Tsusho Metals Limited.

Category 3 members, "associate trade clearing members," and category 4, "associate brokers," are both members of the LME but are limited in the transactions they can make, often to only what is called the twenty-four-hour inter-office market, which connects clients to a broker via telephone who then quotes a price, while at the same time indicative prices are being shown on a screen. If a deal is struck, the transaction is considered a real LME contract. It is a way of including more clients in the day-to-day business without disturbing the exclusiveness of the ring.

Interestingly, category 5, "associate trade," is home to most of the world's largest mining companies, including Freeport-McMoRan. This level of membership has no trading rights except acting as suppliers. That the mining companies are level 5 members of the LME makes sense because they provide metal but don't buy it. They buy a seat at the table in order to know their buyers.

Above the ring hang two large display boards showing the shifting prices of the day. Outside the ring, behind each member's ring seat, are places for assistants to stand in order to pass buy or sell orders into the ring as necessary. A ring trade must be done during a ring session, which are five-minute windows of trading that happen twice a day for each metal represented at the LME. Historically the closing prices for copper from the second session of ring trading—from 3:50 to 3:55 p.m.—set the physical contracts of all worldwide transactions for that day.

Ring trading for all the nonferrous metals happens between 11:45 in the morning and 5:00 in the afternoon within various five-minute intervals called "open-outcry," where men in dark suits shout out a trade. During these short periods, the room is busy with the usual frenzy that any trading floor experiences.

When ring trading, buyers and sellers are dealing in "lots," or twenty-five metric tons of high-grade copper. In the COMEX in New York City, they trade in lots of twenty-five thousand pounds of high-grade copper.

The LME deals in futures contracts for copper based on an actual physical trade of 99.9 percent copper cathodes. These contracts are legally binding obligations for the buyer of the contract to pay a set price upon delivery, which the LME has established as three months from the day it is traded. Referred to by the LME as the "three-month buyer price," this is the price of one metric ton of the metal delivered in three months' time. This lag between purchasing and delivering came about after the Suez Canal opened in 1869. With the invention of the telegraph and steamboats, the delivery time for copper became a more exact science. Members of the ring settled upon three months, the delivery time of copper from Chile, already a major producer by that time, to London. By locking in a price, copper merchants could eliminate the risk of spot prices of copper being higher than when they ordered it three months prior. This simple financial tool, still in use today, allows businesses to have some known stability in their copper supplies.

As for the rest of the metal exchanges in the world, once the LME sets the global spot price, stock traders in Toronto, Chicago, Brazil, India, and Tokyo will begin trading their own lots of copper and also begin speculating on the rise and fall of the prices set at the LME. These traders are hoping to profit by gambling on whether the price of copper set by the LME will rise or fall by the end of the hour, day, or week, depending on the transaction. Often they are not actually dealing with physical copper, only its speculative price. They buy and sell their shares long before any copper would be due.

In addition to controlling the buying and selling of copper, the LME conducts a market of last resort, which is a constant supply of copper, usually somewhere between 350,000 and 500,000 tons, stored in six hundred approved warehouses in the United States, Europe, the Middle East, and Asia. In the United States, warehouses are located in such places as Long Beach, New Orleans, Baltimore, and Detroit. This store of copper is rarely used in fulfilling orders. Instead, it acts as a buffer to the market, but for a price it can be used to fulfill any orders on any given day if needed. Usually this occurs when there is a tightening of supply and those traders who have purchased copper cathodes sitting in LME warehouses can, and do, sell at high spot prices, which can earn the holder of the copper a substantial profit.

In December 2010, as copper hit a new record of almost $10,000 per ton, there was fear of a physical shortage. This spike in price resulted in what is known as backwardation, meaning a copper futures contract price is lower than the expected spot price at the contract's maturity, which is contrary to the normal way of doing business. The markets interpret this as a strong indicator that there will be a short-term supply shortage. One of the reasons for this specific backwardation was that J.P. Morgan—category 1 ring member—purchased nearly two hundred thousand tons of the copper in the LME warehouses, roughly 50 percent of the world's exchange-registered copper stockpile, an amount worth about $1 billion. When the purchase was originally made, copper traders did not know the buyer was J.P. Morgan and feared that a single person, or company, was trying to corner the market. The reaction in the copper market was quick. Prices went up. Then on Monday, December 6, a J.P. Morgan spokesperson stated, "As one of the leading firms in base metals and as a Category 1 ring dealing member of the LME, we are expected to make markets for our clients."

One interpretation of "making markets" for their clients is doing something called "short squeezing," trying to take advantage of a lack of supply while there is an excess of demand, which will then force up the price of copper. By controlling a large supply, Morgan put itself in a position to sell futures contracts of copper at a higher price, thereby "squeezing" those traders who had bought "shorts" or, put another way, those traders who bet the price would go down.

The LME has strict rules on squeezing the market, but it does not limit how much any one member can buy of any metal. It instead relies on market forces to make anyone squeezing the market pay a hefty price for the risk. The biggest tool to discourage trading partners from squeezing, or for that matter, ever attempting to corner the market, is making any copper bought in LME warehouses available for sale in short-term periods at an agreed-upon limited profit margin. Thus no one is able to corner the market, which could be done only if someone hoarded vast quantities of copper, enough to drive up the price with little regard for profit margins on the amount of time the supplies were held. The LME also makes the trader who is buying LME-warehoused copper pay the insurance, storage, and financing costs of those supplies, all of which can easily strip away any profit gained in temporary price differentials. J.P. Morgan didn't actually take the copper out of the warehouses, but it did temporarily exert a large influence on the copper futures market. And since the demand for 2011 was expected to exceed supply by around 450,000 tons, it is fair to assume the company sold its copper quickly and turned a profit. Since J.P. Morgan most likely distributed these copper shares among various clients, tracking the sales would prove impossible.

Basically, the LME has evolved into a gentlemen's collective where controlling the copper market from the supply side is almost impossible. As a member-to-member trading institute, the members all basically know what copper the others have, or will have.

However, that doesn't mean people haven't tried.

The most famous case in modern history is Yasuo Hamanaka, who acted as the head of the metal trading division at Sumitomo Corporation, a Japanese trading house and the same company, incidentally, that has a 15 percent stake in the Morenci mine. Hamanaka, once known as "Mr. Copper," tried to corner the world copper market by constantly manipulating the supply, and thus the price. He bought and sold tremendous amounts, all in a scheme to profit on price changes in the futures market. At one point he controlled 5 percent of the world's supply, which made him arguably the largest holder of copper. The reason 5 percent ownership can drastically alter the global price is that copper cannot be shipped to and from countries in a short span of time to meet any shortages (which is where the LME warehouses play a role if needed). As with many commodities, if the price of copper rises in the United States due to a shortage, there is no immediate way to stop this rise by injecting more copper into the market. It would take months, if it were possible at all. So holding 5 percent of the world's supply in various warehouses and in futures contracts allowed Hamanaka to manipulate the market at the LME to benefit Sumitomo's bottom line. He did this for ten years.

Playing this game has serious pitfalls. And in 1995 certain conditions changed in the international copper market, catching Hamanaka off guard. China began mining more copper, thus adding to the world's supply, permanently. Also, new technology was beginning to allow leaching stacks, which had been dormant for years, to begin producing copper once again at a profitable rate. Hamanaka was left with too much copper in his portfolio and no way to sell it at the false high price he had set.

His game of false pricing fell apart, and in the end he was arrested and served eight years in prison. Sumitomo estimated its loss on the copper market at $2.6 billion. Sumitomo accused J.P. Morgan, the Swiss-based bank UBS, and Chase Manhattan Bank of helping Hamanaka finance unauthorized trades and colluding with the false rise in prices. In 2002, Chase paid $125 million to Sumitomo; UBS paid $85 million in 2006. Twenty companies that had bought copper at inflated prices between 1993 and 1996 sued J.P. Morgan for $1 billion, all alleging the bank was in on the scheme to artificially reduce copper supplies and drive up prices. The lawsuit was settled on May 29, 2007. How much J.P. Morgan paid out remains confidential.

As a result of Mr. Copper's actions, the LME changed its policies regarding day-to-day trading. Although still perceived as an old boys' network, the LME is now more transparent as a result of the Hamanaka affair. Along with the inclusion of daily reports on trades, they introduced interoffice telephone trading, which is open twenty-four hours a day. The LME also added an electronic trading platform, called the LME Select. All these steps allowed more transparency in the fast-moving ring.

The copper cathodes that the LME deals in are the same kind that roll out of Morenci and other mines in Arizona by the truckload every day. In southern Arizona, these trucks can be spotted on Highway 10 between Wilcox and Phoenix, hauling dozens of flat three-hundred-pound one-square-meter slabs of 99.9 percent copper. From the mine, the cathodes go in various directions depending on market conditions and preexisting orders. They could be headed for an LME warehouse in Long Beach, but this is rare. If mining companies are shipping their cathodes to LME warehouses, that indicates an excess supply of copper on the market and most likely a falling price. Why? Because when supply and demand are in sync, the copper leaves the mine for foundries or mills where it is melted down once again and reconstituted into the shapes—billets, cake sheets, ingots, or wire rods—that are used by fabricators to make actual products.

By actual products, I mean something that has a shape or use that we are familiar with. When Toyota buys copper to put into its Prius cars, it doesn't buy it from Freeport-McMoRan or the LME. Instead, Toyota buys its copper parts from a fabrication company that already bought the copper from either a mining company or a mill to reshape yet again into a product that Toyota has ordered. At this company, the copper is then manipulated into the shape, size, and for the specific use that Toyota needs: a coil, or maybe as part of the braking system.

When a company in Thailand or South Africa or Italy buys copper to make copper piping, it goes through the same process. It buys from a middleman supplier of copper rods, ingots, cake, or wire rods. Orders are placed a month or more in advance. Because copper is preordered, getting large amounts quickly is difficult for any company, in any country.

It is no surprise that China is the home base for the largest collection of metal fabricators in the world. Thus if a company in Argentina needs copper fixtures, it doesn't call the LME. It most likely calls a fabricator in China who has the copper on hand and can make the product needed and ship it across the ocean.

In Phoenix, the Industrial Metal Supply Co. buys copper sheets from Revere, the same company founded by Paul Revere, America's most famous silver- and coppersmith. Located in Rome, New York, Revere buys cake sheets from a mining company and then reshapes them into flat rolls to sell to various metal companies. What is the difference between Revere and Industrial Metal Supply? Size. Revere is dealing with larger-scale projects, including architectural surfaces, electronics, and power generators. Industrial Metal Supply can deal with small orders, say, an artist looking to buy half a sheet of copper for an installation.

"We get our copper by the sheet from Revere, and then we are able to make products to sell to our customers per order," says a spokesman from Industrial Metal Supply. "I can sell copper by the pound. As you work back up the supply chain to the mining company, they are restricted by needing to sell by the ton."

I ask how he deals with the fickle nature of the prices of copper on any given day.

"I lock in a price with a futures contract. I don't like more than three months' worth of copper in our inventory. And the prices and profit margin are so tight that when I take a large order, I get on the phone and immediately call New York. I get a quote and tell the client a price based on the actual price of copper at that moment. I then buy at that exact moment on the phone. I lock in the shipment, which then allows me to know I can afford the shipment."

What does this mean to me, when I walk into Home Depot and purchase two $4 brass nipples—made of copper and zinc—to connect my hot- and cold-water copper flex pipes to my hot-water heater? It means the copper in those nipples has traveled thousands of miles by train or truck from the mine, to the foundry, to the wholesaler, to the fabricator (and melted down several times along the way), to the supplier, and finally to the store where a worker placed it on the shelf. All this is lost on the average consumer, such as myself, who walks in one Sunday morning with an iced tea in one hand and my daughter in the other, trying to keep her from pulling everything off the shelves. Attempting to stay focused on my mission of getting to the plumbing section, I pass through the lighting section where I ponder how much copper wire is dangling from the ceilings of all those displays. Given that Freeport is the world's largest producer of coiled copper wire, it is entirely possible that most of that copper came from Freeport's mines here in Arizona, was then shipped to China where it was used in the making of the light, and then shipped back to the United States, eventually to sell in a Home Depot store. Leaving the lighting section, I walk through home appliances, daydreaming of getting a dishwasher for our house. Here, hidden inside the guts of all these appliances is more and more copper, likely in the form of heat sinks inside the refrigerators, washers and dryers, microwaves, and trash compactors. Again I think how I can't escape this metal but rarely ever see it.

Finally I arrive in the plumbing section, where copper is on full display. I am bedazzled by all the brass fittings. There are valves, hose clamps, inverted flares, drain cocks, hose bibs, push-on hose barbs, brass adaptors for pipes, compression fittings, PVC copper–threaded valves, 90-degree brass elbow valves, couplings, locknuts, brass caps, and, finally, my half-inch nipples.

John Tilton, an economics research professor at the Colorado School of Mines, has been studying the macrodynamics of copper pricing for decades. He is also a part-time copper consultant to the government of Chile, which runs the largest copper business on Earth.

"In the short term, say, 2012 to 2013, copper prices will most likely rise," says Tilton. "This is mostly due to the shortage of copper and because some of the bigger mines are producing less. But in the long term, say, ten to fifteen years, I am confident the price will come down lower because the price of copper is far beyond the cost of production. This profit margin will invite new competition, and the appetite for expansion will be ripe. Also some new mines will come online in that time, and new technology is making extraction of lower-grade ore more and more possible."

Trying to guess how much copper to produce or how much to cut production cannot be easily predicted by a single day on the stock market or what happens in the ring at the LME. Expanding mines takes time. Firing personnel during a downturn is relatively easy, but getting the labor back in place when the demand increases almost always causes a drag in supply. Added to this is the fact that copper is an actual physical commodity, meaning that when an earthquake damages the large mines in Chile, which happens from time to time, copper prices spike due to resulting constriction in supply. All this makes the mining business seem like a slow-moving cargo ship that has only so much ability to maneuver quickly, the ship that takes five miles to come to a complete stop and twenty minutes to change directions.

As of 2011, the known total supply of copper in the world was around 940 million tons. By today's consumption and production levels, that is enough for sixty years. Chile accounts for one-third of the world output of copper, making copper to Chile what oil is to Saudi Arabia. It *is* the national commodity. During the Vietnam War, copper exports accounted for almost 80 percent of the nation's export earnings. Today it accounts for 17 percent of the GDP. With reserves of over 100 million tons, and another 150 million tons identified for possible mining, Chile will continue to be the world's leading producer of copper for decades. The United States is second or third in production, depending on the year and what mines are online, but instead of exporting copper, we are forced to import nearly 40 percent of our current copper from places like Chile, Indonesia, and Mexico. The reason? Like China, our demand for copper far exceeds our own domestic supply.

Currently the world uses about twenty million tons of copper per year, with mines accounting for sixteen million of those tons. To make up the difference, the market taps a consistent source that does not come directly from mines: scrap metal. Every year in the United States, as much copper is recovered from scrap as is extracted from mines. And because copper does not decay and can easily be cleaned of impurities using secondary smelters scattered throughout the United States and the world, copper is the most sought-after metal for scrap yard owners.

One day while visiting Flagstaff, I decide to visit the Northern Arizona Metal Recycling scrap yard. I am here on a family vacation because Flagstaff is one of the places my wife and I are thinking of relocating if we decide to leave Bisbee.

Scrap yards are unique in that no matter where they are located, they almost always resemble the aftermath of a tornado, where bits of homes are scattered everywhere, seemingly in no particular order. Yet there is a strategy to this chaos. The piles strewn about the yard are separated into brass, iron, steel, bronze, copper, and tin. Then there are the piles of parts of cars, refrigerators, heaters, lawn chairs, engines, sewing machines, lamps, and almost anything that has metal in it.

To most it looks like junk. To a scrap yard owner it is money in the bank.

I walk to what appears to be the only structure on the premises, which I barely see hidden behind piles of junk. In front of me two Navajo men are selling a truckload of mixed metal parts. One of the men reaches into an open window on the side of the shack and collects a wad of cash.

I step up to the window.

"What you got?" asks a young man named Dean, staring down at a calculator on his desk. He's wearing a shirt with no sleeves and a cowboy hat.

"A couple questions," I reply.

He looks up for the first time and shrugs his shoulders, as if confused by my purpose for standing in his window. I tell him I'm interested in how it all works, how this yard of junk makes him money.

He stands up and walks out the door.

"Welcome to the yard," he says proudly, surveying the tons of metal in front of him. "Really, I'm just a middleman, a very small middleman. There are many of us. And then there are bigger middlemen.

"I just take whatever they bring," Dean continues, pointing to the steady line of people walking up to the window, some holding pieces of pipe, others pointing to a truck loaded with parts of machinery and broken-down homes. All the casual interaction makes it apparent most of his customers are regulars.

Dean explains that the large box of copper pieces in front of the office is worth roughly $3 a pound. The box weighs around five hundred pounds and is filled with copper wire, pipes from homes, and various pieces of appliances.

"I see you paying everyone here, but how do *you* get paid?" I ask, noticing for the first time several men throwing pieces of appliances and engines from one stack to another, separating various types of metal.

"I will drive this box of copper down to Phoenix to a bigger scrap yard and they buy it from me," he says. "They are the bigger middlemen."

We stand for a few moments listening to metal banging against metal. The yard is so packed with scrap metal there is barely enough room for a car to turn around once it's entered the parking lot.

I ask Dean if he knows where his copper scraps will eventually end up.

"China, I imagine. Everything goes to China," he says.

He is almost right. In 2008, almost 70 percent of the world's scrap copper went to China, which also maintains a sizable copper smelter industry. There are three hundred copper smelters spread across the globe, but the single largest concentration of these smokestacks are in China and Japan. Japan's smelters are known for their almost 0 percent emission of pollution, as a result of very expensive technology that they have installed. China's smelters are known for the opposite.

Either way, according to John Tilton, these smelter operations are not profitable.

"Across the globe, smelting is a losing proposition," he says. "In Chile, which produces the most amount of copper concentrate in the world, they ship all their concentrate on boats to China or Japan because to do it in Chile would cost too much money."

I ask how China and Japan are able to effectively control so much of the smelting business if it is not profitable.

"No one really knows for sure, but the only logical answer is the industry is heavily subsidized in those countries. The governments in China and Japan have deemed that industry worthy of protecting and building up," says Tilton.

By having smelters, China and Japan may not make money in the short term, but as a national strategy it allows them a constant source of refined copper. And considering that China is the world's primary manufacturer of consumer goods, the purified copper is often sold directly to Chinese fabricators, who then make airplanes, cars, computers, and hundreds and hundreds of other products for the world's consumer and professional markets.

Conversely, the United States is the world's largest exporter of copper scrap, an indicator that we use too much and create copious amounts of waste. As China continues to grow, this trend of buying scrap metal will increase, making scrap yards in towns all over the United States more and more hungry for copper scraps.

This hunger for copper has also increased the incidence of copper theft.

At the scrap yard in Flagstaff, I notice a few men who appear to be in need of a square meal holding small pieces of metal. They avert their eyes when I approach them. I turn to Dean and ask about the laws in Arizona intended to prosecute scrap yards if they accept stolen copper.

"Well," he says nonchalantly, "we follow the rules, take all the information we have to, IDs, etc., and only accept nonstripped copper wire, but that is all we can do. We want copper just like the next guy. It sells."

Driving away, I stare at the electrical lines that follow the road, the same scene along almost every road in the world. Inside all those lines is copper. Even the lines that hold up the utility poles, usually doubling as grounding wires, have copper in them, which is a reason they are also being cut down.

For a thief hoping to steal that copper, the job seems straightforward. Find a dirt road, get a truck and a ladder, and follow the telephone lines a few miles until you're out of sight. Stop the truck, raise the ladder, and begin working. The lines go on for miles, as far as the horizon. There is as much copper as one can steal. In two years, copper rose from less than $2 a pound in 2009 to a record high of $4.60 in February 2011. During this period, copper theft spiked. Many thieves are caught and sent to jail, but there is a risk in stealing copper far greater than a jail sentence.

In the United States, between 2006 and 2008, forty-four deaths were directly related to copper theft, all due to being electrocuted while trying to steal copper wire, which is often still hooked up to the electrical grid. In 2008, just outside San Diego, a sheriff's deputy stood near a telephone pole in the desert. A ladder was propped up against the pole. Strewn on the ground below were cutting tools and a scorched body. Two power lines had been cut. This scene could have been classified as "mysterious." But the deputy had seen it before. The police reported no suspicion of foul play. The case was closed before they left the scene of the grisly death. The man died alone in the cold desert, zapped by ten thousand watts as he touched a live wire while trying to strip copper wiring from a telephone line.

Copper theft is quickly shifting from petty crime to a major priority of local police across the world. In the last several years, coinciding with China's continued ascension, copper theft is becoming a budgetary problem in many cities. Thieves, like water, tend to follow the path of least resistance. Stealing copper means hitting what is called "soft targets," a police term for places that are not guarded. In the past, whenever I read about these copper thefts, I always assumed they were drug related. Many are, but recently copper thefts have become very sophisticated, indicating a more nuanced and structured force behind the thefts than petty thieves. The incidents may seem minor and affect only single individuals in the community—stealing copper wire from an abandoned building or a few copper pipes from a construction site—but in the last decade copper theft has taken on a new dimension: stealing the infrastructure of cities.

On October 3, 2011, two men drove to a rest stop outside Flagstaff in a van with a false decal slapped on the side identifying them as working electricians. They wore matching patches on their clothes further signifying they were legitimate laborers. In less than forty-five minutes, they gutted the rest stop of hundreds of feet of copper wire.

"They destroyed it," says Gerry Blair, the spokesperson for the Coconino Sheriff's Office in Arizona. "They probably got a thousand dollars' worth of scrap copper, but it will cost us ten thousand dollars to replace all the ruined machinery and wires. It's always the destruction that costs us."

I ask him if he has seen an increase in copper theft since 2010, when the price of copper began a steady upward climb.

"I would say a trend is happening," he says. "And we don't

know for sure, but these two guys we caught may be linked to even more thefts in the Phoenix area. These aren't amateurs. They had all the correct tools. They had scouted the place. They are pros."

In the last decade, according to a 2008 FBI report, thieves have become so sophisticated that they use databases to track foreclosed homes, unfinished subdivision lots, and electrical substations, all popular targets for large unguarded quantities of copper. More than thirty states have a law in place regarding scrap copper, which forces scrap yards to check seller identification, to pay with checks instead of cash, and to register the seller of the scrap metal. In 2009, three scrap metal yards in Arizona were charged with knowingly buying copper that had been stripped from houses. They were each convicted of a Class 1 misdemeanor.

The conservative estimate of the annual damage done to the country's infrastructure hovers around $10 billion. And this doesn't include copper stolen from homes, which are the most frequent target. Most of us think of our homes as our most valuable possession. We see the house as a shell, with nice couches, beds, and fully equipped kitchens. We don't pay much attention to the guts of the house, the wires and pipes hidden in the walls, attics, and basements.

The $10 billion figure addresses the larger problem, like when three hundred feet of copper wire from a Federal Aviation Administration tower in Ohio is stolen, potentially interrupting normal communication between in-flight aircraft and ground control.

Or when farmers in Pinal County, Arizona, took a $10 million loss on their infrastructure when thieves stripped the copper from their water irrigation wells and pumps. In Somerset County, Pennsylvania, the thieves opted not to steal the wire from a 120-foot radio tower and instead stole the entire tower. During the night they cut it into pieces and drove it away to be melted down for scrap.

One of the largest users of copper is the technology sector, and in a twist of irony, in Menlo Park, California, thieves targeted the future home of Facebook, stealing thousands of pounds of copper wiring from the construction site.

One theft with far-reaching ramifications was discovered too late when a tornado threatened the city of Jackson, Mississippi, on April 4, 2008. Five tornado-warning sirens failed to activate that day because the copper had been stolen from the sirens.

Copper theft occurs everywhere. Perhaps the most affected country is South Africa, which loses upward of $1 billion a year to thieves. One syndicate stole thirty miles of telephone line in a single night. The cables that run the railroads in parts of South Africa have been so damaged that shipping containers that used to take twenty hours to cross the country now take forty. As a response to the problem, Cape Town created a special police force called Copperheads, whose sole job is to prevent copper theft from their vital infrastructure. So far they have had moderate success, but they admit that catching the thieves is like a "balloon effect." As soon as they push on one side of the municipality, the thieves react and hit the other side.

Scrap copper has evolved into such a profitable business that there has been a worldwide crackdown on the cartels that manipulate the price of scrap copper to their benefit. In Korea, the government fined twenty-five scrap metal processors for price-fixing. In the United States, there are eight secondary smelters, used for melting down scrap metal. Three of those scrap metal processors have racked up fines totaling $23 million for bid-rigging and price-fixing. And in South Africa, thirteen scrap metal processors are at the center of a price-fixing scheme after a four-year investigation.

John Tilton talks to industry insiders continually. He is regarded as someone with intimate knowledge of what affects copper pricing and in turn copper mining.

I point out that he is able to predict the short-term and long-term price but doesn't have much to say about prices five years from now.

"I have no idea," he says. "If I knew that, I would be the oracle of copper. That is the sweet spot for copper producers, and no one can figure it out."

Today, most economists who study base metals agree there is a general forecast for a shortage of readily available copper over the next decade due to the fact that many existing mines will play out and new mines take so long to come online. This projected gap in the copper supply will most likely drive up the price and force existing mines to produce even more. This is where existing mines, even if dormant, like Bisbee, will begin to look more and more attractive to major mining companies. With plenty of copper left in the hills around Bisbee, it may be only a matter of time before the blasting begins.

8

Pebble Mine

Mining is like a search-and-destroy mission.
—Stewart Udall, former secretary
of the interior for John F. Kennedy
and Lyndon B. Johnson

I am on the way to the airport. I am flying to Alaska, where I have
worked as a commercial fisherman every summer for the past
several years. But I am not going there to fish this time. I am going
because there is talk of developing one of the world's biggest copper and gold mines near the watershed of Bristol Bay, which is
home to the world's largest sockeye salmon run, with almost forty
million fish returning every summer. I am familiar with many people fighting against the potential mining operation and am on my
way to hear firsthand what would happen if the mine opens.

Driving toward the airport, I glance down at the coins on my
passenger seat. I remember hearing somewhere that pennies contain almost no copper. In fact, they are 97 percent zinc and only
copper coated, whereas quarters are almost all copper.

In the last several months, my mind has become consumed by
what copper *is,* and I find even the smallest details fascinating.
Every coin has copper in it. Every house has, on average, four
hundred pounds of copper pipe and wiring. Since 1963, it is estimated that more than 30 billion feet, or 5.5 million miles, of copper plumbing have been installed in the United States. Every 747

jet airliner has 135 miles of copper wire, weighing nine thousand pounds. The Statue of Liberty weighs in at a hundred tons of copper. A Triton-class nuclear submarine uses two hundred thousand pounds of copper. And recently I found out that there is thirty-three hundred pounds of copper in the *radiator* of the Caterpillar 797, the mining trucks in Morenci.

Over the years, there have been attempts to replace copper as the main electrical wire in homes, but so far nothing can beat copper's low price and high conductivity. In the 1970s, due to a spike in the price, there was a move to substitute aluminum for copper. That adventure nosedived after a few houses burned down when the aluminum caught fire while conducting electricity. Of all the minerals that fuel our current way of life, copper is the heavyweight. It alone, not gold, silver, zinc, cobalt, or any other mineral, is most responsible for creating what we like to call civilization.

I veer north, toward Tombstone, home of the daily O.K. Corral gunfight, bison burgers, and lots of T-shirt shops. Once a genuine silver-mining town, Tombstone shut down for all practical purposes by the end of the 1890s, when the mines flooded. Since then, Tombstone has slipped into role-playing what it used to be. Men dress as cowboys with fake guns and walk the streets waiting for the next gunfight show to begin. Women prance around town in corsets and low-cut dresses acting like Big Nose Kate, the tough bar owner and girlfriend of Doc Holliday. Like clockwork, a gunfight happens around high noon. No one dies, and the tourists take photos and the actors dust themselves off and get ready for the three o'clock show.

The airport is still an hour away. As I drive, I see the country around me differently, perhaps for the first time. A hundred years ago, small mines dotted the landscape. Today they are all still there, hidden off the trails, some surrounded by wire, some open shafts that fall two hundred feet into darkness.

To the east stands the iconic Cochise Stronghold, the proud and violent rock formation that acts as the face of the Dragoon Mountains, where Chief Cochise used to stage his raids. Today people go to the Dragoons to camp. Illegal immigrants walk the remote trails on their way to points farther north. On the back-

side of the mountains is the town of Pierce and a ghost mining camp named Courtland. I play basketball with a local man
named Jimmy who spends several weekends every spring digging
in Courtland for azurite and malachite, two valuable minerals
that are prevalent in southern Arizona. A Haida from the Northwest, Jimmy has fallen in love with the desert and has a passion
for rocks. He goes alone into the slopes of the Dragoons, digs for
three or four hours in a hole that he has been digging for years.
He wears safety goggles and a long-sleeve shirt. His tools are a
shovel, raw strength, and his wits. Since Bisbee has a population
of rock hounds, who are always on the alert for rumors of gold,
copper, or other minerals, Jimmy doesn't trust anyone with the
actual location of his dig. So, after pitching out dirt and rock with
a shovel, he spends the last three hours of his day covering the
hole back up. He is almost sixty, lean and taut. I have no idea if
he makes much money from this labor, but like any prospector,
from 1880 or today, the thrill of finding something that no one
else has fuels his passion for living.

Finally I get to the airport, get on a plane, and twelve hours
later land in Dillingham, Alaska. I walk through the one-room
terminal to the pay phone. I call the name penciled into my tat-
tered notebook.

A woman asks, "Who are you?"

I tell her I got her number from a friend in Naknek who knows
her husband and that I was supposed to spend the night at their
home.

"He's down at the nets. But I'll come get you in ten minutes."

Of course she didn't question my intentions. Why would she?
In the Alaska bush, a mutual friend is a key to the front door.

I ask how I will recognize her.

"I have red hair and I'm fat," she says with a laugh that reminds
me I am back in the land where no one cares what you look like,
only if you can hack out an existence in a place that tries very
hard to push people away.

In a few moments, a woman with flaming-red hair, wearing
sweatpants and rain boots, enters the terminal. There are several
young fishermen staggering about, greenhorns lost in their first

117

moments of getting ready to do one of the hardest jobs on Earth. She walks straight toward me.

"I'm Ginger, Terry's wife. Come on, then, let's get out of this dance hall, shall we?"

At home, Terry Hoefferle, her husband and the man I am meant to meet, hovers at the kitchen counter with a king salmon half as tall as himself and easily weighing fifty pounds.

"Biggest one I can remember," he yells at his wife, not a mean kind of yelling but the kind that develops over years as people lose their hearing.

He lays the monster on the counter and slowly begins to fillet the meat, being careful not to nick the stomach. It is a female and she's carrying thousands of eggs, which Terry tenderly puts into a basket. He will later soak them in brine and use them for trading with natives.

"You got boots?" he asks me.

"I do," I reply.

"Well, let's go, gotta bring the net in a bit. It's a holdover tide," meaning the ebb tide will be weak, allowing fish to continue to push upriver against the current and into the hundreds of nets put out by locals.

We drive past the headquarters of the Bristol Bay Native Corporation and the Kanakanak Hospital. A few miles later we turn onto a dirt road. The rain begins, as it always does in Alaska, and we park next to a thicket of alders.

"Hey, bear, hey, bear! We're coming so get the hell out of there!" Terry screams at the top of his lungs. He's pounding his fist on the truck hood. The rain falls harder now, but we are both veterans of Alaska, and so we act like we are enjoying a warm day in Puerto Rico, as opposed to a freezing afternoon in Bristol Bay.

Walking near a river during salmon season in Alaska causes an impending feeling of a large predator waiting, lurking, and stalking you. The grizzly bear may not attack, this time, but the pucker in your ass is undeniable. And your eyes, ears, and each and every pore are suddenly awake and alert. You are not what it wants, but there is a chance you may find yourself between the bear and the salmon-thick streambed.

Still yelling, we reach the river and quickly begin to heave Terry's net up toward shore, wrapping the excess rope around a series of stakes that hold the net in place as the tides rip back and forth.

"Here is my question," Terry begins, unprompted. "Why would you risk a known sustainable resource for one that will only last fifty years? And if there is a bad accident at the mine, it may kill the fish. Why risk a resource we already have with absolute certainty?" he asks, pointing toward the river.

"These salmon have been feeding people in this region for thousands of years. And we've been making money from them for more than a hundred. That could go on for hundreds of years, unless someone fucks up and puts a bunch of toxins in the water."

Terry is lamenting about Pebble mine. The nonexistent mine is on the lips of everyone who lives within two hundred miles. There are signs in yards, bumper stickers on trucks. Commercial boats have NO PEBBLE painted on the side. The issue divides homes, families, and marriages. One man I meet doesn't speak to his father-in-law anymore because they disagree on the mining issue.

The battles are happening in thirty-odd villages spread out over ninety thousand square miles. All this over a mine, which, if built, won't be in production until 2015, or later. But if built, it will be the largest source of copper in North America. The deposits are truly staggering. The estimates indicate approximately 80 billion pounds of copper, 100 million ounces of gold, and 5.6 million pounds of molybdenum. Calculated at today's market rates, the deposit comes out to be worth anywhere between $300 and $500 billion over the seventy-five-year life span of the mine.

"I know it is a lot of money, but the vast majority of that money will go to shareholders in other countries, people who will never know or care that they killed a way of life for us, and our planet," says Terry as we heave the net farther up the shore. I stare out toward the flat gray horizon of Bristol Bay, a one-of-a-kind fishery that is home to half the world's known salmon runs. The sockeye run is worth upward of $400 million each year to the local economies through fish tax, fishermen's wages, and secondary incomes from shipping fish, canning fish, and the many other ways fish are brought to market. Stretched out over the life of the mine, this equals around $22 billion over seventy-five years. This is a lot of money either way. A fundamental truth is that the big money tends to win the fight. A second truth, of equal value and importance, is that sometimes the underdogs win. And when they do, life feels a bit sweeter.

Just like the salmon heading upstream to their spawning grounds, this is the time of year I have always traveled north. Commercial fishing is the most difficult job I have ever done in my life. Each day begins a brand-new cycle filled with pain, crappy food, too much booze, and a dizzying buildup of sleep deprivation. And I can't get enough of it.

There is something pure and simple about working so hard and falling asleep feeling honest about the day's effort. I imagine miners working the underground tunnels of Bisbee feeling the same way. They could be heard at the bars all over town at the end of a shift, saying thing like, "I may be poor, dying of lung disease, and pissed off at the management, but by golly I'm an honest man doing an honest day's work." Of course the difference between fishermen and miners is that the majority of fishermen work for themselves, whereas miners have always worked for the owners. One thing they have in common is that when they die on the job it is usually in a dark cold place where no one can hear you scream.

I'd long heard about the possibility of the mine, but was so busy fishing I didn't take the time to learn about it. And then, like all my fellow humans, I tuned in once it affected me. Because Bristol Bay lies far away from any urban environment, remoteness has always been its biggest asset. It makes buying beer or any flown-in food a very expensive endeavor, but it has also been the saving grace of the fishery and the wild lands that stretch backward from its shores for hundreds of miles. Out here subsistence living is not a myth. This is the kind of place where Farley Mowat could live for several seasons and write five books on how the Native Alaskans have been eking out an existence for seven thousand years, living on fish, moose, caribou, and berries.

If built, the mine will be fourteen miles from Lake Iliamna, the largest natural sockeye salmon hatchery on Earth. Historically, half the sockeye in the Bristol Bay run come from creeks and rivers that flow from Lake Iliamna. That is twenty million fish a year.

I have read vast amounts of literature from the mining companies hoping to operate Pebble mine. The ore body was discovered in the 1980s by Teck Cominco, which after several years of digging holes decided the deposit was worth around $10 billion, not enough to justify the costs associated with building a mine this remote, and near a fishery. Cominco sold its shares of Pebble mine to Northern Dynasty, a junior mining company from Vancouver. Northern developed the site further and quickly realized the deposit was worth much more than Cominco had estimated. It also knew it couldn't carry the entire cost of developing the mine, so the company reached out to Anglo American, one of the heavyweights in the global extraction business, known for its platinum and zinc production, and oh, they own half of De Beers diamonds.

Based in London, Anglo has started a new publicity campaign to win over Alaskans. You see it on billboards and small pamphlets in Anchorage: "Coexistence. Mining and fish can live together." I am not a scientist, but I know that slogan is pure nonsense. Sure, mining and fishing can coexist, until they can't. And then when the dam breaks, or the guy driving the bulldozer falls asleep and dumps toxins into the river, the slogan will change. My best guess is that it will want us to relate to it not as a company but as people trying their best not to ruin everything in sight.

After a short nap, I wake to the sound of gunfire directly outside my cabin. I throw on my Levi's and open the door to see Terry standing on his porch with a .22 rifle, staring at me. He looks pissed.

"That's your wake-up call. We leave in half an hour."

And that is an Alaska bush alarm clock.

By the time we arrive, fifty people crowd the upstairs of the volunteer fire department garage. And although it nears 9:00 p.m., the sun hovers on the horizon, seemingly forever. On a table near the back of the room are coffee and cookies. On another table sit pamphlets showing the danger of the mine.

The woman speaking is Carol Ann Woody, with a PhD in fishery science who used to work for the U.S. Department of Fish and Wildlife, until one day she spoke too loudly about how this mine was a bad idea.

"I was pushed out," she told me earlier that day. "I mean there is a longer story, but that is the short story. So now I work for the opposition."

Woody speaks to a room packed with fishermen from all over Alaska and from the Lower 48, as well as local residents. This date, a few days before the official launch of the fishing season, was chosen specifically to reach out to nonresidential fishermen, a large but usually silent group of stakeholders in this issue. Most of the crowd wear jeans and sweatshirts and are covered in some oil or grease from fixing an engine or repairing fishing gear. The mind-set of a fisherman reflects that of most Americans and most human beings. The fishermen are much more concerned with how many fish they are going to catch on opening day than with Pebble mine, because one impacts their lives right now and the other is a hypothetical danger that is years down the road.

Carol Woody is joined in her presentation by David Chambers, who besides having an MS in engineering and a PhD in environmental planning from UC Berkeley, has an engineering degree in physics from the Colorado School of Mines and is the president of the Center for Science in Public Participation in Bozeman, Montana. For two hours the two try to convince the crowd that the danger lurking years down the road from a hard-rock mining operation will eventually destroy the bounty they take on their opening day of the season.

To begin, they present a horror slide show detailing what has already occurred around the world with hard-rock mining, specifically copper: tailing dams breaking, rivers choked to death by sulfuric acid runoff, and entire vistas replaced by a gigantic hole in the ground. Woody explains how as little as two parts per billion of copper above normal background copper (meaning naturally occurring copper) in the water can make a salmon lose its sense of direction. To illustrate her point, she shows a video of a young salmon smolt in a water tank darting around at great speed. Then the equivalent of one part per billion of copper is dropped into the tank. Within a minute the young salmon is docile, almost still. She explains this makes the fish easy prey. While copper is natural in many rivers in Alaska, it is the addition of processed copper from the tailings that is the potential killer of this fishery.

A slide pops up on the screen showing a mine in Spain where the tailing dam breached, leaking tons of toxic sludge into a river and killing everything downstream. In China, a dam holding back the toxic tailing sludge breaks and empties into a river, killing all aquatic life.

The exact scope of the Pebble mine is not yet known, but that has not stopped the companies that control Pebble mine from floating several ideas of how they will build out the mine site. One is to build three earthen dams near the mine, one of which will be 720 feet high and 4 miles long, which would rival the heights of the largest dams anywhere. Behind these dams would be ten billion tons of waste rock collected over the seventy-five-year life of the mine, the equivalent of three thousand pounds for every person on Earth. There will also be containment ponds, used to dilute and store waste. The pit will be two miles wide and two thousand feet deep. The tailing compounds will cover seventy-five hundred acres. This will occupy more than ten square miles. The vast majority of the waste will be in the form of pulverized rock, much of it laced with barium, cadmium, chromium, cobalt, iron, lead, nickel, selenium, and arsenic, all naturally occurring by-products of mining for gold and copper. And all of this activity will be within fourteen miles of Iliamna Lake, where tens of millions of salmon smolts live while awaiting their downstream journey to the ocean, and whose water feeds forty thousand square miles of watershed. Rational minds must ask why a state would even consider allowing this in a place that has an 8,000-year-old history of fishing for salmon, 125 years of that as a successful commercial fishery that adds more than $400 million a year to the economy.

Then someone mentions the fact that this area of Alaska has a history of violent seismic activity, and the room goes silent.

After a long pause, Chambers, who has a calm way of lecturing, puts his hands on the podium and smiles slightly. He is a quiet man whose expression hints of someone who knows more than he is telling you but who knows his duty is to get the point across in the simplest terms.

"I have found that what a miner defines as risky does not always line up with what you or I find risky. Each party has their own standards for acceptable risk."

This statement, I realize, is the closest Chambers will ever come to painting a picture of doom. He refuses to pound his fists or raise his voice in order to make his point. He is a man of rational thought, long taught to follow science. He is doing his best to tell this room that science is leading him to conclude this mine is a disaster in the making.

I look around the room and see heads shaking. One fisherman gets up and grabs another cookie and cup of coffee and heads for the door. His season begins soon, and all this talk is not helping him catch fish.

Someone from the back of the room mumbles, "I was here on Good Friday and ain't no way this will survive anything like that."

On March 27, 1964, Good Friday, an earthquake shook Alaska for almost five minutes. The quake registered 9.2 on the Richter scale, making it the second-largest earthquake in recorded history. It moved Latouche Island forty feet to the southeast. The Pacific plate moved thirty feet under the North American plate. The energy released from this violent Earth sneeze was ten million times more than the atomic bomb that destroyed Hiroshima.

The quake was so intense it produced what is known as "earthquake liquefaction"—the soil suddenly changes from a solid state to a liquid state. In Anchorage, ninety miles from the epicenter, entire neighborhoods simply turned to sand and washed away. On Kodiak Island, two hundred miles from the epicenter, some land areas rose thirty feet into the air, permanently. Tsunamis raced up the Prince William Sound, killing dozens and wiping out the town of Chenega and severely damaging several other villages. In Valdez, the wave measured over one hundred feet high and instantly killed twenty-eight people working the docks that day.

Maybe the mining companies aren't aware that the Pebble mine site sits on top of the Lake Clark, Castle Mountain, and Denali fault lines. Or that Alaska itself sits in the Pacific Ring of Fire, a zone of geological and seismic activity. Eighty percent of the world's largest earthquakes and volcanoes occur in this horseshoe-shaped zone, running north from Indonesia, up the coasts of Japan, along the Aleutian chain, to the shores of Alaska and down the west coasts of North and South America.

Will the tailing piles, sitting behind three large earthen dams, be able to handle another Good Friday Earthquake, which liquefied the earth? Of course not. The people who will own this mine live in London, Johannesburg, Vancouver, and elsewhere. What they may not understand or care about is that the earth waits for no one, especially in places like Alaska that sit atop geological time bombs ticking beneath its surface.

Another pointed reminder of Earth's power happened on March 11, 2011, when a 9.0 earthquake hit northern Japan. The tsunamis and earthquake killed almost 18,000 people and destroyed 125,000 buildings. The Fukushima nuclear plant had a partial meltdown of its nuclear rods, and radiation leaked out, creating a dead zone for miles, which will last forever. Here is the interesting detail. Modern-day mines and nuclear plants share the same industry standard when it comes to earthquake-proofing their sites. They build their facilities to withstand a 7.5 earthquake. So far all the plans for Pebble indicate they will follow that industry standard.

Chambers also reminds us that only a hundred miles away from Pebble's proposed mine stands Mount Redoubt, which has been spewing volcanic ash for more than two years. When the issue of seismic and volcanic activity has been brought up to the Pebble executives as a concern about the dams they plan to build, which have to exist *forever,* they say, "We are taking the seismic situation into consideration."

I respect the abilities of structural engineers. Their work dots the planet in places such as the Golden Gate Bridge, the Eiffel Tower, and the Panama Canal, but to build one of the largest earthen dams near one of the most seismically active places on Earth reeks of arrogance, the kind of bravado that created Love Canal, Chernobyl, and the extinction and near extinction of many animals over the last hundred years. If this mine has to exist for seventy-five years, pitched in a daily battle against the geophysics of Earth, there will be no contest. It will be a slaughter. Earth, with its violent tantrums, will win. It always does.

9

Which Side Are You On?

The idea of wilderness needs no defense. It only needs more defenders.

—Edward Abbey, *The Journey Home*

To get closer to the actual mining site of Pebble, I first need to get to the remote native village of Iliamna, the headquarters of the mining operation. If built, Pebble would dwarf anything that might happen in Bisbee, which if reopened would be what copper insiders call a "brownfield," or the expansion of an already existing mine site. What Bisbee would experience in terms of waste rock, pollution, and environmental threats to the surrounding area are minuscule compared to what would happen if Pebble had a mining accident.

The problem is that getting to Iliamna is not easy. The village hugs the western shoreline of Lake Iliamna, 175 miles west of Anchorage, separated from the rest of Alaska by the glaciers of the Aleutian Range. There are no roads in or out, and the village maintains a year-round population of two hundred inhabitants, most of whom are native people. The only way in is by plane, and flights are infrequent.

I wake up on a Monday morning in King Salmon, the airport hub of Bristol Bay, to a downpour, knowing I have little chance of getting out of here. Still, I pick up the phone and call the airport, a single-lane mud patch ten miles north toward the ocean. The voice on the other end of the phone says, "No planes to Iliamna today, but keep calling."

After a few days of waiting, I decide to visit Violet Wilson, a well-known leader of native people fighting against Pebble mine. On the phone her directions are simple. She says, "Look for the sign that says KNIVES AND FURS next to the road."

I borrow a truck and drive across Leader Creek toward Naknek, home base to a substantial segment of the commercial salmon fleet in Bristol Bay. For most of the year, Naknek has a population of seven hundred, but every June thousands of souls descend upon this native village from around the world. For that one month, Naknek becomes an ethnic melting pot, all enticed by the promise of making money. Everyone is here to work, and because the sun doesn't set until around 1:00 a.m., and then for only a few hours, work feels as though it is a never-ending delirious frenzy. I pass cannery workers from Turkey, the Czech Republic, Russia, and the Lower 48 walking along the side of the road, strolling to the pizza parlor, to the liquor store, and back to the cannery. Many are still wearing their hairnets, most have rain boots, and some look like the walking dead, exhausted from the hours this job demands. My window is rolled up, keeping the army of mosquitoes at bay.

After a few more wrong turns, I find the small KNIVES AND FURS sign. I drive up a dirt path to her house, a two-story wood home with a small truck in the driveway. Violet answers the door with a large grin on her small, round native face, and she quickly ushers me into her downstairs living room. There is no place to sit, as it serves as a makeshift gallery. On display are racks and racks of fur, mostly wolf and fox.

Violet is eighty-five years old and was raised in Kanakanak, on the shores of Lake Iliamna, with her siblings, her parents, and a nearby uncle and his family. In 1938, the family came to Naknek for work, but Violet missed being near the lake. In 1948, she returned to Iliamna for a few years before moving to Kodiak, and then again moved back to Iliamna. She tells stories of growing up in remote Alaska without stores, electricity, or any connection to the outside world. They relied on various food sources, but the most abundant was always the summer salmon runs, the same runs she feels will be threatened if Pebble mine is allowed to go forward.

"Archie traps by himself upriver in the winter," she says of her husband, waving her hand among the pelts, all treated and ready for the furrier to make a coat, scarf, or hat.

Nearby stands a table full of knives, all handmade. The prices range from $100 to $400, all pieces of art as well as function.

Upstairs, Violet, who walks with a limp, makes me a tea as we discuss her grandson. Then she sits down near the window and dispenses with the small talk.

"Well, I should start by saying I have had four husbands. Three of them died on me. The first one died in 1964 in a plane crash. Second one died of cancer. Third one died of a heart attack. And now I have my Archie."

I ask Violet if she has an opinion about the Pebble mine.

"I certainly do. It will be dumbest damn thing if they build that mine. Nothing can come of it other than the destruction of our only knowable resource, the fish. We have lived from these fish for thousands of years and can keep doing it."

Archie saunters into the room with a cup of coffee in his hand, wearing denim overalls. Archie smiles in my direction, obviously amused by his wife's passion for the issue.

"I hunt animals for a living," says Archie. "But I love animals. People who don't live up here would get mad at me for killing them, but all I can say to them is you don't live here. We live by the land, and we'll probably die by it."

I ask Violet about the Angasan family, who are known to have a tight grip over the King Salmon Tribal Council and steer the local politics in favor of the Pebble mine development.

"Clair Angasan is my sister," she says, nodding her head in obvious disappointment. "She is married to Ralph, the patriarch of the family. And they won't talk to me. They haven't spoken to me in a few years."

"Why?"

"They say I embarrass them because I don't want the mine to be built." Violet slowly shakes her head. "We are blood family, but she married into the family that has all the power in this area and they shut me out."

I ask if there is a chance they will ever see eye to eye.

"I don't think so," says Violet.

"They are lazy," says Archie. Violet nods in agreement. "Those people are proud to be the last frontier of socialism. They like free lunches and these Pebble people feed them so many free lunches they forgot where they came from. And there is not much anyone else can do about it."

I ask if there is an argument that the mine will do good things for the region.

"No. I raised five children by fishing on these rivers. Fishing was the only income I had for the entire year. And these people that are for the mine, well, they never liked the hard work of fishing and they really enjoy the free money from cozying up to the mining company. They don't care about this place," says Violet, her hands gesticulating.

"So we wait for them to get fat and then fall apart. But I tell you what, the only way that mine is going forward is over my dead body," she says, pointing her finger in my direction.

Powerful families controlling entire villages is nothing new. However, in Alaska, the circles of power are tighter and virtually impossible for outsiders to penetrate. The tribal councils—sometimes also called village councils—do not answer to any state regulatory power. There may be a municipal government that runs a particular town, but the village council doesn't answer to it. Instead, its control can be far greater because it controls the village land, tax structure, and decisions on anything on that native land. So in many towns of the Alaskan bush there is a shadow government that operates outside the normal town structure of mayor and city council. It exerts a great deal of power when someone wants to buy the native land of that area. This partially explains why the Pebble Partnership (a joint ownership of Canada-based Northern Dynasty and London-based Anglo American) feels confident it can succeed in building this mine. It has been slowly gaining allies in the right places—by infiltrating the families that dominate the village councils—even though the vast majority of the population in the villages or towns is against the mine.

Before Alaska became a state in 1958, this governing structure of small native villages was even more powerful. They had to restructure again once oil was found in Prudhoe Bay in 1967, which created a need to run a pipeline from the northern tip of Alaska to Valdez, a deepwater port on Alaska's west coast. This necessitated quick action by Congress to address the native people, who had been promised lands under the Alaska Statehood Act in 1958. On December 23, 1971, Richard Nixon signed into law the Alaska Native Claims Settlement Act (ANCSA), which established thirteen native corporations to manage the $962 million allotted to the nearly eighty thousand Alaska natives. This money was to be distributed over a set period of time, to both individuals and local villages. In addition to the money, ANCSA was put in charge of forty-four million acres, or about 10 percent of the entire state.

Inside the structure of ANCSA is the establishment of two hundred Alaska Native Regional Corporations, which are responsible for allocating money collected by the thirteen larger Native corporations. Of course, whoever controls the local village councils, which were created to govern the land and local laws of small villages, would have great influence on the flow of money and power, which is based on their allotment of money from the larger village corporations. The purpose of these multiple layers was to make sure native people were in place to always protect their rights and their land. The truth is that in many villages members of the same family often dominate the councils, holding everyone in the village hostage to their decisions.

I contact a member of the Angasan family and tell him I have just spoken to Violet.

"I have nothing to say about the mine. We are waiting for more information. If you want to contact me again, call my lawyer," he says and hangs up.

After several days I get a call from the airport. A plane is headed to Iliamna to pick up a fisherman wanting to get to Bristol Bay. The flight takes less than an hour and covers a vast tundra and raging rivers. Down below, the gently sloping earth is flat, hammered horizontal by the slowly receding glaciers that covered this land eight thousand years ago. As we approach the village, the mountains rise sharply to the west. Below, the Newhalen River explodes with Class V white-water rapids. The water flows into the lake, thousands of gallons per minute. I imagine it full of salmon fighting the current to get upstream, always looking for the feeder creeks where they were born. Salmon spawning: ancient, simple, and yet complex enough that no one can fully explain how it works. It's hard to imagine that the yearly cycle of a fish is the reason people have lived on the shores of this lake for thousands of years.

Iliamna, Alaska's largest lake, measures one thousand square miles, eighty miles long and twenty-five miles across, or roughly the size of Rhode Island. The locals believe a monster swims in these waters. Thirty feet long and black, it resembles, they say, a sleek whale. It is vicious and is known to attack the color red, which is why no boats on the water have the color of blood painted on the side. The name itself, Iliamna, stems from the Athabascan words "Nila Vena," which mean "island's lake," most likely referring to the size of this body of water. It is also only one of two lakes in the world that maintain a healthy population of freshwater seals.

The three helicopters parked on the Iliamna village runway are the first clue that someone else is here. An outsider.

From the airstrip I can't see the mine site, but I know that the largest undeveloped deposit of copper in the Americas is fourteen miles from the lake, itself home to the largest sockeye salmon incubator on the planet. These two large resources are both real and both valuable. They are also incompatible. I know the usual ending of this story. The fish lose, the money wins, and the company that extracts the copper moves away never to be seen again. I'm here to see if there is one chance in hell this place can create a different ending.

"You have arrangements for housing?" asks the pilot as he scratches his beard on the way to a building that looks like a small warehouse but doubles as the terminal.

"I do not," I reply.

"Transportation?"

"No."

"Well, you better get something because you don't want to be outside after dark. Bears, cold, and all that," he says and grabs a cup of coffee. The pilot, dressed in loose-fitting jeans, a dirty jacket, and slip-on shoes, looks like a man in a hurry to get back to King Salmon where at least they have bars. Iliamna is a wet town, common in village Alaska, which means you can bring booze into the village but the nearest place to purchase the stuff is a hundred miles and a $300 plane ticket away.

Looking back toward the runway, he points at a man exiting a black pickup truck that has pulled up next to his plane.

"Ask him. He's an Anelon and has housing and transportation. Shit, they have everything," the pilot says, referring to the family that dominates the village council and almost every facet of political power in Iliamna.

Walking back to the tarmac, I extend my hand to the man standing near the back of the pickup.

"Tim Anelon," the man says. With him are a few young boys loading ice chests and duffel bags into the plane.

"Going fishing in Naknek," Tim says.

I couldn't help notice that he was wearing a NO PEBBLE MINE hat. I know his family is pro mine, or at least pro money from the prospect of a mine. I ask about the hat.

Laughing, he says, "I take this hat fishing so I can get it slimed with fish guts, ruin it."

I smile, but not much.

"But really, I have not made up my mind yet. My mind is open."

This is a popular line among those in favor of the mine, who know that most of their neighbors are not. To mitigate backlash, they insist they are waiting to hear all the facts before they make up their mind.

I ask about housing and transportation.

"You can take my truck for $100 a day," he says. I accept.

"And you can stay at my house for $125 a day," he offers. I am intrigued. Maybe I will find out something by staying at his house, driving his car. Maybe I will find some secret document on his kitchen counter, a ledger for millions of dollars from the mining company. So I agree, but under the conditions that I may find another car and other lodging. He ignores me as we enter the small air terminal building, where he makes a short phone call.

"There is a girl who looks after my house. I just told her you are coming. You have satellite television in your room and everything. It is very comfortable."

He walks with great confidence, with the strides of a man who doesn't have a worry in the world. As he approaches the plane, I walk toward the truck.

"Hey," I yell out, "which house is yours?"

"Past the dump on the left. The only two-story house you will see." He points north.

"Where do I put the money?"

"Leave it in the glove box of the truck. And park it here when you leave. Keys in ignition. No one can steal it, right?"

"What color is the roof of your house?"

"I don't know." He laughs.

"What color is the siding?"

"I don't know."

He waves and gets in the plane. They are in the sky a few minutes later. I start the car and can't help but laugh. Does he trust me with his car and house because that is his nature, or does he trust me because there is no way to steal a car from here and because he is an Anelon and ripping him off would only result in trouble for me?

I take the road toward town, which it turns out is the only road. From a bird's-eye view, the road would look like a circle with a tail. The circle loops from the airport around the town and back to the airport, with a few side roads to houses. From ground level, the low scrub pine trees and high grass easily hide any evidence of a road unless traveling on the two-lane pavement. Once the circle is complete, a tail of pavement points north. Here a dirt road continues for thirteen more miles into the mountains, following the Newhalen River to the Athabascan village of Nondalton, a subsistence village that has a long history of refusing any and all outside influences into its way of life. And the rumor is that they hate the Anelons.

Up the dirt road, I find the house. I take note of the blue roof and gray siding. It all appears brand-new. What kind of person doesn't know the color of his roof? There are ATVs in the yard, a brand-new truck, and a snowmobile, all signs of wealth in rural Alaska. In the back are several dogs barking. It is a team of sled dogs, all of them staked down.

A small native girl answers the front door. I guess she is around ten years old. She ushers me inside. A young boy joins her immediately, probably three years old, and then another boy, around the same age. In the kitchen is a sixteen-year-old girl. The babysitter?

"Is this Tim's house?" I ask the older girl.

"Yes," says the ten-year-old girl.

"Did he just call saying I may be staying here?" I ask.

"Uh-huh. He called me," says the same young girl.

"How long will he be gone?"

"About two weeks or more."

"Do you have a phone?" I ask.

She takes me into a bedroom that she says is mine. A plasma television hangs down over the foot of the bed from the ceiling, like something you see in a cheap hotel room. She shuts the door and returns to a living room of screaming kids.

There is no one to call, but I have to catch my breath. I don't know where I am going to stay tonight, but I know it won't be in a house with four young children who aren't mine.

"Is there a store in town?" I ask the girl. She nods and says it's down by the lake.

I tell them I won't be back and walk out the front door.

A poster at the market reads:

Arsery Melognak, age 81 died December 16, 2006. Walking on roadway and struck and killed. Driver who hit him didn't stop. Unsolved. Iliamna Troopers. 907-571-1871

135

No one knows what happened. It is a mystery to some. His wounds suggested a car, or perhaps a snowplow, hit him. This poster is a plea for a tip even though I meet several people who believe they know how he died. They suspect that Ted Anelon, who is the snowplow driver for the city, may have hit Mr. Melognak. I was told that, after finding the body, the state trooper went to the city yard to examine the snowplow, but there was no evidence of an accident. That does not resolve the issue to those who still believe an Anelon mowed him down. This death and the fact no one has been indicted is insight into how the village feels, like a fiefdom of people waiting for the next move by the Anelons.

The reason this family has so much power has nothing to do with its popularity. That, I quickly deduce, is nonexistent. Any people I ask—the cashier at the store, the person buying frozen meat, or the woman who runs a bed-and-breakfast nearby—all have the same response when I ask about the Anelons. "I don't like or trust them but can't say anything because they control everything."

Members of the Anelon family make up the entirety of the executive body of the Iliamna Village council: the president, vice president, secretary/treasurer, administrator, assistant to the administrator, and environmental program coordinator. With this lock on the village council they control any and all decisions regarding any native land surrounding the village. The mining company needs to build a sixty-six-mile road from Iliamna to a deepwater port in Iniskin Bay. Some of that land is state controlled and some is federal. The Pebble Partnership can deal with those two entities using money and cronyism, which have long dominated Alaska politics. Alaska has a long history of allowing the foxes of the mining industry to control the henhouse of the permitting process. So the state land should be acquirable through normal channels. The tribal land, near the village, is trickier. Without this land, which can be accessed only by the blessing of the village council, the company cannot build this road and that means it cannot get the copper to market.

The Anelons also control the Iliamna Native Corporation, which the Pebble Partnership uses for many of its services, from shipping gasoline across the lake to trash collection and housing. The only true competition in town to the Anelons is John Baechler, who owns the Iliamna Lake Lodge, the largest lodge in town, which he rents out exclusively to Pebble workers. Locals estimate he rakes in around $50,000 a month. He also takes people up the Newhalen rapids and runs a sport-fishing lodge on the lake. He has known the Anelons for years.

"They are fucking crooked," he says to me. We are standing in his shop, just outside the lodge. "They are like the mob and Taliban in one. I'm not sugarcoating this one. I am telling you, this is a family that will squeeze the fucking blood out of their own family members if they could. But their little empire is coming unraveled as we speak. As we speak."

From the outside, the Iliamna Lodge looks like a slightly worn-out Motel 6, in a deserted tourist village of Maine. The paint is peeling and the architecture is simple, yet it's effective against wind and rain. The windows are double-paned and none are cracked. Signs on the doors say for employees only, which means employees of Pebble mine. Evacuation plans plaster the hallways. Each room has two or three single beds, allowing for almost thirty lodgers. Upstairs there is a large room, with brand-new floors and enough tables to seat almost 250. A dinner menu features prime rib, king crab, and top-shelf vegetables, sauces, and desserts, all luxury items in the Alaska bush.

"I bought all the kitchen supplies and everything else. Don't want anyone having anything over me," says John, who is tall and lean, and speaks with the air of someone who is confident he is in the right. He tells me he came here thirty years ago and married a native woman and has kids. He isn't going anywhere.

I ask if he has any moral conflicts with taking money from the company backing a mine, which may end up killing this place.

"I'm making a fortune off this Pebble mine gig and that's great. I can retire in Costa Rica. Today. I got no problem with that. If they want to pay, I will take it. But I hope it gets spread out a bit more. It would, but that Anelon family sucks everything up that Pebble gives to this village and shares nothing. And everyone knows it. And here is the funny part, Pebble knows it. I'm sure they do. I'm sure they also hate the Anelons. But that family controls the land so they continue to pay them. But I say if you keep sucking their dick for five more years, they will bleed you dry. Buy the fucking land now. Ask them how much and get it over with and then ignore them."

We walk outside, where he and a friend are fixing one of his jet boats that run the rapids. He also has a helicopter he leases to the mine along with a fuel service. I ask about what it is like to live here for thirty years.

"Fine. But the native bullshit, it can be too much. When the IRS calls and tells them they owe money they act like they can't talk and speak in that slow click-click of native talk, acting innocent, like, 'I didn't know, I am just a dumb native.' Then when the IRS calls and says hey we've got some for money for you, they respond in perfect English and say send it to this address."

I ask him if he wants the mine to go into operation.

"I'm not saying the mine is a good thing, it might not be. I mean, who the hell actually wants a monster Walmart in their front yard, right? And if there is a disaster, it will ruin everything. That is for sure. But until someone comes up with something to give kids a choice around here for work, I'm open to it. For now."

By the time the helicopter travels the fourteen miles from Iliamna to the mine, the temperature has dropped to thirty-five degrees. I sit facing forward next to six other men, all involved in the mining business, either as executives or as lobbyists. The quiet man with the bushy eyebrows sitting in the copilot seat is John Shively, CEO of the Pebble Partnership. The Partnership serves several purposes. One, since it is based in Anchorage, it allows both Anglo American and Northern Dynasty to say they have an "Alaska presence." Two, it allows personnel to be in Alaska to deal with the permitting process, which at this point is their main focus. Third, and most important, it acts as the mouthpiece for the mining companies and deflects direct heat away from the mining executives in London and Vancouver who actually call all the shots. In many ways, the Pebble Partnership is a media outreach program in support of the mine development. Shively was specifically hired to act as the narrator of the story from the mining company's perspective. It is his job to sell media slogans like "Fishing and mining can coexist."

These helicopter tours are given from time to time by the Pebble Partnership in order to educate interested parties on the details of Pebble mine, albeit from their perspective.

"At first they wanted to call it the Pebble Beach Mine," yells another man, with a shock of white hair under a baseball cap. "'Cause the landscape reminded everyone of Pebble Beach golf course," he continues, now overcome with laughter. My first reaction to the man is that he smiles too much, for no reason, like a car salesman when you step on his lot, even by mistake. He sits directly across from me talking into his headset, which I hear in my headset, along with the other passengers.

"But in the long run they thought better of it and just named it Pebble," he says, delivering his well-practiced punch line. This is Steve Borell, the executive director of the Alaska Miners Association. These associations are common in states such as Nevada, Arizona, Montana, and New Mexico, where hard-rock mining is a major economic player. His job, as he puts it, is to "protect the Alaskan miner from the government." I am about to ask who protects Alaskans from the Alaskan miners, but I already know the answer.

For the most part, mining executives think in terms of stark black-and-white choices. "If it hasn't come from a tree, then it came from the earth" is one of the universal laws in the mining world. Also, that mining is the basis of all things in modern society. Food for the most part comes from nature, but even then machinery plays a large role. And all metal and plastic machinery comes from the earth as oil or a mineral. So to a miner there is no real choice whether to mine Pebble for gold and copper. We mine, that is a given. The only issue to be worked out is one of politics with the locals and the state. How much money must be exchanged, how much public relations work must be done?

From atop the mountain we look down into what looks like a giant tundra meadow nestled below. The mine site will sit in the cradle of two major drainages, the Nushagak and the Kvichak, which feed into Bristol Bay. There are also two distinct headwaters here: Upper Talarik Creek and the Koktuli River, both of which begin their lives near where the mine would exist. According to the mining company, it has not officially submitted a mining plan, one of its defense mechanisms against criticism of Pebble. Their logic is that without a mine plan, there is nothing to criticize. Yet in 2006 it did submit two thousand pages of plans outlining its calculations of water displacement associated with the mine activity.

In those plans, both the Talarik Creek and Koktuli River would disappear if Pebble is built in order to clear the groundwater from flooding the mine. This is one of the most destructive results of building an open-pit mine. Once the mining begins, the process mirrors a large toilet bowl that wants to constantly fill up with any groundwater that surrounds it. To keep it out of the mine is impossible except by pumping. For Pebble to operate, all the water in the surrounding area must be drained in order to create a safe environment to work. This water must be either diverted downstream or used directly in the mining process.

Meanwhile, while the groundwater must be diverted in order to mine, a stable source of water is necessary in order to process the ore. The mining companies in charge of Pebble have applied for the rights to nearly thirty-five billion gallons of ground- and surface water per year, almost four times as much as Anchorage uses per year.

There are many factors that make mining possible, but arguably none is more important than water. At Pebble, water will be used in all steps of processing the ore and for carrying the copper slurry in pipes along the road from Iliamna to the deepwater port. It will also be used in the concentrators and leaching fields. Where that water would come from is not certain at the moment.

Borell seems overly excited to explain in vague terms how this mine will be "the safest mine in the world." Being that everyone else on board the flight is either a mining executive or a mining lobbyist, Borell tends to speak directly at me, actively trying to bring me into the light.

"They have spent more than seventy million dollars study-ing the environmental impact of the mine," he says, as if that has anything to do with how the mine will behave once active. The logic is seductive. It goes something like this: After sums of money have been spent to scientifically predict the environmental impact of the mine, the mining company then provides an abun-dant amount of data hoping to prove without a doubt the mine is safe, by the sheer act of proving it is paying so much attention to the potential environmental impact. The fallacy in this logic is that none of the environmental studies done *before* the mine is built will be able to predict how the tailing dams will hold up against the first earthquake, or how the salmon will react when the first truck carrying sulfuric acid drives off a bridge into a salmon feeder creek. Mining companies don't run those models, or if they do, they don't release them to the public.

The tour lasts over an hour as we fly around the mine site. Below are a few drill holes and temporary offices. "Every sin-gle thing you see has been flown in by helicopter. We have not made a footprint up here worth mentioning," says Gernot Wober, a Canadian geologist and the director of site operations for Peb-ble. "We have increased safety measures by adding thirty percent to costs. No one in the mining world does that," he says. Again, more of the same logic that says spending money increases the chances that this mine will not adversely affect the surrounding environment.

He goes on to explain that the mine will need a power grid equal to the one that services all of Anchorage, and that the per-centage of gold in the Pebble site measures at a one-quarter gram for every ton of earth extracted. The copper will measure out to be three pounds per ton of rock mined. The waste is estimated around ten billion tons, which will sit behind several large man-made earthen dams for the rest of time.

Borell, the Alaska Miners director, picks up the conversation during a lull, as we all stare in awe of the sight before us. There is nothing but wild land as far as we can see. Glacier-topped moun-tains crowd the horizon. Below, moisture trickles off the side of a mountain, the birthplace of a river.

I ask my first question. "How far are the nearest salmon-spawning grounds?"

"The nearest salmon-spawning grounds are less than half a mile," says Borell with his large smile, as if this answer is a plus. Hard-rock mining has destroyed virtually every known source of groundwater near open pits throughout the world. There are no examples of open-pit mining of copper that don't result in some destruction or displacement of the groundwater. And this mine will be built on tundra, which is basically a sponge-like crust.

As we fly off the mountain, we pass two small ponds that will be drained for the mine. Like a tour operator on a Disney ride, Borell speaks into the microphone while looking directly at the mining lobbyist from New Mexico. An ally.

"But in no way, no way, will this mine ever threaten salmon spawning. No way. We will make sure of that," he says, like a parrot reciting his master's voice.

On the way back to Iliamna, we fly by a large fishing hole on the Newhalen River. Gernot, the mine site supervisor, looks at me and says, "I caught a huge trout off that rock right there last summer." For the entire tour the hosts have been steadfast in their attention to detail. They speak of the ore in the ground as a resource but of the land as an asset for all to share. They talk as if the mine is an *addition* to the landscape, something that will make it even more wondrous and enchanting. Like all good salesmen, they downplay the opposition and its senseless resistance to a project that will benefit all Alaskans and Americans. They speak of the environmentalists as patsies for big-money lodge owners who want their own private nature preserve at the expense of good jobs for locals.

What they never mention is the damage that will be done. When asked about the tailing dams or the waste created, they nod and say things like, "We have our jobs cut out for us, but this will be the safest mine in history."

I begin to think about their attention to the details. They push this meticulous awareness as a sort of example of what devoted stewards of this land they will be. For example, when I first arrived at the Pebble offices at the airport, we were given a safety course, which included a video of mine safety. The most exciting aspect of the presentation was the explanation that every working crew on the mine site has "bear guards." These guards, armed with shotguns, protect the miners from any possible bear attack. The motto was clear: "We don't want to dispatch a bear, but we will because people are more important." I found "dispatch" a strange word to use in place of "kill," but then again miners like using words like "dispatch," "footprint," "mitigate," and "enhanced."

After the video on safety, everyone was given a safety vest and wraparound glasses for the helicopter ride. Before leaving the building, we all signed a large stack of documents. The binder of paper laid out all the regulations and rules of being on land controlled by the Pebble Partnership. Along with the standard waiver for accidental death, no smoking or drinking alcohol, and no liability clauses, it contained a single piece of paper that said that no guest or employee of Pebble Partnership is allowed to fish, hunt, or otherwise use the land in any way, or take a single thing that may infringe upon the subsistence livelihood of the native people who live here. When I signed the paper, I asked one of the employees how serious this was.

"Dead serious," was his reply. "You violate that rule and it can be immediate termination of employment."

This is on my mind as Gernot points out where he caught a monster trout. I remind him about the rules of infringing on the subsistence way of life for the native people. I ask if he signed the same piece of paper I did, which clearly prohibits fishing on this river. "Of course," he answers and does a double take out the window, collecting his thoughts. "It was one time. I was away on vacation in Canada and then flew back up on my own dime and not on company money or time. So I was just a tourist."

As I said, miners think differently from everyone else. No matter how nice they are, or how reasonable they sound, in the end they will take what they can get.

Before flying out, I drive Tim Anelon's car down the only road that leaves the village of Iliamna. It hugs the Newhalen River for thirteen miles and then ends. The directions are to follow the river and don't take any side roads until I find myself at the edge of the water. Across the river, I will see Nondalton, an Athabascan village of three hundred people with a deep-seated dislike of the Pebble mine proposal.

I park next to several other cars, all empty and pointed toward the river. One vehicle has the markings of a state trooper. I look around, expecting someone to pop out of the bushes, but there is no one there. Here the river is a mile wide, with a bluish-green murky color from glacial mineral deposits. There are a few houses on this side of the river, and there are few small homes visible on the opposite bank. There is not one soul in sight.

I wait for a few moments, taking in the rush of the water and staring at the surrounding mountains.

And then, as instructed, I yell at the top of my lungs.

The only way to access Nondalton is either to bring a boat or to arrive at the side of the river and whistle, yell, or wait until someone sees you and taxis you over in his boat. The river itself is only twenty-five miles long, beginning in Six Mile Lake and flowing south to Iliamna Lake. Down where the river meets Lake Iliamna, there is the Class IV–V section where John Baechler leads tours for hard-core river rafters. For local teenagers with cars, Nondalton is literally the only place to drive, and then, like me, they have to wait for someone to come get them in a boat.

As far as we know, the Amazon is the last place where there may still exist a few tribes of people that have yet to make contact, lost in the hidden world of the jungle. This may be true, but when I travel to a place like Iliamna and the surrounding landscape, I wonder if there is any other place as remote as this. If I walk an hour off this road, I will be where no one has walked in a thousand years, if that.

I am hoarse after a few minutes, feeling both foolish and rude to be yelling in such a place of immense quiet. No one comes for the first hour. Then a boat appears on the river, making its way toward my side. The skiff makes a soft landing and Clyde Trefon, a native of Nondalton taking his sons out for an afternoon cruise on the river, says hello. I ask if I can catch a ride across the river, back to his town.

"Well, that all depends now, doesn't it," he says, his eyes hidden behind wraparound sunglasses. Clyde is trim and taut, and his voice clips in a tone of anger mixed with playful sarcasm.

"What side are you on?" he asks, playfully but not quite.

I tell him I'm talking to everyone about Pebble.

"Well, I didn't think you were here for a vacation. Are you for or against Pebble?"

"My instinct is very against it, but I am also very open to hearing all sides."

"Fair enough," he says as we push off from the shore.

If there is a bedrock of resistance against Pebble mine it is anchored in villages like Nondalton, which of all the surrounding villages is perhaps the most united and vocal against the mine. It makes sense. Iliamna is the base station to the mine site because it has the airport and lodges, but Nondalton, as the crow flies, would be the closest village to the mine. The villagers would feel the direct impact without many of the benefits. Sure, a few locals could be hired to drive some trucks, empty garbage, or do various custodial jobs for $20 an hour, but overall there is not much for this village to gain. For a village that exists almost entirely on subsistence hunting, gathering, and fishing to survive, the mine offers nothing of value.

After a quick ride upriver, we circle back toward shore, the same shore I just left. I realize he has no intention of taking me to his village.

"Can't take you there today. There is a funeral," he says.

Back at shore, Clyde notices the truck I drove to the river's edge.

"Tim's truck," I say sheepishly.

"I don't mind Tim so much," says Clyde, "but the Anelons in general, they are fucking horrible greedy bastards who will end up killing each other," he yells. "*And* they are my goddamn cousins."

Clyde goes on to explain that he quit drinking five years ago, and that single act has gained him lots of enemies in town. By not drinking, others who do drink think he is judging them. "I don't

145

give a shit what they do, I just don't want to do it no more," says Clyde.

I ask if he would take a job at Pebble, if it were built.

"I got friends that have got jobs doing stuff, and that's fine. Tim's son has a camp across the river. Good person. He works for the mine but lives here. Just trying to make a dollar and live. I get that. I just hate when these people from Anchorage, or Vancouver, or wherever want to come here and bullshit us with pamphlets and graphs of how good it is going to be. I know the caribou are moving away 'cause of the drilling they are doing and because of the helicopters. I know the fish will die the first mistake they make. I don't need no graph to tell me how it is all going to work, 'cause these kinds of projects never work anywhere in the world. They are designed to make people money, not satisfy the locals."

The locals live a life that most would find difficult, if not impossible—the isolation, the reliance on their native skills to hunt and provide for their families, and the lack of immediate medical help. Take Clyde. He has had nine children. Four have died. One from SIDS, one from dwarfism, one from meningitis, and the last one in an ATV accident while a cousin was driving.

When it comes to his thoughts on the outsiders who would work at the mine, Clyde tells me a story of his aunt, who has a fish camp next to his on the river. She married a guy named Mike, a white man who works for the mine. One summer day the husband brought out some Pebble employees to enjoy a day on the river and fish.

"So I come out to fish and see these guys with their goddamn poles in the water and I say, 'What in the fuck do you think you are doing?'" Clyde screams. His boys explode in laughter at their dad's expressive language. He looks at them and screams in joy, "Oh they know. They were there."

"And?" I ask.

"And one man says to me, 'Oh, Mike says it's okay.'"

At this point Clyde shifts his feet and gathers even more steam in his storytelling.

"I said, 'Mike is a fucking asshole. And you have two choices.

146

My gun shooting you in the ass or the state troopers coming here and arresting you. Either way you are getting off MY LAND.'"

I ask what they did.

"Oh, they left. Fast. All these fuckers sign a piece of paper that doesn't allow them to fish our rivers, or hunt our land, and here they are drinking beers and watching their pole jiggle up and down with our fish. If I was on their property in whatever fucked-up place they live and they saw a native man on their land, they would call the cops, right? Well, what I see is a white man who works for the mine who is not supposed to fish our waters. So get the hell out, all the way out."

Around eight o'clock I tell him I have to return to Iliamna for the night. We shake hands.

"I wonder. What would you have done if I said I was in favor of Pebble?" I ask playfully.

"I would have shot you in the ass with my shotgun," he screams, followed by a burst of laughter. His boys chime in, as do I. We were in hysterics at the thought of me being shot in the ass on the side of a river in the Alaska bush.

It seemed funny at the time.

10

$300 Billion vs. a Fish

There are some ideas so wrong that only a very
intelligent person could believe in them.

—George Orwell

A few days later, I am in a room on the second floor of the Mil-
lennium Hotel in Anchorage. Waiting. The hotel is near the
airport, and my window faces a large circular pond where dozens
of float planes are parked, idly waiting for their next departure
into the hinterlands of Alaska. The hotel, popular with travelers
stuck waiting for an early flight to the Lower 48, has a 1980s feel
to it, with worn-out yellow-and-brown carpets and fluorescent
lights in the hallways that are either much too bright or dark and
flickering.

To kill time, I am reading a book by Farley Mowat titled *No
Man's River,* a tale of his journey on a remote river in northern Canada in the late 1940s, a time when places were still hidden from modern society. Where living off the land was the only
choice. This story gives me a familiar longing for a time long ago
when surviving the cruel elements added up to something. Feats
of survival were the measure of a man's worth. Of course what
is often forgotten in such a haze of nostalgia is that their deaths
were also often cruel twists of fate at the hand of nature.

I just returned on a chartered jet from Iliamna, courtesy of the
Pebble Partnership, with the mining executives who took the heli-

149

copter tour of the Pebble mine site. Everyone but me had been overcome with glee as we flew above the untouched land. Where they saw the future sites of leaching piles and crushing plants, I saw tons of waste bleeding toxic chemicals into a pristine water-shed. They saw copper being shipped to an insatiable China and I saw a fishery experiencing the beginning of the end.

I am never quite sure how I am able to get on planes and heli-copters with such people, meaning why they allow me to tag along. I have always enjoyed meeting people I would normally never know. No matter how much I disagree with their perspec-tive, I like the educational process of hearing them out. Besides, in this case I find it illuminating to see up close the public relations machinations of the mining industry. How they strategize. How they work extremely hard to convince people, just enough peo-ple, that they are doing the right thing. They knew I was a writer. They also knew I was a commercial fisherman. Thinking back, I can only assume I was granted access because I was from Bisbee, a town steeped in mining history. Either way, it didn't take long until they saw me as one of them, a company man.

I put down the book and scan through my notes from my trip to Iliamna. I look at the shorthand: money, dirty politics, fighting families, an unsolved murder, wild land like no one can imagine, a helicopter ride to a deep valley circled by windswept mountains where, depending on the market, a potential *half a trillion dollars* in gold and copper sit thousands of feet straight down.

Finally, the phone rings. It can be only one person. No one else knows I am here. John Shively, CEO of Pebble Partnership, tells me he can meet for drinks in the hotel bar in twenty minutes. We tried to speak after the helicopter mine tour but that turned out to be impossible due to his schedule. We had agreed to meet in this hotel upon returning to Anchorage.

I slap some water on my face and down a second cup of black tea. With notebook in hand, I race downstairs, reminding myself what I know about John Shively. He is originally from Goshen, New York, and attended college at the University of North Car-olina, Chapel Hill. His forty-plus years in Alaska date back to 1965, when at the age of twenty-two, he sat in the back of a classroom and listened to a guest speaker talk about VISTA, Volunteers in Service to America, a program designed to be John Kennedy and Sargent Shriver's U.S. counterpart of the worldwide Peace Corps, both fighting poverty. The speaker said something that day that convinced Shively that he needed to join up. He wanted to go places he had never been and make a difference.

A month later he landed in Bethel, a remote Yupik city in western Alaska. After six months working for VISTA there he migrated to Yakutat, an isolated city tucked in the lowlands along the Gulf of Alaska, two hundred miles northwest of Juneau. He stayed at this post for nineteen months. His last stint with VISTA had him "strapped to a chair," as he would later tell me, in Fairbanks, where he acted as a supervisor for the volunteers in the Yukon River region, Kotzebue, and the North Slope district. Then, from 1986 to 1992, he joined NANA Regional Corporation, a Native Alaskan–owned company, beginning as a vice president and eventually becoming the chief operating officer. As COO, he oversaw the development of Red Dog mine, the world's largest zinc mine, located in the extremely remote De Long Mountains ninety miles north of Kotzebue. After leaving NANA, he became the commissioner of the Alaska Department of Natural Resources from 1995 until September 2000. He also served as the chief of staff for Alaska governor William Sheffield in the mid-1980s. Still, his work with VISTA seems to be his personal calling card. Without it he would be just one more executive drone, here to exploit the natural resources in the great hope that a buck invested is worth ten in profit.

Shively strides into the hotel's bar wearing shorts and sweating profusely. He explains he rode his bike to the bar. He also drives a hybrid Toyota Highlander and later tells me he owns an organic farm in Nebraska. I cannot tell if he cares about his carbon footprint or is careful to project that he is environmentally correct. I decide it is too early to judge. Besides, I know he has spent most of his adult life as a registered Democrat, and he voted for Obama, a fact that puts him at odds with almost all of his mining colleagues, and that he has been an avid bike rider for two decades.

"It gets better gas mileage," Shively answers, when I ask why he drives the hybrid, giving the smartest and most reasonable answer possible. I decide to hear him out.

He orders beers for both of us. For a man holding the reins of control over the most controversial project in Alaska since the oil pipeline, he seems remarkably at ease talking to me, a writer who has told him up front that as a commercial fisherman in Bristol Bay I fear that Pebble mine will destroy one of the greatest resources left on Earth, the wild salmon.

Shively stands five foot eight, with sturdy legs and blue eyes that seem to twinkle and frown at the same time, like a man caught between laughter and remorse, which ends up looking like a self-conscious nervous state of mind. Intelligent and judicious in his responses to my questions, Shively has been described as being politically astute, or as his enemies like to say, "crafty" or "shifty." But those same people also say, "You won't catch him saying the wrong thing, ever." When I've mentioned his name to the more vocal opponents of the mine, the characterizations can get more colorful. One person who had known Shively for almost three decades warned me to be very careful around him, and that "he represents the same old crusty white mining executive double-talk while at the same time they have crews raping the place and leaving us with a fucking disaster."

Of course one of the things Shively is most known for is lying . . . and then getting caught. In 1985 when he was the chief of staff for Democratic governor William Sheffield, he lied to prosecutors investigating the governor regarding some altered documents and building leases. Because he was not under oath at the time he lied to the prosecutors, he did not face perjury charges. He was then given immunity from prosecution and later testified truthfully in court that he did the altering, allegedly under direct orders from the governor. Soon after admitting to lying, he resigned his post. Then Shively trashed the prosecutor as being on a witch hunt against the governor, who later barely survived being impeached by the state legislators.

Shively seems like someone who doesn't like to lose. Ever. As for his experience in mining, he openly admits he has none.

"As a CEO I hire people who do know," he replies when I ask him about his mining background.

His most direct involvement in the mining business was his work for NANA, when he helped build the Red Dog zinc mine in Kotzebue, a mine that a federal judge ruled in 2006 had violated the Clean Water Act 618 times, by pumping more pollution than its discharge permit allowed into Red Dog Creek.

"We had some problems, but they eventually got fixed," he says about the Red Dog pollution problems.

I pause, making a mental note that he basically dismissed what has been a major pollution issue in Alaska for almost two decades. This "problem" of violating the Clean Water Act is exactly what worries so many people if Pebble is allowed to open. For a quick moment I think of Bisbee and how small a mine it would be in comparison to Pebble and yet how similar problems would exist.

Sensing the subject was done as far as he was concerned, I ask about his role at Pebble Partnership.

"I don't think of myself as a miner," he says. "I think of myself as a community developer. That is my emphasis, always has been. And I knew I was going to catch a lot of heat for this job. I knew I would be attacked, which really didn't bother me, but I didn't want it to hurt my family or those close to me."

Maybe that is why his wife spends most of her time on their farm in Nebraska. "I go there quite a bit, just to get away from Anchorage. It can be a bright light here, and I wouldn't be doing this job, which I don't really need at my age, unless I really thought this mine could help the region and the native people who live there."

Everything about his body language and facial expression makes me believe that he means what he says, which isn't to say what he says is true. But I believe he believes it. I tell Shively of one man's interpretation of "community development," a line the Pebble Partnership uses often in selling the idea to the public.

The man had said, with spit flying from his mouth, "They are doing community development if it means developing the most corrupt families in the area, paying off friends, destroying the land, hiring locals to clean toilets, and leaving a toxic pile that will one day destroy the water. I guess that's one way to define community development."

Shively seems bothered by his critics, but their statements do not paralyze him. It's clear he wants to be liked, but that is not what drives him. He is more than capable of putting in the hours at the office whether he is liked or not. "I can take it. I am used to it. And I believe in what I'm doing. But sure it would help if I wasn't demonized."

When pushed on the topic of copper mining, he, like most mining executives today, points out that President Obama's initiatives to build more wind and solar farms will ultimately lead to a shortage of copper, a vital element in these technologies. "My hybrid car has twice the amount of copper than other cars. This green technology will take an enormous amount of copper to build, much more than is used in today's power plants. The reality, and no one wants to be honest about this, is that copper doesn't come from a tree. We have to dig this stuff out of the ground."

The fact that every copper executive repeats this mantra means more than likely it is a talking point, long ago developed by people sitting around a room in London or New York figuring out how to sell hard-rock mining to the general public. Sixty years ago, the talking point was war. We needed the copper for the war, which was true. Then in the 1960s and '70s, it was a need to own or control our resources, anything to have an edge over the Soviet Union. In the 1980s, the copper market fell to pieces, all but destroying most copper towns in the Southwest. When it came back, the slogan for more mining hung its hat on jobs. *We will give you jobs.*

Today, the message is finely tuned to a quickly evolving audience. One, there are jobs, which is always a plus in today's weak economy. Two, copper is the engine of green technology, a useful talking point against environmental blowback. The third, and newest component of today's industrial message, is advertising the intention to leave the community better than when the mining company arrived, which twenty-five years ago would never have been considered a component of the talking points.

I ask Shively a simple question that addresses what Cynthia Carroll, the CEO of Anglo American, said regarding the company being "a good neighbor" of the region.

"How can Anglo American say on the record that 'We won't mine where we aren't wanted,' when all the polls tell us that the overwhelming majority in Bristol Bay don't want the mine?" I ask.

Shively nods and straightens his back. He's gearing up, ready for some verbal ping-pong. "I agree and will continue to agree one hundred percent with that statement, but only when we actually have a mine plan. People are stating they don't want the mine when they haven't heard the plan. *When* the mine plan comes out, and then it is obvious no one wants the mine, or it threatens the fish, then I don't see how the mine can go forward."

Clearly he has a politician's mind, which means he can't respond to a question with a simple answer. Instead, he delays the answer, which is not really an answer because he has basically said there is no question to address, yet. The problem with this is that once a mining plan is in play, the permitting office in Juneau will be loaded with ex–mining lobbyists, and approval of the mine will happen long before any popular outcry can possibly stop it. And he knows this. How? He used to run that same office when he was commissioner of the Department of Natural Resources. He and Anglo are depending on this strategy to push this mine through. And one more thing of particular interest. In Alaska, the party asking for a permit is responsible for paying the billable hours that the DNR spends working on that task.

I ask, "Isn't it a conflict of interest that the people in the permitting office, empowered to give Pebble Partnership the permits, are also being paid by Pebble Partnership to do the work?"

"I don't think it makes a difference. In fact, they might even delay the process in order to make more money. Milk us," he says, raising his eyebrows while taking a sip of beer.

"Sure," I begin, "in the long run that is expected, milking you, but what is also expected is that they will ultimately approve the permits needed to get this mine up and running because you have been paying the bills."

"I can only submit the permits to the proper channels that the

Alaskan government has established. If we are also required to pay their billable hours, then we will do so."

"But how is it possible to avoid conflict of interest?" I ask.

"Alaska is just making sure the folks taking up their department's time for a permit are footing the bill and not the taxpayers," he answers.

I take a moment to register what one elderly Alaska native told me when I asked him about this permitting process, and how it seemed like a recipe for nepotism, cronyism, and legal bribery.

"Well," he said with a wide smile, "I think you just described Alaska politics since the white man got here."

I am in the room with a big fish. These people don't come to the table with weak cards. They stack the deck. One way of doing that is by hiring people who think like they do. People like Ken Taylor, the former deputy commissioner for the Alaska Department of Fish and Game, who acts as the Pebble Partnership's vice president for environment. This is the same Ken Taylor known as Sarah Palin's "point man" on the status of polar bears, which he thought were not endangered by global warming and did not need protection. These are the same bears that are drowning at sea, unable to find ice.

I shift gears and begin to talk about community development, Shively's specialty. I tell him of my time in Iliamna and what John Baechler said about the Anelons. He smiles and takes a moment to respond.

"We live in a democracy and I don't choose these people. I don't choose how the local process works. If the villages elect these people to be the ones that represent them, then that is who we will conduct our business with."

So far he is proving to be both cagey and diplomatic, two traits of any good CEO.

"Okay, so how about this?" I'm hoping to appeal to his devil's advocate gamesmanship. "What if Anglo decides to not be a good neighbor and develops a mine that obviously threatens the fishery?"

"I'll leave the project," he says without hesitation. "Look, no one is more concerned about the fishery than me," says Shively.

"You gotta be concerned about the region. If we are going to mess up the fish or the water, then we shouldn't put a mine there. But until the science and the mine plan are fully developed, I won't know. I didn't need this job, but I saw it as an important opportunity to change the economy of a region that could really use some economic stimulus."

On that point we agree. The region is economically depressed, with most incomes tied directly to fishing or the occasional shot in the arm from tourists. The stimulus he talks about so frequently includes jobs for about six hundred to one thousand people, with a base salary of about $80,000 a year. That is far above what people in the region make today, but there are no promises locals will get the majority of the high-paying jobs, and if other mines are any indicator—and they usually are—many jobs will be outsourced to hired professionals transplanted to the area.

Shively and I start our second beer and talk about our mutual, but respectful, hatred of each other's favorite college basketball team, his being North Carolina and mine, the University of Arizona. No matter how many beers we share, this will always divide us, and perhaps bond us; sports has a way of doing that.

"Do you think you will still be with Pebble Partnership when this mine actually gets in operation? If it ever does?" I ask.

"I'm pretty sure someone will be spreading my ashes by the time that happens," he says with a chuckle.

I have to admit I find Shively likable, funny, and insightful, which makes me feel only more sorry for him, because I can't help but think down deep he knows he should turn out the lights in the office, close the door and throw away the key, drive to the airport, and board the next flight to Nebraska and ride his bike along dirt roads on his organic farm.

He steps away to the bathroom and I think of Wadi Faynan in Jordan. It is a copper mine that has been dormant for two thousand years, since the Romans abandoned the site. Today all the surrounding vegetation and livestock—that eat that vegetation— still show dangerously high levels of copper in their tissue.

Shively returns, and I remind him that he has called some of the environmental groups that oppose the mine "environmental terrorists." He says they are the ones that are using false information to spread lies about the mine.

"For them it is not about science, it is about stopping us," he says, his face tensing up, becoming hard like a steel plate. It is the first time he is not smiling.

"Well, the science says this mine is a danger to everything around it," I say, offering up the obvious.

"No. We don't know the science yet. That is the point. And stopping us before we can assess the science is sabotage," he says, almost willing me to understand his point of view.

In the dictionary, "delusion" is defined as "a false or mistaken belief or idea about something" and "a persistent false belief held in the face of strong contradictory evidence, especially as a symptom of psychiatric disorder."

I am still not sure if we just have different opinions or one of us is delusional.

And then he says something that proves what I suspect is true of anyone who occupies these CEO-type jobs, people who usually abide by the adage that to win the battle is more important than to be right. They eventually buy the company line to the degree that they just start to sound crazy. I bring up the *Exxon Valdez*, the ultimate sin of environmental damage in recent Alaska history.

"I'm not so sure the spill actually hurt the salmon run at all," Shively says, smiling, as if he knows a few scientific facts that I don't regarding the destruction of the Prince William Sound coastline. "Or if there was damage, there doesn't seem to be any real sustained damage today."

I am shocked he has said this out loud, and to me. I know salmon, and I know fishermen who live in the region that was destroyed by the spill. While it's true that twenty years later the pink salmon run has begun to recover, most of that recovery is due to hatchery fish released into the Prince William Sound. The herring, which was the backbone of the local fishermen's livelihood, has yet to show any real sign of recovery. Countless other species have never recovered. To even hint that the spill's long-term effects are negligible is borderline psychotic and definitely delusional. To utter these words as a company man fighting to open a mine in a volatile region, near salmon-spawning grounds, makes my head spin. I figure he is just reaching, grasping at straws. I force myself to believe that when he goes home and kisses his wife before going to bed, he finds himself looking sideways in the mirror just before lying down. At that moment he nods at himself, just a little. He may even chuckle, and why not? He is getting a huge paycheck for his favorite vocation: fighting. Part of me imagines he doesn't believe half of what he says, and when the time comes to break ground on the mine, he will quit. Maybe he will cite personal family reasons and bow out. Maybe he will circulate rumors that he was always against the mine but took the job to make sure it was held to the highest standards. Sort of a Trojan horse that always had the best interest of the region in mind. Publicly he will thank Pebble for the opportunity and hope the region profits greatly from the project.

I have to tell myself this as I sip my beer because otherwise I have no choice but to break this beer glass on his face.

On the long flight home I realize that writing about saving wilderness is difficult. How do I explain to people that they need to help save a place they will never see from an encroaching monster that has no fixed face? The mining company, the CEO, the permitting process, and the ubiquitous advertising campaign are all arms of the same murky creature. I am not certain how to tackle this task, but I am certain no one should go to the place I have described beyond the shores of Iliamna, except those who already know where it is because their grandfathers showed them. No more geologists, biologists, archaeologists. No more people studying a place that needs only to be forgotten by outsiders. No one needs another report to figure out that the price is too steep to swap this swath of wild land for a mine. Or that if this region is opened up to a mine it will be permanently altered, and eventually destroyed. Eight thousand years of a cyclical routine broken forever.

Once home, my wife quickly hands me the baby. Tired from running the house for so long, she postpones any talk about

159

Alaska for a few days. I have missed my family for three weeks and I am quickly transformed from worrying about Pebble mine to worrying about my young kids. And loving them. Then one night after the children are tucked into bed we open some wine and talk about Alaska and Pebble. She knows the issues and is worried. She worked three summers in Alaska, one in the waters off Homer counting whales, and she has a great passion for preserving wild Alaska.

"Well?" she asks.

"It's a battle," I answer.

"Who do you think will win?"

"I usually would say big money, but in this case there is so much resistance and logic to saving the place that it might work. The mine just doesn't make any sense. At all."

We talk a bit more about it, then seamlessly switch topics to immediate issues facing our life. We pour some more wine and laugh as we catch up on the town gossip. Not once do we mention the mine in our town or if we want to move. We invite the blinders of denial because we want to keep enjoying our town.

Once sleep comes, we do what most sane people do. We cuddle up with each other and create a shield against the never-ending clatter of the world.

11

Superior

A mine is a hole in the ground owned by a liar.
—attributed to Mark Twain

Pondering something as invasive as a mine reopening on the edge of town can be overwhelming, and for the longest time I managed to push it aside and just keep on enjoying where we lived. Things even felt normal for a while. The summer after the soil was replaced, I planted a new garden. My wife and oldest daughter, who was beginning to enjoy vegetables, ate the salad from the yard. No one got sick. Our second daughter rolled around in the dirt, oblivious of all the history of the ground below her. The best part was that we got to relandscape our property on Freeport's dime.

Some of the younger guys I play basketball with on Sundays eventually went to work for Freeport, mostly doing reclamation work. I waved to them in their Freeport trucks as they went house to house digging up poisoned soil. One went to work for Freeport in Douglas, where he tells me he works on a small crew using bio-leaching, a relatively new technology, where living microbes are inserted into the copper slurry. Instead of using sulfuric acid on a large leaching field, the microbes eat the sulfide, and then the organisms are extracted out in a smelting process, leaving a pure copper solution. They all tell me the same thing when I ask about working for the company. They like the pay.

161

After returning from Alaska, I read about something in the *Arizona Daily Star* that once again reminded me exactly where I live. It's called TENORM, or Technologically Enhanced, Naturally Occurring Radioactive Materials. Ever since the late 1990s, the EPA has stated that copper-mining wastes constitute the largest quantity of metal-mining and -processing wastes generated in the United States. They also concluded that one of the results of copper mining is TENORM. Nearly all rock has low doses of radioactive material, such as thorium, radium, and lead, and traces of uranium and polonium, a natural occurrence of Earth being formed, but when rocks are then violently dug out of the earth and pulverized, it can become a real health problem. As of now, no one seems prepared to state if there are any damaging long-term effects of being exposed to this low dosage of radioactive waste.

I never heard any of the Pebble mine opponents mention TENORM, but it could be the most viable argument why a mine as large as Pebble should never exist at the headwaters of a healthy salmon run.

And with ten active copper mines within a few hundred miles of our house in Bisbee, I don't feel I need to wait for the official government report to tell me that the exposure to radioactive waste, however small, is harmful. I am also beginning to think more and more that moving may be our only choice.

Besides, the rumors of the mine reopening are whipping up a frenzy between those against it and those for it. Recently Freeport has begun holding town hall meetings where they hand out food and drink while making experts available for our questions. One man, standing in front of a graph, talks about water issues. He says, "We are creating more efficient flows for the rain runoffs to alleviate sulfuric acid runoff." Another expert, a geologist, talks about the sulfuric acid plume that extends from tailing piles five and six, toward the Mexican border. A hydrologist who was hired to work on this problem told me, "We have dug multiple wells to stop the plume, but eventually those will fill and it will continue south toward the aquifer."

When I ask about the fact there is no stopping this underground river of poison from getting into our town's aquifer, he explains that the company has located new wells outside the plume's path that will be tapped at the right time.

The ugly truth is we have very little power over the slow trickle of these toxic plumes. Water, aboveground or below surface, will always run downhill, no matter what we do to alter that fact. Thus, the sulfuric acid will eventually reach the aquifer. The question is not if, but when.

In Tucson, the mercury is already above 100 degrees and it's not even noon. Here, the concrete will keep the temperature above 100 until after midnight. This time of year all across the desert the pressure begins to rise between the ears and sweat pools in every crease. In Bisbee, south and higher in elevation, the monsoon rains have already begun. Flowers grow wild out of the cracks in the retaining walls and are suffocating the neighborhoods with their musk. But in Tucson and points farther north, the rains have yet to begin. Water-soaked cumulonimbus clouds are beginning to take shape on the horizon, but until the skies open up, partners hug their sides of the bed, waiting for the rains to come before they mix their sweat.

I drive north on I-10, a four-lane strip of melting pavement, through the heartland of everything dismal about Arizona. The air-conditioning in my small truck broke a month ago, and I feel as if I'm stuck in a tin can hurtling toward the sun. It may be my imagination, but the heat seems to be lengthening the crack in the windshield that swirls in an S formation from top to bottom. That crack started when a rock bounced off a mining truck near the remote town of Bagdad in northwest Arizona.

I drive toward the mountains, hoping I can get there before my radiator explodes. I can't help remembering something the guide for the Bagdad mining tour told me. He said he worked in the mine all his life so his kids would be able to go to college and get out of that town. He didn't want them to live the life of a miner. When I asked where his four children were today, he tilted his head and pushed back his hard hat.

"All here, working in the mine," he said with a tone both disappointed and yet at peace with how the cards had played out.

My destination is the Copper Triangle, a 180-mile loop that weaves through the Pinal Mountains, a small range between Tucson and New Mexico.

The most productive copper region in the United States, the Triangle has a long history of mines opening and then closing and then opening once again. Like Bisbee, all the towns in this loop were built for the sole purpose of extracting copper from the earth. Mining towns tend to exist in this state of flux, and maybe that is what I am feeling as I drive: not knowing if the mine in Bisbee will open again, bringing daily explosions, dust, trucks weighing hundreds of tons, leach ponds, a small population explosion, and a long ugly erosion of all the reasons I moved to Bisbee ten years ago.

My first stop off the highway is Florence, a gateway town to the mining communities in the mountains beyond. Florence has a sign on the edge of town that reads, ANOTHER ONE-STREET TOWN IN ARIZONA. There are actually several streets in Florence, each one leading, one way or another, to one of nine correctional institutions, including a county prison, a federal prison, three state prisons, and two private prisons. A small but important detail is that Arizona's only gas chamber and execution room exist here. There is a vent on the outside of the gas chamber that releases the gas and final breath of the condemned. As for mining in Florence, it consists of men and women who have spent their adult lives bouncing between jobs at the prisons and commuting to the mines. Either way, they are in uniforms, on a strict routine, and counting the days, months, or years until they can get out. I drive on, hoping I never have to take a job in either a mine or a prison.

As I climb in elevation, the temperature drops. I am mesmerized by the surrounding flora that has adapted to the desert heat, roots burrowing deeper and deeper into the earth forever seeking a trickle of water. Flowers bloom, the paloverdes litter fluorescing yellowish green blossoms over the desert floor, and white flowers drip off the top of saguaros.

About one hour northeast of Florence, tucked against the mountain of Apache Leap, is Superior, a mining town named after Lake

Superior. The name owes its origin not to the lake itself but to the money that flowed to this area from the mining companies that started in Michigan, home of America's first copper rush. To take root, Superior, like many other Arizona mining towns, depended on the money from companies like the Lake Superior Silver Mining Company. I always have to remind myself that Michigan, not Arizona, used to be the king of copper. It makes sense that as Michigan began to close up shop in the 1860s, the money followed the trail west, to the new mines in Nevada, Montana, Alaska, and Arizona.

As the story goes, as it always goes, prospectors found silver, some gold, and then copper in Superior. Soon the mines were built, along with bars and brothels, and—presto!—another mining camp was born. The unique aspect of mining in Superior is that all the mines are underground. The head masts of the mines are visible from any vista in town, massive rusting steel reminders that shafts ten feet wide drop thousands of feet below the surface.

The closing of the Magma mine in 1991 marked the beginning of the downward spiral of the community. As with Bisbee in 1975, the survival of the town hung by a thread, mostly buoyed by retirees and families too stubborn to leave. In its heyday, there were twenty-six bars in Superior and plenty of families taking the hour-long trip to Phoenix to shop. Today Superior resembles places like Ajo and Mammoth, busted copper towns where long-time residents squeak by on fixed incomes and memories of when the mines meant better times. The only steady flow of visitors to these outposts are stray tourists looking to fill up their gas tanks, take a few snapshots, and get back on the road to civilization.

It doesn't take much to see that Superior is broken, a shell of a town compared to what it once was. The old Main Street has buildings built a hundred years ago, many of them with broken or boarded windows. I think of Bisbee and wonder what makes it so different from this town, both victims of boom and bust. Bisbee is a struggling but viable town. In Superior there is a spooky feeling that no one runs the place.

I see a few signs of life, though. Three cars sit outside the old miner bar and there's some fresh spray paint on the plywood boards that cover the buildings. The graffiti is almost entirely in support of a new mine, called Resolution, which will sit a few miles from town in a popular camping area called Oak Flat. If all goes as planned, production is still several years off. Still, it doesn't take long to realize that most of the town's population wants the mine to open, with the great hope that it will impede the erosion of this place. One sign states in bold red letters, WE SUPPORT THE MINE. Other slogans are "Resolution has our support" and "Miners are our lifeblood." Just past this block of abandoned buildings sits Resolution's local company headquarters.

The company is a consortium of Rio Tinto, the British-Australian mining conglomerate, and BHP Billiton, based in Australia, the largest mining company in the world. Although smaller, in the Resolution partnership Rio Tinto is the majority shareholder of the mine, with a 55 percent ownership. Together these two mining companies have an estimated value of more than $250 billion, and they have come to this broken town with the promise of extracting one of the largest sources of copper in North America, and possibly the world. The deposit, some 1.5 billion tons of 1.5 percent copper, is huge, and the mine, if built, will be active for almost a hundred years. This is high-grade ore, and if the mine advances to full capacity it will be capable of producing 25 percent of the U.S. copper demand for several decades. The town smells money.

The Resolution office smells of new wood, new carpets, and the unmistakable fragrance of ink toner and copy machines. The several cubicles that lead to a supervisor's office are broken up not by the usual white fiberboard but by a rich dark wood and lovely opaque glass. Not a speck of copper has been mined yet, but the face of Resolution looks younger, more attractive, and sexier than anything else in town. In every town I have visited with mines hoping to go online, such decorative offices always exist. It is good business to look prosperous and optimistic. The various maneuvers companies make during this long process of permitting and readying the mine details is like a playbook written by some mining deity in the 1950s. The companies tend to sponsor most town events. They join the local Rotary club. When it looks like a mine will be built, they make sure to build a park or two, usually with an environmental emphasis. They donate new computers to the high schools and throw a few bucks at the local hospital. Cynics say they are buying off the locals. Realists say, yes, that's true, but that is how things get done in towns with no other steady supply of benefactors.

Inside, I speak to an attractive young lady who knows nothing about mining but is more than happy to give me bundles of literature, which she offers repeatedly. When I ask about certain specifics regarding the new mining operation, she smiles and refers to the pamphlets. It's like calling customer service for any utility company. They speak in a calm monotone as they repeat the useless options. I know the routine and I don't have the energy to ask her any more about the mine. Giving up, I ask her where the mayor of town spends his days. She jumps at the question, pleased at last to know the answer.

"Oh, Mayor Hing. He is probably at the grocery store."

A checkout clerk directs me to the meat section of the store. A man with Asian features slides out from behind the butcher counter, where he was busy cutting up pieces of steak for his customers. He wipes his hands on his bloody apron and extends his hand to mine and says, "Hello, I'm Michael Hing, the mayor."

Before I can shake his hand, a woman steps up and asks about the young man who is the regular butcher.

"He's been AWOL for a few days," the mayor says, shaking his head, as if saying that he's worried, but not really.

Michael Hing has a relaxed smile and a distinct Chinese lilt to his voice. He is in his third term as mayor and is a second-generation Chinese American.

"I am for the mine. I mean, I am for preserving the earth but I am for jobs, and this town needs jobs," says the mayor, as he explains his position on the mine.

"Our country is at war," he continues, "and we go to these wars for resources, oil and whatnot. But we have a great resource right here, so why not go get it? I am excited and proud that this copper has been found in Superior."

The Hings are invested in Superior. For almost a century the family has lived and worked here, though never in the mines. The first Hing, Michael's grandfather, migrated from China to Superior in the early 1900s and set up a kiosk near the mine entrance that sold tobacco and various small items to the miners as they entered and exited the underground shaft. By the 1950s, the town was a thriving copper center and Michael's father built a grocery store. He called it Save Money, which remains the name today. The mine shut in 1991, but the store is still here and it is the only grocery store in town, other than a few convenience stores and several liquor stores.

"Since the mine closed in 1991, everyone asks how I am doing," says Mayor Hing. "I tell them I am busier now than when the mine was open. Why? Because no one can afford to leave town to buy groceries, so they buy mine. Me and my family are fine, but the town is not."

When I ask if the mine has given anything to the city, the mayor tells me that the mining company has contributed $400,000 to the city each year to help finance schools, parks, trails, and other civic projects. It also gave another $100,000 to the fire and police fund, which covers any and all costs of those agencies responding to issues directly related to the mine.

I step outside and pass more boarded-up shops and homes. One street over is the road that links Superior to Phoenix, an hour away, all of it downhill. I look down that highway and my reaction is to build a large gate. Down that road is unbearable heat and sprawl.

I walk into the nearest bar and order some Mexican food and a beer. So far everyone in town has talked about Oak Flat and the mine. Some cars have bumper stickers that state SAVE OAK FLAT. Others, I LOVE MY MINER. An association of rock climbers has become a stakeholder in the mining process, hoping to save Apache Leap, one of Arizona's most fabled climbing spots.

I decide to stick my head in the snake pit. I ask the bartender about the mine and Oak Flat. She immediately points at the man sitting a few stools down, sipping on a beer.

"Charlie, what do you think of losing Oak Flat for the mine?" she yells in her East Coast accent.

"Stupidest thing I ever heard of," he yells, straight ahead, lost in an afternoon beer buzz.

I slide down next to Charlie.

"I've worked in the Ray mine all my life. Maintenance," he says.

The Ray mine, an enormous open pit, is eighteen miles down the road in the heart of the Copper Triangle and only a few miles from Hayden, home of one of the only remaining smelters in Arizona. Ray is the state's second-largest producing mine. In operation almost a hundred years, the mine has many more years before the ore plays out. Most Arizonians don't know where Ray is or that it even exists. Occasionally it makes headlines, like in 2008 when a young miner was electrocuted while moving the cables that operate the massive loaders. Then the headlines move on to another story and the machines keep cranking out the copper at Ray, twenty-four hours a day.

"Hate that mine and the company, but when they pay eighty thousand dollars a year, well, I become a goddamn hypocrite," Charlie says, mumbling to himself. "So, basically, they pay me enough so that I turn my back to all the shit they do."

I ask him what kind of shit they do, and he just shakes his head, as if the story is too long and too convoluted to be told once again.

Charlie and I have another beer. The bartender chimes in to say, "I like Oak Flat just the way it is. And they promise lots of jobs, lots of money, but you know what, the companies that own the damn thing are not even from the United States. So the money ain't staying here."

I think of the $500,000 the mayor said was staying here, but then again this civic infusion of money rarely trickles down to a bartender or the guy sitting at the bar.

A man in a large white straw hat and goatee sidles up to Charlie, and upon hearing the words "Oak Flat" blurts out, "Shit, this town is dead already. Mine or no mine."

My food comes and I rest it on the bar. Charlie tells me about working at depth, almost one thousand feet down in the mines.

"Hot, hot, and more fucking hot. It's brutal. They do it in

South Africa, but shit, they don't seem to mind. That's why I work maintenance. I want to quit, but I bought a car, have an ex-wife and kids, so I'm in it until they kick me out."

I tell him that in Bisbee we still think we actually have a say in what the mining company will do, partly because the residents can't imagine anyone doing anything to "their" town to alter it in a negative way. No matter that Freeport owns all the land and if it wants to reopen the mine not much the locals say or do will be able to stop it. Call it delusional, but it's a necessary ignorance.

Charlie wakes up from his beer, ignoring my rants on the plight of Bisbee.

"And then," shouts Charlie, "in fifty years when the underground mine goes dry, they will suddenly decide to have an open pit in Oak Flat. Bet on that. That is how they operate. They just wait for the original protesters to die. Man, they grind you down."

With the sun setting, I race up Queen Creek Canyon, which begins at the very edge of town. I enter the canyon, sheer red walls over five hundred feet high. I quickly gain elevation, as if riding up a corkscrew. If I stare straight up, I see the sky shining a deep cobalt blue through a small window in the slot canyon. The rock formations jut up in dramatic spirals, each one a perfect perch for a red-tailed hawk or golden eagle. The journey through this narrow slot is three miles long and just wide enough for a two-lane road.

When I reach the top of the canyon, the world immediately flattens to a mesa full of Arizona oak trees and large round boulders. Still, the thing that dominates the view is a brand-new 150-foot A-frame steel structure plopped on top of the ridgeline. Next to it stands a rusting steel structure, a relic from the mine that worked this mountain until two decades ago. This is shaft number 9, which drops three thousand feet straight into the earth. For twenty years, since mining stopped here, number 9 has been filling up with rain runoff, creating a reservoir large enough to supply a midsized city for a year. But for the last few years, in anticipation of reopening the mine, miners have been pumping all the water out of the hole into a pipe, which goes around Queen Creek Canyon, around Superior, and down into the water-starved

Quail Creek area for farmers to use. The reason they are bypassing Queen Creek? The water's nitrate levels are too high, which is bad for indigenous plants and humans but good for budding agriculture, which needs an abundance of water. How long will it take to empty the shaft? At 2,500 gallons a minute, 24 hours a day, for 365 days a year, it will take three years. The goal? To drill to the five-thousand-foot level and use the old shaft as an air duct situated side by side with the new shaft, to be called number 10. As the water is emptied in the number 9 shaft, miners have already begun the "prefeasibility" phase and are working on the new shaft, which extends downward under the brand-new A-frame. The shaft will eventually reach seven thousand feet deep, the starting point of the new mine.

This will not make it the deepest mine in the world. That title currently belongs to the TauTona gold mine in South Africa, with a depth of 12,672 feet, or 2.4 miles. But mining seven thousand feet underground has its share of problems. For one, the temperature of the rock hovers around 130 degrees, creating a constant life-threatening situation for the miners. Expensive air-conditioning units must be installed, along with "cool rooms" for the workers. By all estimates it will take twenty minutes for miners to descend the seven thousand feet, and another twenty to get into their safety gear. This potential loss of productivity is causing some Arizona politicians to call for an increase in the time an underground miner can be on duty. Currently it is eight hours, but in response to the demands of Resolution mine, and perhaps because of the influence of Resolution, the company, there is an effort to change that to a twelve-hour shift. And this is an example of the long view that mining companies take. Even if the company clears all the environmental, political, and economic hurdles, its miners won't reach the richest part of the copper vein until around 2025.

Contrary to Charlie's claim, there is no open pit in the plans. So far. In mining linguistics, the technique the company will use to mine the ore is called block caving. Although most of the hard work is to be done underground, there are consequences for the surface area. To achieve successful block caving, the miners must dig to a level beneath the desired ore body. Then under the ore, an entire infrastructure, including train tracks, is put in place. Tunnels are built up and into the ore body, large enough for earth-moving loaders. Once all that is in place, the miners blast the ore body from below. Like poking at a bloated piñata, they will prod and poke at the earth, allowing gravity to do most of the work. The ore will fall like candy into their waiting machinery. Still deep underground, the ore is crushed and readied for conveying to the surface.

Currently the plan is to use all the waste rock to reclaim the adjacent Magma mine, which closed in 1991. In theory, this is an efficient and creative way of getting rid of the waste rock. However, there are always drawbacks when blasting away billions of tons of earth. The real disadvantage of block caving so deep in the earth, and for so long, is that in years to come the rock and soil that is displaced underground will eventually cause a collapse, resulting in a permanent and irreversible subsidence in the surface land. By all estimates, the surface of Oak Flat will collapse at least three hundred feet, making the area a permanent sinkhole.

I veer my car away from the A-frames and drive east a few hundred feet into the rustic Oak Flat campground. There are sixteen campsites, all of them primitive setups. No facilities are located here. No bathrooms, no ranger station, no barbeque pits. There is no fee to stay, which anyone can do continuously for a maximum of fourteen days. Toward the rear of the campground I find a sidetrack that leads through the trees to a well-hidden campsite. I set up camp with a clear view of the number 9 shaft. For centuries, Apaches used to come sit under the shade of the Arizona oak trees and perform healing ceremonies and mash acorns into a stew. Today, families from surrounding towns come here to camp and take their children for walks in undisturbed land. This is the Southwest as people far and wide dream of it. Burning sunsets, wide-open vistas, cactus poking out the sides of mountains, and red rocks standing on one another. One can imagine Wile E. Coyote popping out from behind one rock only to fall a thousand feet into the abyss.

For the executives of Rio Tinto and BHP Billiton, all that stands in the way of the mine going forward directly under this campground is the fine print on executive order PLO 1229, signed by President Eisenhower in 1955, supposedly at the request of his wife, Mamie, who once camped in Oak Flat and thought it was worthy of forever saving against any potential mining activities, which would have been very active at that time in Superior, a few miles away. The presidential order specifically prohibits mining activities in the Oak Flat area. By law there can be no building upon this land or anything done to it that will alter its current designation as a public campground.

At the behest of Resolution Copper, Arizona senators John McCain and John Kyl, along with several members of the House of Representatives, have repeatedly introduced versions of the Southeast Arizona Land Exchange and Conservation Act. These are all intended to allow Congress to overturn PLO 1229 and place Oak Flat under the sole ownership of Resolution Copper. In exchange for Oak Flat, Rio Tinto and Billiton would arrange for the transfer of fifty-five hundred acres of high-priority conservation lands in Arizona to the U.S. government. Also, low-interest loans would be made available to Superior for various purposes.

The critics of the land swap say this is an end around for Resolution that allows the company to sidestep strict EPA rules when mining on federal land.

"If they wanted to try to do this the right way, they would go through the National Environmental Policy Act," said Sandy Bahr, director of the Sierra Club of Arizona.

For the Sierra Club and others, the main problem with the land swap act is that in all the bills introduced to Congress there is no mention of any mining specifics. It is strictly focused on swapping land. There is no language that would hold Resolution Copper responsible for violations of various environmental standards. It is as if the mine is not important in the language of the bills, when building the mine is the only reason members of Congress have been trying for so long to push this land swap.

Some in Congress are using the Resolution land swap bill to argue the time has come to alter the 1872 mining law, which, if not changed, will allow Rio Tinto and BHP Billiton, two of the world's largest mining companies, to pay no royalty tax on the metals it extracts from U.S. soil.

Another issue for some opposing the land swap is Rio Tinto's mining practices around the globe. Most egregious, the company faces charges in U.S. federal court of genocide and war crimes for actions it allegedly took while running a copper and gold mine in Papua New Guinea in the 1980s. On October 25, 2011, the Federal Appeals Court in San Francisco reversed a lower court's ruling to dismiss the case. Judge Mary Schroeder wrote in her ruling, "The complaint's allegation that Rio Tinto's 'worldwide modus operandi' was to treat indigenous non-Caucasians as 'expendable' justified restoring the genocide claim to the case."

The case stems from the Panguna mine, where locals complained they were forced to live in slave-like conditions. Acts of sabotage began to occur at the mine, and it is alleged that Rio Tinto coerced the national military into suppressing those who were calling for even more acts of sabotage. By 1989, the mine was shut. By 1997, ten thousand civilians had been killed as a result of the military actions on its own people.

The judge went on. "The complaint alleges purposeful conduct undertaken by Rio Tinto with the intent to assist in the commission of violence, injury, and death, to the degree necessary to keep its mines open."

The entities hoping to extract the metals under Oak Flat are in boardrooms in London and Melbourne, but it is the politicians in Arizona who are vying to get credit for allowing the mine to go forward.

One former member of Congress, Representative Richard "Rick" Renzi, tried too hard in his attempts to get the swap to happen. He is now awaiting trial on charges related to his involvement in the land swap. Reportedly, Renzi sold land he owned to a James Sandlin. Then Renzi tried to arrange a land swap on behalf of Resolution with land Sandlin owned. After that announcement, Sandlin sold the land for an inflated price. A mysterious $200,000 was then paid by Sandlin to Renzi, who failed to report this income in formal disclosure forms. The land swap bill that Renzi tried to pass was never enacted, but on February 22, 2008, a federal grand jury in Arizona indicted him on thirty-five counts, including conspiracy, wire fraud, money laundering, extortion, and insurance fraud. As of 2012 the trial was still pending.

Washington politicians and Resolution Copper quickly put the Renzi scandal aside, and since 2008, Senators McCain and Kyl have introduced several more bills to Congress that would legalize the land swap. The Senate has never taken up the legislation. However, Representative Paul Gosar, from Flagstaff, introduced the most recent bill in May 2011, the tenth in six years. In July it passed the House Committee on Natural Resources and on October 27 it cleared the House. Now it is awaiting a vote in the Senate.

Standing outside my tent, the view is impressive: Apache Leap to the west, high riparian desert to the east, and in between nothing but a landscape that hasn't changed since Kit Carson rode his donkey over the same square footage.

By sunset, thunder roars all around me, lightning erupts in violent bursts. It is July in Arizona in the mountains. Rain is guaranteed, and it will fall with a punishing strength, as if reminding all those who walk these hills that nature has the upper hand.

The white streaks of electricity sweep up Apache Leap, a mountain range that towers over Superior like a cathedral spire. This cliff face has seen mining companies come and go over the last hundred years. It has witnessed the human population below expand and contract depending on the price of copper. In the distance, the light at the head mast shines bright. There is a constant hum. Buried far beneath this mountain, and in the land all around, copper remains king here. There never seems to be a shortage of the mineral, only the means to access it.

As I sit and stare up at the light show, I do a mental inventory of everything I have with me: car, cell phone, tent, flashlight, tools in the back of the car, notepad and pen, camera. Other than the pad and pen, everything has copper in it, and I am certain plenty of copper was used in the making of the pad and pen in the form of electrical wiring for power. Then I think of my family in Bisbee, hunkered down in our 110-year-old house that has plenty of copper in it, but unlike most people's homes, mine not only has copper products throughout, it was built *because* of copper. It was built for the sole purpose of providing someone working at the copper mine sleep and shelter before going back underground and digging for more copper. Tonight, as the winds blow the rain into Oak Flat, as my wife and kids sleep in our house in our peaceful town, I try to imagine the life stories of all the people who lived in our house before us.

The sky clears and the stars shine brightly. I imagine I can hear the voices of the keepers of this place screaming in the wind. The language? Yavapai Indian.

Legend has it that in 1871, during the last Indian Wars, the U.S. cavalry had a band of warriors on the run through Oak Flat. Surrounded by an overwhelming force, the Apaches became trapped between the soldiers and a fifteen-hundred-foot drop-off. Instead of surrendering, they leaped to their deaths, their bodies coming to rest in what is now the town of Superior. How many died that day? They say seventy-five, but no one really knows. Today rock hounds routinely scour the base of Apache Leap for obsidian, which they carve down into small drops of stone, calling them Apache teardrops, for those who died that day.

I wake early in hopes of walking overland and getting as close to the A-frame as possible. As I walk through a field of boulders, I imagine that something far more sinister is happening on the hill in front of me. Maybe they are mining uranium or building a missile silo. Maybe they are building a secret bunker for the Desert Oval Office.

And then I spot a wire on the ground running toward the mine. It looks like a telephone wire, brown and small. Harmless? I'm not sure, so I follow it, climbing more boulders and down small rock faces. Everyone I met in town spoke of how they enjoyed bringing their kids out here to camp, to play in this natural playground. Everything I see now will collapse three hundred feet and forever be blocked off with a tall chain-link fence with signs that read DANGER! MINE. As I chase the wire, bouncing through the landscape like a young boy, I think that losing this place will be sad.

The closer I get to the mine, the more treacherous the terrain. I watch the wire stretch down a steep canyon into a dry wash bed below. What is this wire? If I splice into it, will I suddenly be linked into secret conversations between mining executives who want to destroy the world?

That is what I am thinking when I spot a man a hundred feet in front of me with binoculars and a handheld radio. I duck behind a boulder but can still hear his conversation. His outfit resembles a birder's, but birders don't have the kind of walkie-talkie he is carrying. Staying still, I hear the voice on the radio become louder as he gets closer to my location.

"He's directly to your right, just look right, you should see him," the voice on the radio says.

I'm busted. I figure them to be either federal rangers for the campground or private security contractors for the mine.

The man looking for me can't find me, and the voice on the radio shouts at him. "Near the rock, the white one. No, the other white one! He's right there!"

I stand up, knowing he isn't a ranger because a ranger wouldn't care if I was climbing boulders.

"Nice day for a walk," I say.

"What are you doing here?" the man asks, his radio in hand.

"Birding. Did you see that pyrrhuloxia? Or the black-headed grosbeak?"

The man stares at me. I scan him for a gun but can't see one, at least not from ten yards.

"What are you doing here?" I ask, returning his question with an air of neighborly innocence.

"I didn't see any birds," he says and walks away.

Feeling that some secret cactus camera is monitoring me, I push onward. After all, this is my campground, a federally owned campground, at least for now. I am now on my hands and knees and following the telephone line as it inches closer and closer to the mine. I know there is a road somewhere to the north and am determined to connect with it. Then, the thin brown line disappears into a sandy wash. I shoot forward, more determined than ever to find where the line surfaces. With the brush scratching me, I try to ignore my growing thirst under the rising desert sun. A fallen tree tears open my pant leg. So I sit down, but not before scanning the ridgeline for the man with the radio. Up close, the A-frame from the mine looms over the top of me, like some Japanese horror-flick monster waiting to reach down and eat me alive. I am near, but what is the point? They already know I am coming. At least Mr. Edward Abbey had an element of surprise with his characters in *The Monkey Wrench Gang*, the iconic novel published in 1975 about a gang of desert rats determined to stop the machines of the industrialized world from digging up their desert. They put sugar in gas tanks of bulldozers and tore out radiator hoses from dump trucks. They acted fast and were always long gone before the workers discovered what had happened.

I have nothing on me to do any real damage. Besides, *they* have the brown wire on their side. Right then I know I should double back to cut the wire as a small gesture to Abbey and the Gang. Who knows, maybe that wire is the link to everything that happens up at the mine? The Rosetta stone of Resolution.

A truck roars past, sending a shudder through my spine. I stand up and realize I am five feet from the mine road. Exhausted, I climb up to the road and walk back toward the campground, away the mine. I don't cut the wire, which I begin to regret. Along the way I pass several mining vehicles, and the drivers all wave. They always wave. And I wave back, which I immediately regret. I don't regret waving to the driver; he is just putting in his time to collect a paycheck. I regret waving at the actual truck and the logo on the truck, for it makes me feel as if I am complicit in the work being done here. As mines go, I'm not sure Resolution is a bad idea, but I feel the act of waving is like a vote of unreserved confidence.

Another truck passes and I don't wave back.

12

A Miner's Friend

A fanatic is a man who consciously overcompensates a secret doubt.

—Aldous Huxley

Phoenix, Arizona, rises out of the ashes like a bolt of hot white light, and in the summer is often the recipient of a haboob, an Arabic word meaning strong wind, when sandstorms blast the city with a wall of sand ten thousand feet high and fifty miles wide. The downtown feels hollow, and that feeling seems to grow by the year as people seep out into the suburbs, where the abundance of foreclosures makes buying a home easy picking. I go there only when necessary, for instance, passing through on my way to the Grand Canyon, or Flagstaff, or California.

Before the settlers arrived in Arizona, the Pima ran an efficient society built around the Phoenix region, using the water from the abundant Gila River to build a sizable farming empire. Then the pioneers and prospectors started riding mules back and forth from New Mexico and California looking for gold and other riches. It wasn't long before some of those people realized that dry heat is different from the heat on the East Coast, and the rest is history. Today the Gila and all other sources of water are long gone before they ever reach the valley of the sun.

The first time I spent more than a day in this sprawl of urban diarrhea was in July 1991. I was standing at the far end of the airport runway working as an assistant director on a car commercial. It was 115 degrees and the soles of my shoes were melting into the tarmac. I knew then I would never live in this city and am always shocked that people actually do reside here. Traveling here for any purpose always takes a day to prepare for the traffic, the heat, and the maze of endless blocks that all seem to end at a medical clinic, a gas station, or a big-box store.

This time I travel to downtown Phoenix to visit the Arizona Department of Mines and Mineral Resources, located in a building with a life-sized mural of a mining dump truck on the back wall.

The man I am to meet, Mr. Nyal Niemuth, sits behind his desk on the second floor. It takes only a few seconds of shaking his hand for me to know that he loves his job. So much so he can't stop talking about it. Physically he resembles a college professor and possesses a full beard and sparkling eyes. He speaks quickly and wears a permanent smile, one that says he's very pleased with himself. His job title is Chief Mining Engineer at the Department of Mines and Mineral Resources. Nyal explains his role as part tour leader, part cheerleader, and part record keeper. Simply stated, he lobbies for the development of mining throughout Arizona.

Outside temperatures climb above 110, while we sit comfortably in the air-conditioning, which I remind myself has several feet of copper tubing running throughout its white plastic shell. Piles of literature detailing how the mining industry drives Arizona's economy are spread throughout the office. One piece of paper has a sketch of an infant with numbers all around and arrows pointing at the body. It states that every American born will need 1,398 pounds of copper, 773 pounds of zinc, 32,654 pounds of iron ore, and 578,956 pounds of coal over the span of an average life. I note that the Mineral Information Institute produces the piece of paper.

I tell Nyal I just drove in from Superior, where the battle over the Oak Flat campground seems to be the focus of all conversations in the town.

"Well, if the greenies and Sierra Club types would just stop being hypocrites for one second," Nyal says, "we could begin mining what could be one of the largest deposits in the world."

I tell him I met with the mayor, who owns the supermarket in town, and that he is all behind the mine.

"Everyone should be," responds Nyal. "We all need copper. *They* can't tell us not to mine and then talk on their cell phone and use their computer in the same breath. They all have copper in the house, their cars, their phones, their television. Everything we use in modern society probably has copper in it."

I feel for my cell phone and hate myself for even having one. I don't know how to text, never have. I try not to use the phone much, mostly for family communication. Still, there it is, hot against my thigh, copper and cobalt burning and dissolving into my tissue, as if to remind me that the man has a point.

I ask if mines are inherently dangerous.

"I know people who don't wear seat belts," he says, while offering me water, for the second time in thirty seconds. "People engage in dangerous activity every day. They smoke cigarettes, a known killer."

He continues on with other examples of irrational behavior: drinking too much, not exercising, eating too much meat, flying in airplanes, and riding a bicycle without a helmet.

"I understand all those examples," I say, "but is mining dangerous?" For me the question is just a beginning point of a conversation. Not for Nyal.

"China kills up to five thousand people a year in mining," he says, standing straight up and ramping up his voice. "In Arizona we might have lost one person last year. So if we allow all of our mineral extraction to happen in other countries, countries like China, aren't we a participant in these deaths? Aren't we contributing to dangerous workplaces for miners and in some cases children?"

I understand Nyal's point, and perhaps even agree with his thesis, but something about his delivery reeks of a practiced speech. In fact, I have heard it before from almost every mining lobbyist over a two-year period.

* * *

The image on the state seal of Arizona tells the story of the territory in 1912, the year Arizona was admitted into the Union. On the seal, a miner with a pick and shovel stands in front of a dam holding back an abundance of water. Nearby are orchards, cattle grazing, and a quartz mill. This scene represents what are known as the five Cs in Arizona: cattle, cotton, copper, citrus, and climate. Even though cattle, citrus, and cotton are all still commercially produced in Arizona, climate and copper are the true fuel in the state's economic engine. The climate, which, because of drought conditions, may end up being the one thing that finally obliterates Arizona, keeps attracting people looking for a good suntan, well-watered golf courses, and cheap homes. This influx of older citizens has in turn created a large health-care industry to look after them as they sicken, often after chasing a good tan in the desert.

And then there is copper, which pumps more than $9 billion into the state's economy each year in the form of direct and indirect taxes, wages, and various fees.

"When you fly over Arizona what do you see? Highways, mines, or farms?" Nyal asks.

I tell him I see a mishmash of desert, mountains, and forests.

"Not mines, that's for sure," he says, stepping on my answer. "You see cities and highways and deserts and farmland." Then he continues on, as if used to speaking to people like me, people who don't work in the mining business. "Mines use so little of our state's space and yet are the number-one source of income. And all our modern-day products use copper, a mineral we are lucky enough to have in abundance here in Arizona."

Yet even though billions of dollars flow through Arizona as a result of the copper mines here, there is potential for more direct money flowing into the state's coffers. Not from opening more mines, but from amending the 1872 mining law and allowing the state and federal governments to collect a royalty on minerals taken from land owned by them.

I ask Nyal about this concept, and he suggests we walk the Arizona Mining and Mineral Museum together. We walk, he talks. He can't stop talking. About mines. About minerals. About all those "greenies and do-gooders" who want to stop every mining project in Arizona. In between his insults to Sierra Club types, he points out various minerals, all behind glass, all from Arizona mines, and all of them beautiful enough to take home and put on the table as a conversation starter.

When I first entered his office, Nyal told me he had only a few minutes, but after an hour he shows no signs of stopping. He speaks quickly and with a hint of defensiveness, as if used to being on his heels when speaking to large groups, like religious people can be when asked to justify their actions using the Good Book.

"I was born in South Dakota," he says as we walk up and down aisles of glass cabinets with minerals staring up at us. He is explaining why he got into the mining profession. We walk on. "And every winter the land would freeze and every spring as the land began to thaw I would notice the rocks that had been frozen in the ice begin to move as the temperature rose. The rock was slowly sliding 'cause the land was thawing. I used to watch the rocks move. Like magic. This fascinated me. I guess I am a rock hound."

We step in front of a piece of uranium, in the form of yellow-cake, nicely separated from me by a piece of thick glass.

"Do you feel sick? Do you feel like you are dying?" Nyal asks with great enthusiasm, as if by saying yes he would be thrilled.

"No," I say, staring at the uranium.

"No, and yet when we want to mine uranium here in Arizona there are all sorts of roadblocks. They say it's dangerous to mine. Nonsense."

I point out that many people did die from mining uranium in the 1950s in the race to arm America with nuclear weapons.

"Yes, but you know why?"

I thought I did, considering I just read the very informative and engaging book *Uranium* by Tom Zoellner.

"Because it's radioactive," I answer, with no trace of irony.

"No," he says, laughing at me as if I had been fooled, like everyone else. "They died because back then the miners smoked. Yep. They smoked, and when you smoke, the nicotine and carcinogenics allow uranium particles to attach to your lungs." He said more, but I really don't know what. Why listen when the man is trying to convince me that miners in uranium camps got radioactive cancer due to smoking? By now I am used to this, the talk of people selling you something. Nyal is selling mining in Arizona, one of the largest employers in the state. That he is selling it by saying uranium mining is safe is, well, insane.

"I love mines," says Nyal. "Love them."

His passion makes me think of him as a young teenager, watching rocks move at a snail's pace in the melting snow in South Dakota, an image that would forever set this man upon his destiny of being a rock hound. The innocent joy of his curiosity is charming. Even insightful. His determination to mine at all costs is not.

As he bounces around the museum pointing out rocks, minerals, and facts about various mines in Arizona, he keeps telling me that he loves mines, and that the pros far outweigh the perceived cons.

"A mine means we are progressing, digging our future out of the ground," he says, pointing at a large globule of blue-and-green rock.

When we arrive back in his office, it has been well over an hour and he hasn't stopped talking at me.

"Is there ever a mine that doesn't make sense to build?" I ask.

He tilts his head to one side and pauses, as if I am speaking a different language for the first time and he is caught off guard.

I repeat the question.

"I know of times when a mine should not have shut down. Is that what you mean? For instance, San Manuel shouldn't have shut down as early as it did. There was plenty of ore left in that mine, and they shut it down. A big mistake."

I nod and then repeat the question. Is there ever a mine that should not be opened, whether because of environmental, political, or social reasons? "I mean if a company wants to open a mine in the middle of a city, smack-dab in the middle of downtown Tucson, would that be a mine that should not open?"

Nyal looks at me one more time and then, with a slight squint-ing of his eyes, looks at his computer and begins typing. He con-tinues for almost thirty seconds.

"Nyal?" I ask.

"Good luck with your book," he says and returns to his com-puter screen.

I stand and extend my hand, thanking him for his time.

He never looks up from his computer, his fingers typing away furiously.

He is still typing as I walk into the hallway, still feeling caught off guard that I had just been dismissed.

Dazed, I begin to project my own amateur analysis of this man's thought pattern. He likes rocks, big trucks, big cranes, and big holes in the ground. But to reduce his fascination with min-ing to a boy's fantasy would be incorrect. When his fantasy inter-mingles with the personal life stories of miners, and histories of individual mines and the towns they built and then destroyed, it becomes easier to find myself fascinated with the allure of his endless joy. I just wish he realized the full scope of his fantasy, that mining also cripples people and places and uproots entire populations of people and nature alike. We may have to mine in order to *be* a modern civilization, but that doesn't mean we have to mine at all costs, which I am beginning to feel is the only choice most proponents of mining would like to us to believe we have.

I step outside and the sun bakes everything in sight. Phoenix. This city does not belong here. Nothing human belongs here. I get back into my copper-lined car and turn on the air-conditioning full blast. Sweating and navigating Phoenix traffic, I think back to how I got myself into this mess. Basically by allowing some soil experts to scratch below the surface of my garden, I have ignited a debate inside myself. How can I be thankful for the ways copper makes our lives simpler, while at the same time being extremely nervous about the people in charge of extracting it from the earth? Copper mining by its very nature is a destructive force. By har-nessing our resources in this manner, we enter an unspoken con-tract to ruin our aquifers, add to the problem of global warming, and be responsible for the massive displacement of billions of tons of earth.

My phone rings. I am told the meeting is set for sunrise tomorrow morning on the San Carlos Apache reservation. I pass my exit for Bisbee and keep driving east on Highway 10. I'm headed back up into the Copper Triangle. It is time to meet the chief.

13

The Chairman

One does not sell the earth upon which the people walk.

—Crazy Horse

The chief is actually not a chief. He is a chairman and he arrives just after sunrise, wearing black jeans, black boots, a black long-sleeve shirt, and a black skullcap. At the base of the cap is a small eagle feather that bobs back and forth as he walks. I am sitting in the nearly empty coffee shop of the Apache Gold Casino, located on the edge of the San Carlos Apache Reservation, seven miles from the mining hub of Globe-Miami. The chairman walks across the casino floor with a slow but confident stride. Chairman Nosie, pronounced NO-See, takes his job seriously. He is not a chief because he is elected in a straightforward voting process. He does not see his job as just being a figurehead, or even a mayor. He sees himself as a caretaker, one whose responsibilities extend far beyond the white man's borders of the reservation. His critics think he takes himself too seriously, that he has a chip on his shoulder. They may be correct. Or he may have history on his side. After all, he is the first descendant of Geronimo ever to be chairman of the reservation.

Before he can sit down, two people get up from their slot machines and stop him, shake his hand, and smile. An employee of the casino stops the chairman. His body language is deferential and respectful. They nod and part, and the man in black strides to my booth and sits down across from me. He extends his hand and gives me a firm handshake.

"I am Chairman Nosie, the elected leader of the San Carlos Apache tribe," he says.

"It's a pleasure to meet you," I say.

"So why are you here?" he asks, wasting no time.

I tell him I want to hear his side of things. I know what Resolution, the company that intends to build a mine under the Oak Flat campground, has to say. It says what all mining companies say—that the mine will be compatible with the surrounding environment and economies, that it will bring the region lots of jobs, including to his tribe. But we all know that mining companies import employees from elsewhere to fill their well-paying jobs and that they ruin everything in sight of the mine.

He seems interested but not convinced that I legitimately care. The waitress delivers a round of tea and coffee. For minutes, or what seems like minutes, he stirs a few packets of sugar into his coffee. All I can hear is the spoon touching the cup and the monotonous clinking and clanking of the slot machines. This isn't Vegas. The casino layout consists of one room in an octagon shape with the café, bank, bar, and bathrooms sitting on a level higher than the slot machines, which sparkle and glimmer while pinging out the familiar noise of one more coin going into the slot. The gambling crowd consists of a few locals, easily spotted by their darker skin, dark almond-shaped eyes, and expressionless faces. They are joined by a smattering of retired snowbirds who live in RVs nearby. All of them slouch on stools in front of slot machines, drinking coffee out of Styrofoam cups. Losers, and the occasional winner, tossing pennies, nickels, and dollar bills into the machines one motion at a time, hoping the machine tilts for them.

Finally the chairman looks up from stirring his coffee to look me in the eye.

"Where do you live?"

"Bisbee."

He stops drinking his coffee. "Born there?"

"No, but have lived there almost a decade and there's talk of reopening that mine."

"Do you work for Resolution?"

I tell him I work for myself.

"We are a sovereign nation and we don't have to speak to the mayor of Superior, the bosses at Resolution, or even the state of Arizona. We deal with representatives from Washington. Only."

A man comes to the table to speak about his art, how it reflects the struggle of the Apache nation. He believes the fight for Oak Flat is important because it defines who they are. He leaves a phone number on a piece of paper for me and walks away.

"I have not given an interview in a long time," the chairman says as he gently reaches for two of my books that I have brought as a gift. He turns them over and scans the blurbs and synopses.

"I have turned down dozens, hundreds of interviews. I won't talk to any of the newspapers in the state."

When his secretary called the night before to confirm the meeting, she told me the only time he could meet was at 7:00 a.m. the next day. I had been calling for a month and wasn't about to miss my chance. I drove for several hours last night, passing through Mormon farming country and into Geronimo, a town that sprawls with no particular purpose other than being the last town before the reservation begins.

The San Carlos reservation is one of the poorest Native American Nations, but it is also one of the biggest. It covers 1.8 million acres in a remote area of Arizona, on a road rarely driven by tourists. Eighty percent of the population live in poverty. Seventy percent are unemployed. The average life span of a male is fifty-four years. Alcohol and drug use are high.

Unlike many other reservations in the Southwest, which were designed to contain various tribes on land where they had historical ties, the San Carlos reservation was created as a large outdoor jail, where any and all Native Americans, regardless of tribe, were sent once the U.S. government decided they were too troublesome to deal with. This is where the army put the Indians whom they could not contain, conquer, or kill outright. In the beginning, the captives were kept at Lake San Carlos, a muddy swamp full of mosquitoes and disease and exposure to unbearable summer heat. For army soldiers, Lake San Carlos was equal to being assigned to Siberia. For the Indians, it was a death camp. The result was that both the captors and the captured hated the place, and one another, with a passion.

Today, in Bylas, the first town inside the reservation border, both sides of the highway are littered with plastic bags, plastic soda bottles, and plastic wrappers. Most of the housing consists of four rooms in a concrete shell or mobile homes. In either case the yards contain a smattering of junked cars, dirt, chain-link fences, dangling plastic, and broken dreams.

"I will tell you a story that explains why I don't do interviews," the chairman says and takes another long sip of coffee.

"An old friend of mine from high school came to visit me a few years ago," the chairman begins. "We weren't that good of friends in school, but still I know him. Over the next year we spoke a few times, casually, in social settings. Then one time he asks what my plans are regarding the Resolution mine at Oak Flat. I ignore him. As the chairman, I have a duty to be careful who I speak to regarding the Oak Flat issue. Then he asks again. And again. I continue to ignore him. Then one day he shows up at the tribal office wanting to see me. I left him in the lobby for four hours before I finally agreed to see him. He asks a few personal questions, as if we are good friends, and I cut him off. I ask him if he was paid by Resolution people to try and find out information from me."

The chairman paused, as any good storyteller would do at this moment.

"And then he admitted that he had been paid by the mining company, and that he felt terrible. He said he was in my office to admit this and ask for forgiveness. I told him I can forgive him and have no problem moving on, but that he is never to speak with me directly again. That is who these people are. They lie for a living. They lie like a politician. I have no reason to speak to them. None. I know what they are going to say. They will talk about numbers, statistics, and promises of a wonderful future. This is a very old story for us Apaches. They think we don't understand the details or the impact the mine will have on the local economy. We understand everything."

To his critics, Nosie's mission is one of aimless protesting. They say he is a man who likes to hear himself talk. To his supporters, he is a breath of fresh air. He was once arrested for walking on the University of Arizona's land atop Mount Graham, regarded as the spiritual home of the Apache people. The university had built a telescope on the mountain and thrown up a large fence. Nosie saw this as a direct violation to a well-known holy place of the Apache. He went to court and was hoping to take the case up the ladder to the state supreme court. But after hundreds of supporters showed up on the first day, it became obvious that the effort to convict the chairman of an Apache Nation for walking on their own sacred land was a publicity nightmare the state didn't need. All charges were soon dropped.

To the Apaches who think like the chairman, desecrating Oak Flat is nothing less than sacrilege. It is a mortal wound to the earth, one that cannot be healed.

"The Apaches are a race of benevolent mystics," says the chairman, as he takes another long sip of coffee.

"In the Apache religion," he continues with a fluid sense of pride, "we believe we are blessed to be caretakers of what God gave us in this land and that we must honor that gift. To do anything else would be an abandonment of our beliefs."

Over the course of several hours, the chairman will say many things along these lines, and after a while I get lost in the fog of conversation. At times I catch myself wondering if he truly does like to hear himself talk or if he is really telling me something.

We slowly edge out of the casino, where he is approached several more times to buy jewelry, physically support an elderly lady, and shake a few hands. The startling blue sky is a reminder that casinos easily erase all consciousness of life outside their sealed domes.

Looking back at the casino, I ask Nosie about the importance of this place as a source of income for the tribe. He waves his hand dismissively. He says let's go for a drive.

"They want to destroy Oak Flat, as if it is just another piece of empty land no one cares about. In our language, Oak Flat is known as Chich'il Bildagoteel, or Red Medicine Place," he says as we hop up into his large black truck.

We cruise south toward San Carlos, the central town of the reservation. Out here the desert is never far away. It lurks at the edge of every town, every vista. On each side of the highway, the desert is ready to reclaim the land as soon as the locals let down their guard. We pass a dusty home, next to another one, and then another. I notice there are no plants in the yards, not a single blade of grass. Each home looks like its neighbors. I tell the chairman that I have traveled throughout the Southwest, and this desolation of home ownership, at least in the yards, seems universal to Native American tribes.

"To an Apache, everything you invite into your life becomes your responsibility. Our children, our friends, our cars. If we bring a tree that was taken from another place, we are then responsible for displacing that tree and must care for it like a family member. People don't want that responsibility."

As we drive away from the casino, the air-conditioning is so cold I plug the vent with a shirt. The chairman doesn't notice.

"I have read that the mining company likes to say you are a hypocrite because you drive a fancy big truck, which has lots of copper in it, and yet you resist a copper mine because you personally don't like it. They call you a NIMBY," I say.

"NIMBY?" He smiles in my direction.

"Not in my backyard," I reply.

He laughs. "Do you know why you see big expensive trucks on a reservation of poor people?"

I shake my head.

"Because we don't own our homes. The government does. So we have no equity and the bank won't ever give us a loan on a house we don't own. My wife has worked for the IRS for twenty years and we can't get a loan because we don't technically own our house. On reservations we aren't allowed to. But banks will give us big loans for cars because they can come and drive away the car if we default. As for the copper in my truck, I don't know about that."

Nosie turns the black truck down a dirt road. "We are going to the lake," he says, as we drive straight toward the mountains.

"I see my role as chairman as a chance to remind ourselves that we come from a strong people, a history of protecting our land, of honoring this earth. If we do that, then we are in tune with this world," he says as we stop by a lake that has gone dry, except for a small section of water to the north that sits behind a concrete dam built to capture water destined for agriculture crops near Phoenix, seventy-five miles to the west.

He walks ahead of me, up to a monument overlooking the lake, which appears more like a mud reservoir. The sides of the lake are well defined, each one a steep ridgeline that circles the lake. One hundred and thirty-five years ago the ridgelines would have allowed cavalry soldiers a clear shot to the gathered Native Americans below. No one knows how many were killed here, but it would have been a turkey shoot. Geronimo escaped from here three times, each time returning of his own free will in order to be with his family. Then the army killed his family. Upon his final escape, he terrorized the army for another decade before surrendering in Skeleton Canyon, seventy miles from Bisbee.

"I want to make this spot a place where all Apache people from San Carlos are proud to bring their children," Nosie says as he lays out his master plan. "This will become a place where Apaches can find their center."

On August 14, 2009, police and Secret Service agents surround the high school gym in Superior. A local crowd is filling the gym in anticipation of the arrival of Senator John McCain and Ken Salazar, the secretary of the interior. They are coming for a town hall meeting to hear the community's thoughts on the proposed Resolution mine.

Outside, Secret Service agents are baking under the desert heat in long-sleeve button-down shirts and sports coats, with twisted cords of earpieces dangling from their ears. Some hold cell phones over their heads looking for reception. Near the door of the gym, a frenzy of television crews pace the sidewalk waiting for their intended subjects. In the parking lot, a few protesters hold signs that read SAVE OUR OAK FLAT. Right next to them is a woman with a sign that declares ACORNS WON'T FEED US ANYMORE, referring to the Apaches' claim that the mine will destroy Oak Flat, the place they have traditionally gone every summer to harvest acorns for ceremonial rituals. I grab a seat on the bleachers directly behind an elderly Apache woman dressed in traditional costume. I notice that Chairman Nosie is not here. To my left is a man with a white beard, overalls, and a baseball cap painted red, white, and blue. To my right are a husband and wife with two small children, each one with a balloon, as if this were an outing at the county fair.

The Washington politicians are late, and the room is hot, so it is decided to have a few locals keep the audience engaged. The first to speak is Mr. Hing, not the mayor but the mayor's father, who used to be the mayor of Superior. He's an older man with a crick in his back, making him lean forward. Like a Chinese Don Rickles, he comes out fighting.

"Let's talk about culture," he begins, with direct aim at the Apache stakeholders. "I stopped using chopsticks when I left China. So stop talking about the acorns and get a fork," he says to a roar of laughter and a few hisses.

I think back to my time spent with his son, the current mayor, in the meat section of the Save Money grocery store. He told me his grandfather was the first family member off the boat, not his father. So I make a note to myself that this man, with a thick accent, never left China to begin with. He was born here.

After Mr. Hing's stand-up routine comes Hank, the president of the chamber of commerce, who points out that his father, who is eighty-five, was a miner and has lived his whole life in Superior. Hank says a few more things about how mining is good for Superior before noticing a growing number of people in blue suits gathering near the side door. He wraps it up and quickly exits.

The politicians enter stage left to a roar of applause. I've learned to withhold any applause until politicians deliver on their promises. I haven't clapped in years. Senator McCain, nicknamed "the Maverick," strides in, his right arm locked against his side, a result of being tortured in Vietnam. He looks over the crowd with his steely eyes. He is not a politician I would want to meet. I imagine in the quiet of night he is a bitter man who has spent his whole life trying to impress his father. And failed. Next to him is Ken Salazar, a western man, one of us. He wears a cowboy hat and bolo tie.

The first ten minutes are dedicated to the local, state, and federal politicians thanking one another for, well, one another. The first rule of politics is to make sure to cover all flanks, especially anyone who may become your enemy.

The interior secretary's first solo act is to march out a few of the elderly Apache women, who get a standing ovation.

One woman, who identifies herself as the descendant of a famous Apache tracker for the U.S. cavalry, takes the microphone and goes after Mr. Hing. "You said you threw away chopsticks and picked up a fork. I guess that is where the term forked tongue came from."

The crowd erupts in a loud mix of laughter and boos. The show has officially begun.

The temperature keeps rising as more and more bodies pour in the side doors. Tables with literature for and against the Resolution mine at Oak Flat line the walls. Television cameras take it all in. A few Tea Party types walk the edge of the crowd, seemingly looking for a reason to shout out.

The politicians promise to take into consideration all interested stakeholders. With that in mind, someone shouts, "It's an underground mine. So what's the problem? Drink a beer and shut up."

Senator McCain urges the restless crowd, most of whom support the mine, to calm down. He says level heads will prevail. He is in charge of making the land swap with Resolution Mining that will give the state of Arizona an excess of five thousand acres of prime real estate and in return Resolution gets Oak Flat.

The town hall circus ends and the politicians storm out the side door into a fleet of SUVs headed toward Phoenix. The crowd disperses except for a few dozen people who walk onto the gym floor like fighters racing from their corners. I join the stampede.

A Native American woman smiles glowingly as a Native American man points his finger in her face and screams, "If this goes through, this blood is on your hands. You know that. You are Native American. How can you do this?"

He keeps yelling at her and she never stops smiling. When the man turns away, I ask her for her card, which she gives to me while smiling more. It reads: "Resolution Copper Company, Native American Advisor." The cleverness of corporations to use the English language in such nuanced ironic twists seems both disheartening and ingenious. I can't help but think of the rooms of people who create these titles out of thin air. I imagine she takes home a hefty paycheck, or at least I hope she does. It can't be easy explaining away her job to her family and friends, except by using the same line most people rely on, that everyone needs to make a living. I'm sure they pay her enough to smile as she explains to her own people that losing a place they hold sacred will be good for them in the long run.

I wade through the crowd and find David Salisbury, CEO of Resolution Copper, explaining to a journalist how this mine will be safe and exceed all environmental standards set by the EPA. A man screams from five feet away that once the land swap happens, Oak Flat will be considered private land and Resolution won't have to follow the EPA rules. The CEO repeats his statement, "This mine will exceed any and all environmental standards given to us by the federal government."

He turns toward me, as if expecting a question. Instead, I say, "I spent some time with Chairman Nosie."

He smiles and gets a little closer to me. "Ask him why he drives a big SUV," says the CEO. "Ask him how he lives a really comfortable life using copper and won't admit it. And how many of his people actually use Oak Flat?"

"I did," I say.

He nods and lifts his shoulders, as if to say, "See, I told you."

Then, not waiting for another question, he turns and walks away.

Over the years, the CEO has posed these questions over and over to anyone who will listen. It makes me think of how politicians fall in love with a single fault of their opponent. "He is an adulterer," or "She lied on her taxes," or "He hired a undocumented worker to cut his lawn." They find that one thing and then hammer us until we want to believe what they are saying

196

so they will shut up. The problem is that no matter what Chairman Nosie does, or believes, he will have no bearing on how the multinational companies that own the mine will behave once it is opened. That is what is at stake here, not the chairman's choice of car.

Feeling in need of a shower, I walk out of the gymnasium into a bald white sun. I look up at Apache Leap. On the other side several miles to the south is San Carlos Lake, where I stood with Chairman Nosie. He won't come to these meetings, not now or ever.

I remember back to our meeting a few months ago. Before we left the lake, I asked him what he thought are the realistic chances of saving Oak Flat from sinking three hundred feet. He took a deep breath and looked out at the muddy pond.

"There is another word for Oak Flat for the Apache. We say Gan Diszin, 'where God touched the earth.'"

History mixed with tragic irony is thick when one is standing next to a man with the blood of Geronimo in his veins. We are in the exact place where the ancestors of the people in Washington gunned down his ancestors, and now the people in Washington are hoping to trade his people's land to a corporate mining tribe from London and Australia, so they can destroy it. Again.

Sure, the chief drives a Yukon, sucking up the modern-day conveniences like the rest of us. And yes, he is full of anger, righteousness, and a healthy dose of resentment. His arguments for Oak Flat may seem trivial to some—saving an acorn-gathering spot—considering the large resource of copper under the surface, but I would bet my life that the power of his people's knowledge of that land is far greater than anyone's sitting in the Superior offices of the Resolution mining company.

No matter how much New Age babble we consume, or yoga positions we master, we will have no idea of what it means to communicate with an animal or a plant as Native Americans once did. I have tried to communicate with the creatures of the natural world since I was a child and am sure they still don't hear me.

14

Prospector

> The conquest of the earth, which mostly means the taking it away from those who have a different complexion or slightly flatter noses than ourselves, is not a pretty thing when you look into it too much.
>
> —Joseph Conrad, *Heart of Darkness*

He sits behind his desk plotting, reading numbers. He has maps of remote places in mountain ranges few ever travel. He has phone numbers of people in capital cities all over the world. On the wall is a mountain lion, stuffed. A single shot he took years ago. He has bet millions on hunches and made billions for shareholders he will never meet. He has a building at a nearby university named after him. He is the most famous copper prospector in the world and lives in a smuggler's corridor, surrounded by death and crime, in his ranch house in Peck Canyon, a few hours from my house.

To get there, I drive west of Bisbee through the small outpost of Patagonia, a town built as a railroad stop to service several silver- and gold-mining camps near the Mexican American border. Then I turn north at Nogales, take the Peck Canyon exit, and follow the directions to the Atascosa Ranch, a short eleven miles from Mexico. This is remote land, riddled with smugglers, weekend gold prospectors, ranchers, and Border Patrol. As I drive, I remember the night a few years ago when I stopped for a beer in Arivaca, an old gold-mining town forty miles from here. The sign at the bar said guns had to be left with the bartender. Within an hour, a man on crutches was fighting another man, the two of them wrestling on the floor like two snakes slithering over one another. A few minutes later everyone at the bar, except me, retrieved their guns from the bartender and quietly lined up to take sides with the fighting parties. I knew it was the twenty-first century out there on the freeway, but in here was another world. Finally the bartender pulled out a shotgun and told everyone to get out. He announced the bar was closed until noon the next day.

I park in front of an old ranch house and walk, as instructed, into the adjacent guesthouse. An assistant ushers me into a large room, which doubles as an office. A few miners' lanterns decorate the room, along with a dozen or so photos of mining operations in remote places. A glass case of precious gems stands near the back wall. Above it a bookshelf is filled to capacity.

Sitting in a chair behind a large desk is an eighty-two-year-old man, who immediately stands up and shakes my hand. His smile is genuine and his voice raspy but still full of confidence. I take a seat, as well as a deep breath, and race through dozens of questions I have been thinking about on my drive. I have imagined this moment for weeks, and I decide to start with the obvious.

"How would you describe what you do for a living?" I ask, nervous he will think this is shorthand for small talk.

"Well," he says, leaning back in his chair, "I guess you could call me a professional treasure hunter and not a bad metallurgist."

This man is David Lowell. He has explored more than fifty countries in six decades and made fourteen major copper discoveries, including Escondido in Chile, the most productive copper mine on Earth. His discoveries have grossed hundreds of billions of dollars for the companies that own them, and made him a very rich man. He has been called the world's greatest living explorer by many of his colleagues. Yet Lowell wasn't trying to explore the entire world. He set out to discover a very specific piece of it. He wanted to find all the copper he could, and if he found it in places where big mining companies had tried and failed, that made it even sweeter.

"Big mining corporations are not built to make quick decisions. They are not set up to think like a prospector. They make strange decisions, if you ask me," says Lowell, when I ask his opinion of mining corporations.

"I mean, I am in business with many of them, but I wouldn't want to work for them." He laughs. His smile tightens up and his head bobbles from side to side; his face is clearly telling me that he has endured a lifelong relationship that he needs but doesn't necessarily enjoy.

"I was born here in southern Arizona. My dad was a miner. My grandfather was on the coroner's jury for Geronimo," he says, introducing himself as an Arizona native.

He began rock hounding near Arivaca. There his dad mined for gold and David scraped the hillsides for any trace of shining minerals. He began his professional career as a mining engineer for ASARCO in Mexico. In 1961, he struck out on his own as a consultant. His wife didn't trust that he could get any work, so she got a job teaching Spanish. They had three children and their debt and stress increased.

"She didn't want to rely on my hunches. She wanted to make sure our family at least could buy food and pay the weekly bills," he says with a chuckle. "*She* is the determined one."

By 1973, he was working as a consultant for large copper-mining companies and found two midlevel deposits: Vekol Hills and Kalamazoo, both in Arizona. That got him a paycheck, but his wife kept teaching. By 1973, he was working part-time as a consultant and part-time as a pitchman, selling his own prospecting ideas to mining companies. The former would make him a good living. The latter would make him a few hundred million dollars.

As he toiled in the consulting business, he began developing a theory on how to locate large deposits of copper based on understanding the geological patterns of low-grade copper deposits known as porphyry copper. This type of copper is found in trace amounts, attached to other minerals and locked in massive deposits beneath Earth's crust. Most open-pit mines in operation today involve porphyry copper, which explains why it takes one ton of rock to find ten pounds of copper, or a ratio of about half a percent of copper.

Lowell came to realize that 150 million years ago, when copper-producing magma shot up from Earth's mantle, it created a bubble of water, silica, copper, and gold that formed the tip of the molten wave that cooled on its way toward the surface. However, minerals that had the highest melting points solidified first and deeper down, thereby creating a potentially large layer of copper and other minerals that would lie in a deposit mostly untouched by surface mining.

These layers would not be easy to find. Instead of being layered in obvious pools directly under an initial find, the copper, he theorized, would be deposited in concentric rings for several miles outward. He believed these rings would have developed as a result of the process of heating and cooling the minerals. As if that wasn't hard enough for the mining executives to swallow, he threw in a wild card. These halos, he explained (in a revolutionary mining theory he wrote in 1971), would best be seen on a three-dimensional map and could be tilted at any angle. If minerals are already hard to find, this made it even harder. That is, unless you hired David Lowell to find them.

As he sits across from me explaining his theory, which is now used widely in the mining business, Lowell seems slightly amused. He strikes me as a man who knows he has lived a gambler's life but was able to have something most who do this for a living don't have: more success than failure.

"In 1965, I told the San Manuel owners—a mine north of Tucson—I thought they were digging in the wrong place, but they didn't want to listen to me," he says with a big smile. His theory was that the copper deposit that the mining company was looking for was not in any direction outward from the initial find. Rather, he theorized that the deposit had been severed by Earth's surface over millions of years. Instead of being horizontal, the deposit was straight down, extending in halos deep into the earth. The aboveground halos would have long ago disappeared into a placer deposit on the surface, like an iceberg melting at the top but leaving a massive solid piece of ice underneath. The company, Newmont, didn't buy into this theory, so he sold the idea to another company, which proceeded to dig where Lowell told them to. They found the copper. For this consulting he was paid a finder's fee of $120,000.

The phone rings and he answers.

"Excuse me for a moment, I have to do this interview," he says to me.

He is talking to a national news channel about a killing that happened on his ranch last week. Peck Canyon, and specifically Lowell's ranch, is one of the most popular smuggling routes for the Mexican gangs running drugs and humans across the border. His ranch hit the national radar a week earlier when U.S. border agent Brian Terry was killed on his property in a botched ATF operation, "Fast and Furious." This is not the first time his property has made the news. It has a history of blood and mystery, and got its name when Geronimo and his band of Apache warriors killed Al Peck, his family, and a ranch hand on April 27, 1886, on what would turn out to be the Apache leader's last killing in the Arizona territory before his surrender in Skeleton Canyon.

Lowell finishes the phone interview and we talk about the shooting.

"There's been five shootings in the past year. I have found a dead body on our property and seen lots of caches of drugs ditched until they come back for them later."

I can't help but think how Geronimo, copper, and violence all figure into the long, tangled history of the borderland of Arizona, which was still called Mexico 150 years ago. Back then it was clear to Washington, D.C., that obtaining the mineral-rich zone of southern Arizona was critical. The first step was the Gadsden Treaty, which overnight annexed everything south of the Gila River to the current Mexican border, which includes the Copper Triangle, Morenci, and Bisbee. Then, the army had to get rid of Geronimo and his highly efficient warriors. The government accomplished that by shipping him off to Florida. Then copper brought the industrial muscle—railroad, mines, and a large influx of European migrant labor—to southern Arizona. For a while the mining companies had the run of the place and they supplied the world with what it wanted so badly, a cheap and reliable source of copper.

Today, the cartels of Mexico are deftly using these same remote regions to supply America with what it wants so badly, drugs and cheap labor.

Like most people who live here, David and I exchange a few words about the smuggling problem and then move on. This is common among locals. Talking about it seems pointless at times. No one in southern Arizona has a clue how to win this battle. Politicians like to talk about tall border walls and "virtual" security systems, but when a crime syndicate can build tunnels under connecting border cities, complete with railroad tracks, and send submarines into the port of San Diego, the wall and extra cameras on that wall are meaningless. At times it seems unsolvable. In the meantime, hit men from Phoenix, on the payroll of the cartels, will continue to drive vans up and down I-10 shooting other vans full of undocumented aliens caught in a war of revenge and profit. This happens, but no one knows about it because no one but illegal immigrants are killed. A dozen dead Mexicans doesn't get a headline. One dead agent does.

David leans back in his chair and continues to tell me his own story.

"My first real discovery of any size was in 1981 with Escondido." He straightens up, with a proud twinkle in his eyes. If he were a boasting sort, this would be the moment. Escondido, located in Chile's Atacama Desert, the driest place on Earth, is the largest copper mine in the world. Not in physical size, a distinction held by the Kennecott mine outside Salt Lake City. And not in reserves. That is more than likely Grasberg, in Irian Jaya. But in production of copper there isn't a mine even close. It pumps out twice as much as Morenci, America's most productive mine.

He found the mine using his theory, the one that companies respected but weren't sure they wanted to spend millions supporting. Copper mining has existed in the three-hundred-mile-long copper belt of the Atacama for centuries, and several large companies are constantly prodding the region hoping to find even larger deposits. By the end of the 1970s, it seemed no one could find the next "discovery." Then David suggested his halo concept. He calculated that the deposit was there, just not where they were digging. Getty Oil decided to back him. Working as a hired consultant, he methodically increased the range of the probing drill holes, hoping to catch a glimpse of the underground halo belts full of minerals.

"Escondido means 'hidden' in Spanish, and it was well hidden," he says while showing me photos of Escondido on his wall. There are no trees, only vast horizons of empty space. This is our vision of Mars: a desolate stretch of sand with a violent white sun scorching everything below. For sixteen months, twenty-four hours a day, his team drilled holes to a nine-hundred-foot depth. He spent $3 million of Getty's money.

"Biggest financial mistake I made in my life, being a consultant instead of self-financing the dig. But it worked out in the end."

In twenty-five years, the mine has produced almost twenty million tons of copper, with a market value of over $140 billion. To add to his legend, he also found an adjacent deposit, called Zaldívar. For both finds he was paid a flat fee of $4.5 million.

"If I had found it on my own, I would be entitled to a small percentage of profits, or at the very least a very large buyout," he says with a laugh. By any calculations, that would have made him a billionaire.

He didn't make that mistake again. He soon met Catherine McLeod, a Canadian investment banker who helped Lowell become Lowell Incorporated. From that point forward, he would always be a large shareholder in his own discoveries.

The vocation of prospector was born in Europe after the Dark Ages, when the serfs were encouraged to seek out treasures on the noble's land for a piece of the action, an arrangement not so different from what happens today, when large mining firms lease out claims and let small mining companies do the hard work of finding the deposits. Today prospecting is a combination of technology, experience, and, most important, luck.

To get a sense of the corporate notion of prospecting, I had traveled to Tucson a few months before my interview with Lowell. There I visited Richard Leveille, the president of exploration for Freeport-McMoRan.

Leveille is tall, thin, with a full beard. He wore jeans, high-end hiking boots, and a long-sleeve shirt. He looked as if he were ready to walk twenty miles in the 105-degree heat and laugh about it. Like Lowell, Leveille comes from a mining family. He grew up in Nevada, New Mexico, and Utah, with a dad who was a geologist for Kennecott, when it was still owned by the Guggenheim family.

I asked how the junior mining companies play a role in the business of finding copper deposits.

"Well, occasionally, and I mean very rarely, they act as the prospector by finding a deposit," said Leveille. "If they do that, then they raise some money and develop enough of the deposit to attract the big companies, who have no problem buying them out if it holds promise. But in reality, most junior companies are exploring what major firms already know about but don't want to spend the time or resources finding the ore body. They want a junior to do the legwork, while they track the progress. It's just a better use of their money and labor. Then they just come in, buy them out, and start production. That is more common. It is sort of a long-term investment by the majors to allow the juniors to do the scrambling."

Like the insurmountable odds of getting a green light in the movie business, getting a mine in production faces a grim statistical calculus. Out of 1,000 prospects, 250 are green-lit for exploration. Of those, 80 show promise. After more geological studies, 12 merit more investment. Two make the finals, and in the end 1 mine goes online.

"There is only so much economic copper to find in the world. My job is to find it and secure it for Freeport," Leveille said.

By all estimates, at today's rate of consumption, there is enough copper within one mile of Earth's surface to last five million years. The copper is there, but getting to it without going broke is the issue. Freeport, like most of the major companies, has fifty years' worth of reserve, maybe a bit more with the Tenke mine in the Congo beginning to produce large quantities of higher-grade copper.

"Most people see a mine and assume this business is high-tech. Bullshit," he said. "Ninety percent of it is an old prospector walking an arroyo and having a feeling for the ground."

David Lowell is that old prospector, who used to be a middle-aged man on a mission: to find more. And unlike others, he takes the big risks, physically and financially, to follow his instinct.

For instance, in 1991 he began trekking the Cordillera Negra range in Peru. He was looking for gold. The problem was that the Shining Path, the terrorist group, was known to use the area as a base of operation. Americans would not be welcome on their turf. Trying to stay under the radar, Lowell continued his exploration. Paying for the expedition out of his own pocket, he hired five local geologists and for three years looked for what he thought was a large deposit of gold in those hills. After spending millions and based out of a hotel room in Lima, he recruited an old Australian friend who fronted David more money.

Back home, his wife continued to teach Spanish and raise the children. I wonder what the children knew of their father's work, or whether they knew their father was out there, somewhere, chasing his obsession.

Then toward the end of 1995, lab results confirmed that Lowell had found a mother lode. In the end, Barrick Gold bought his company's rights to the mine for $790 million, of which Lowell pocketed $63 million. By the time the deposit was all mined out, it had produced over $11 billion worth of gold.

"I don't dig around much anymore," says Lowell. "Instead, for the last ten years I have done most of my treasure hunting by reading through old files in forgotten buildings in South America. A lot of these big hidden deposits are near the same areas where they found surface minerals years ago. Sometimes hundreds of years ago. I just dig deeper."

As he goes into the other room, I walk around the office, looking at pictures of him in front of his collection of mines. All of them show a gentle-looking man with a relaxed smile. I don't imagine he ever has that other thought, the one that wonders if he is the point man on destroying everything in sight. To Lowell, there is no dilemma in mining. To him, we mine because we are human. He sees life as one big expedition, with him at the front of the line. In space he would be the first to volunteer to get to the moon, to see what was there.

On one hand, I find him fascinating, like a modern-day Indiana Jones who travels the world seeking new treasures. On the other hand, I find him deeply disconnected from the adverse results of his mining claims. He finds the goods, sells them, and keeps going, always eager to find the next trophy. Prospectors by their very nature don't see the physical earth as something to save and behold. They see it as a large map, waiting to be diagrammed, probed, and dug up. I imagine he sees himself as a facilitator of building the modern world. And he would be right. I doubt he has ever lost a night of sleep worrying about the destruction that will follow his discoveries, the villages and communities that will boom from his discoveries, and then bust once they fade away. Or that will benefit from the jobs created yet struggle against greedy corporations to maintain their human rights.

Either way, today Lowell is the CEO of his own equity group that finances his prospecting ideas. I ask if, when he picks up the phone to call his inner circle for money, they ever hesitate on one of his prospecting hunches.

He laughs. "No, not anymore."

He has made millionaires of all his colleagues and continues to make billions for the companies that buy out his discoveries.

In 2002, he visited a copper deposit long abandoned by the Peruvian government. He paid $2 million for the option to mine. By 2007, after tens of millions of dollars to prove the mine was profitable, a Chinese company bought Lowell's company's ownership of the mine for $810 million, with Lowell depositing $80 million for his efforts.

He then sold another deposit in Ecuador to the same company for $700 million.

I ask about the 1872 mining law in the United States that basically allows mining companies to get away with mining on public lands for free. I ask if he finds it strange that in every other country where he prospects, the host country asks for an option or royalty rate for the profits of the mine.

"Not at all. I would find it strange if they didn't," he says.

I ask his opinion about Bisbee, whether it will reopen or not.

"Well, I don't know if it will, but I know where the copper is. I helped find it," he says.

In the early 1970s, he was hired by Phelps Dodge, then the owners of the Bisbee mine, to come to Bisbee for a few days to try to locate a new deposit of copper. He found it and tracked it all the way over the Mule Mountains, ending on the land of a rancher who hated the mining company. He talked to the rancher, local to local, rancher to rancher. "So I go back to the mining company and give them the terms for mining on his land and they agreed."

I ask if there is enough copper to justify a large operation.

"Oh, sure, but it is all a question of economy of scale for Freeport. Is it worth it? I have no idea. But if they dig in the direction I told them to, I get a hundred-thousand-dollar finder's fee. All for a few days' work."

I ask what is next.

"For the last four years I have been prospecting a platinum mine in South America," he says. "Got eight million dollars in so far. It will take a few more years, but I think it will have a huge deposit, maybe half the reserves in the world. Someone will buy it. Or maybe we will just develop and run it ourselves. I'm not sure yet."

This is the first time he speaks of a current operation, and now I see the salesman in him. I am not someone he has to sell anything to, but still his voice gains momentum and his excitement grows with every breath. He is in the business of pitching billion-dollar deposits, and for a split second I want to invest money I don't have in his newest discovery.

We talk a little longer outside. Lowell motions in the direction of the shooting last week that took the Border Patrol agent's life. Just off his main house, he shows me where he found backpacks of marijuana. His wife comes out and tells how one day she was

209

driving down their driveway and a truck was stopped. Men came out of the desert and loaded up the truck with bags and bags of weed. They looked at her like it was just a slight delay in traffic. They weren't scared or nervous. She waited until they drove off and then she went about her day.

I drive away from the home in awe, and slightly disturbed. David Lowell has made hundreds of millions of dollars and by his own account given away much of it. At the University of Arizona in Tucson there is the Lowell Institute for Mineral Resources, funded largely by a donation from the Lowell family. He seems grounded and happy with his successes. Still, this one man has single-handedly been responsible for digging holes one mile wide and half a mile deep all over Earth. And if Bisbee ever reopens, David Lowell will have had a role in making it happen.

Driving, I think how he is a throwback to another era. Aside from the fact that he is shockingly rich, Lowell doesn't seem like a person who needs or desires money in order to survive. I imagine he is much more at home riding a mule to twelve thousand feet to scratch in the dirt for years at a time. He is someone I can't help but admire, but fear at the same time.

So if you see an eighty-something-year-old walking around the hills near your home, be sure to say hello. He will charm you with kindness. He will tell you stories of finding treasures in faraway lands and helping the world grow at a faster pace. But beware if he stays too long. And be very scared if he sets up camp and starts drilling holes in those hills you adore. They may not be around for very long.

15

Freeport-McMoRan

To greed, all nature is insufficient.
—Seneca

Years ago, when I first traveled to Indonesia, my journey lasted three months and covered dozens of islands. I saw Komodo dragons, watched men on horses jousting, and was chased by a pack of monkeys while riding a scooter with a flat tire. On Sumatra, I spent five days hiking to an orangutan rehabilitation center in the middle of a jungle, survived a bus crash in the Goya Highlands, and walked scared all night after the crash through tiger country. I have a deep affection for the country and am still fascinated by its geological, linguistic, religious, and ethnic tapestry. I built my first house on Weh Island off the northern coast of Sumatra. Actually a beach hut, it overlooked a turquoise bay filled with turtles and coral. Within swimming distance was a smaller island with an abandoned prison where, in World War II, Japanese doctors conducted Josef Mengele–type medical experiments on prisoners.

But today I would like to visit a different part of Indonesia, specifically the western part of Papua New Guinea, also known as West Irian Jaya or West Papua. Unfortunately, there is no point trying to get there. No one other than military or mine personnel are allowed anywhere near the mine known as Grasberg, located atop the highest glacier between the Himalayas and the Andes.

For almost thirty years, Freeport-McMoRan has been mining deep in the Jayawijaya Mountains, specifically the mountain of Ertsberg, which means Ore Mountain. First recorded by Dutch explorers in the 1500s, they wrote of seeing a black mountain that had characteristics of copper. The mystery of Ertsberg continued to grow when in 1936 Jean-Jacques Dozy, a Dutch geologist returned from climbing the Jayawijayas, told of seeing gold and copper on the mountain. But it wouldn't be confirmed until 1960, when a geologist named Forbes Wilson, using maps from old manuscripts, took a month to hack his way to fourteen thousand feet above sea level into the glaciers. There he found the largest deposit of surface-level copper ever discovered. The company that sponsored Wilson in 1960 was Freeport-McMoRan, the same company that in 2007 bought Phelps Dodge and now owns mines in Bisbee, Morenci, the Congo, Chile, and in New Mexico, among others. A minority owner in the project is Rio Tinto, the same mining company behind the Resolution mine proposal in Superior, Arizona.

By 1973, Bechtel, the San Francisco–based engineering and construction company, was contracted to build the mine site. Grasberg is still considered by most in the industry the most difficult mine ever developed. A seventy-five-mile road goes from sea level through tropical jungle and rises almost twelve thousand feet. From base camp, two aerial trams courier workers and supplies up a two-thousand-foot rise, from the mine plant, over the black mountain cliff face, and into the mine. Employing upward of nineteen thousand workers and contractors, the mine works like all mines: 365 days a year, 24 hours a day.

In addition to having the largest recoverable copper reserve in the world, Grasberg has the largest-known reserve of gold, and for the last thirty years has been the most profitable mine on Earth. Most mining companies peg production costs at $1.30 per pound of copper. In Grasberg, they hover around 60¢ per pound. With copper selling in early 2012 between $3.50 and $4.00 a pound, this has created an enormous profit for Freeport. This disparity with other operations can largely be attributed to the fact that the company pays the local workers at the mine $1.50 an hour to do the same job for which a worker in the United States would make between $15 and $30 an hour.

In addition to being one of the largest mines, Grasberg is the most controversial, with a history of violence, repression, and environmental disasters unparalleled anywhere else. Grasberg is ground zero for anyone looking for a mining company maximizing its profits at all costs. Freeport knows this and has gone to great lengths to keep any prying eyes out of the area.

The Indonesian military has been suspected by many of the local tribes in numerous deaths over four decades, including the killing of various leaders of the West Papua independence movement and at least one prominent lawyer, who was suspiciously poisoned. Human Rights Watch says ninety Indonesians are in prison for peacefully protesting the mine. And since 2009, fifteen people have been killed and fifty-six injured in shootings, primarily on the road that leads from the sea to Grasberg. In 2011 alone, six people were killed by sniper fire on this road. In addition, the helicopters shuttling mine employees up the mountain stopped flying after being shot at by unidentified shooters.

The *New York Times* did an in-depth investigation of Grasberg in 2005, which revealed that Freeport spent more than $20 million between 1998 and 2004 paying local military officers, police, and government security officials to protect the mine from outsiders and from the indigenous tribes that occasionally act out by killing a miner or blowing up infrastructure. According to the report, Freeport also paid $35 million to the local military to bolster their housing, buy vehicles, and purchase various military "infrastructure." It has been suggested that this spending by Freeport is a direct violation of the Foreign Corrupt Practices Act, which forbids U.S. companies from bribing foreign officials or military personnel. Freeport's defense of these payments is simple. Company officials claim it is the way business is done in that region. Since the 2005 investigation was made public, Freeport has tried to address the issue of paying local military by hiring more private security. In 2010, Freeport reportedly spent $22 million on such security, most of that going to Triple Canopy, a contractor that employs mostly former U.S. Special Forces.

The Clinton administration had taken notice of Freeport's environmental record at Grasberg a decade earlier than the *Times* exposé. In 1995, the administration took the unprecedented step of revoking a little-known corporate insurance called OPIC, or Overseas Private Investment Corporation, which held a $100 million policy on Freeport's Grasberg mine. OPIC stated in a letter to Freeport that "OPIC is terminating the Contract as an exercise of its statutory charge under the Foreign Assistance Act of 1961 to ensure that Freeport's implementation of the Project does not pose unreasonable or major environmental hazards to, or cause the degradation of tropical forests in, Irian Jaya." The report further states: "Freeport's implementation of the Project, and especially its tailings management and disposal practices, have severely degraded the rainforests surrounding the Ajkwa and Minajeri Rivers. Additionally, the Project has created and continues to pose unreasonable or major environmental, health or safety hazards with respect to the rivers that are being impacted by the tailings, the surrounding terrestrial ecosystem, and the local inhabitants."

Freeport immediately sued the U.S. government to reinstate the insurance. The entire issue went quietly away when former secretary of state Henry Kissinger, who was then on the board of directors of Freeport and is currently the director emeritus for Freeport-McMoRan's board of directors, did some backroom politicking. To prove its point of not needing the U.S. government's approval for how it conducts business, the next year Freeport canceled the insurance, stating that the mine had outgrown the usefulness of the insurance policy.

This wasn't the first time Kissinger found himself involved in a country where American-owned copper mines were at stake. In 1973, as Kissinger was serving as President Nixon's secretary of state, Salvador Allende, the democratically elected president of Chile, nationalized all the major industries, including copper mining, which, like today, was the country's leading industry. The action immediately caused enormous conflict with the United States and the American companies that had a large industrial presence in Chile. At that point Nixon made it clear he wanted Allende to fall. When the Chilean military staged a coup, surrounding the presidential palace, Allende gave a speech refusing to resign and later committed suicide. While Kissinger has always denied direct involvement in the coup, declassified CIA documents reveal that the U.S. government was privy to information from those plotting the coup, and Kissinger has been accused by various historians of "influencing" the overthrow. (For a scathing account of Kissinger's involvement in the affairs of Chile, Indonesia, and many other countries, I suggest reading *The Trial of Henry Kissinger* by the late Christopher Hitchens.)

As a result of Freeport's questionable environmental and political history at Grasberg, some large investors have withdrawn their support of Freeport, the largest being the Government Pension Fund of Norway, the world's second-largest pension fund. The fund stated that it cannot ethically invest in a company that consistently violates both human rights and environmental rights.

With the continued reports of these abuses, and the fact that Freeport has, at least in the past, paid the military to guard its vast empire at Grasberg, it is not a stretch to say the company has benefited from the military's acts of intimidation.

Since Google Earth is the only way to see the mine, I take an afternoon to get a closer look. Most open-pit mines have an eerie quality of being the result of an alien civilization, say, a species of giant ants, creating a nest in Earth's skin. Grasberg looks like no other mine. In satellite photos, the mine resembles a massive borehole perfectly carved inside a glacier. The bottom is not discernible. All around the mine, ice lines the jagged peaks of the mountains.

So far no one has discovered the bottom of this deposit, and Freeport has been spending upward of $600 million a year digging underground mines adjacent to the open pit, accessing areas that current mining operations cannot reach. By 2016, and after investing between $16 to $18 billion in the underground facilities, the open pit will phase out and the underground mines will employ the block cave method to retrieve the ore.

From afar, using my keyboard to move Google Earth satellite photos, I can see the large black-and-blue stain that indicates the more than one billion tons of mine waste that Freeport has dumped into the nearby Ajkwa River, which in turn has created an acidic mine drainage plume that extends thirty miles into the Arafura Sea. The runoff continues to grow as Freeport adds almost three hundred thousand tons of waste ore to the tailing stacks every day. To get an idea of how Freeport thinks of what other people think of its Grasberg operations, it is best to hear from the boss himself. When the *Australian Financial Review* asked CEO James Moffett about the damage caused by Grasberg to the surrounding rivers and sea, Moffett responded that the environmental impact of the mine "was equivalent to me pissing in the Arafura Sea."

To no one's surprise outside, independent analysis of the Ajkwa River is not allowed. The Amungme, a local indigenous people, have been pleading to the national Indonesian government for years to punish Freeport for this gross pollution of their water. Their pleas go unheard, and the reason can best be found in the national tax bill of Indonesia. Freeport is the largest corporate taxpayer in the country, which is the sixth most populous nation on Earth. The Grasberg mine accounts for almost a quarter of all the income of the Papua Province and 1.2 percent of all Indonesia's GDP. Since 1991, it has paid $12 billion to Jakarta in the form of taxes and royalties.

This iron grip comes with a cost. In addition to destroying the surrounding environment, the mine is taking its toll on the local inhabitants. With the influx of money, there has been a substantial increase in the importation of sex workers from the outside. HIV/AIDS rates grew by 30 percent in 2011 alone, with the highest increase in the Mimika province, home of Grasberg. Coupled with low wages, there is a strong and constant rebellious local population looking to get paid more, while at the same time insisting that their land be treated better. There is no telling how this will end, but my guess is Freeport will buy itself breathing space with various small donations to the local populations, which the

216

company pays no royalty to, and the mine will be played out long before any of these issues are resolved.

Although Grasberg is Freeport's moneymaking juggernaut, the company is always actively seeking new discoveries with hopes of one day finding a mine that can produce for as long and as profitably as the Indonesian mine. When I visited Richard Leveille, Freeport's president of exploration, in Tucson, he mentioned that the company has around fifty years of copper in known reserve, meaning still in the ground ready to extract. Freeport already accounts for roughly 10 percent of the world's mine output, including its copper, gold, and molybdenum operations, and it expects to increase copper production by nearly 25 percent, or a billion pounds a year, over the next several years. Finding new sources of copper near the surface at a reasonable cost is Leveille's main job. He and Freeport are banking on a deposit that will be their new Grasberg for generations to come. It is called Tenke and is located in the southern part of the Democratic Republic of Congo, also known for decades as the sweet spot of Africa's copper belt. It also happens to be in perhaps the world's most violent country.

The World Bank regularly lists the DRC as the worst place to do business, more difficult than Somalia, Iraq, or Afghanistan. Five million souls lost their lives in the last fifteen years to war. Rape and pillage and murder continue in the eastern part of the country. International companies take long hard looks at their cost-benefit analysis before they invest there.

Freeport-McMoRan decided it was worth the risk and picked Tom Weiskopf, who used to be the site manager of Bisbee, to help get the place up and running. One day I receive an e-mail from Tom in the Congo. He tells me ground at Tenke mine has been broken, buildings are being built, and processing plants are taking shape. The Tenke mine is enormous. Located within a 930-square-mile mining district, Tenke currently produces around 250 million pounds of copper a year. When production hits full stride in the next few years, the output is expected to near one billion pounds a year, which would make it one of the largest copper mines in the world.

Tom also writes about a security course in London that taught him how to avoid being kidnapped. His house in Lubumbashi has a panic button. He travels with armed guards. In 2010, thousands of locals attacked the mine site and its employees. They burned cars and stole computers. The reasons for the riot had nothing to do with pay disputes, often the cause of riots in foreign-owned mines in Africa. Instead, these riots started when locals who mined copper on their own property, or on public land, rebelled against a foreign company coming in and running the show. Also, some were angry that the promise of hiring a thousand locals hadn't been fulfilled.

Maybe it's me, but it makes sense that when a person digs a hole with a shovel and his hands for a decade, making around $10 a day, he gets angry when a foreign company spends $2 billion to start the largest copper mine in Africa in his backyard, which he is now not allowed to enter, and strips away one of his main sources of income. And yes, the company will likely hire around a thousand people, but that is not nearly enough to reduce the poverty in the region or to replace income lost to the thousands of self-employed miners. As for the enormous profits made from this mine, a few dollars will trickle down to the local churches, clubs, and road projects, but the real loot will be deposited in accounts far away.

Hoping to understand how these global decisions made by Freeport may impact the reopening of the mine in Bisbee, I called the mine office in Lowell, a suburb of Bisbee whose original location was devoured when Phelps Dodge began expanding the Lavender Pit in the 1950s. Today, a small portion of Lowell still exists, including a collection of desert-tan buildings that constitute the mining offices that date back to the 1960s and sit within a few feet of the southeastern edge of the pit.

"Are you requesting a donation?" asked the secretary from Freeport.

At first her question is slightly off-putting but then I realize that because Freeport is the biggest donor in town, the staff expects most phone calls from locals to be about donating to a cause.

Since the company took over operations in 2007, Freeport has consistently pumped money into all the right places: the Boys and Girls Club, Fourth of July events, and a large majority of local charities.

As much as I wanted to say yes, I told her an interview with the site manager regarding the mine would suffice. She said she would pass on my request.

I hang up and drive around the pit, heading to the grocery store for dinner supplies. I am delayed at the edge of town due to construction on the state highway. Freeport tore up the road to make way for a drainage system, hoping to relieve pressure from a company-built reservoir to the north. While wondering if I will ever speak to the site manager, I think how Freeport continues to make all the right moves in its efforts to be good neighbors.

There is no doubt the mine reopening would benefit the town in some ways, mostly by giving it a structural and economic boost. The parks are decaying. The outdoor pool funding is so skimpy it opens only one month a year. If the mine reopened, the mining company would likely shell out money to fix these problems.

Still, I doubt that Freeport could help with one of the fundamental problems that weighs heavily on my wife and me. The school district is so underfunded that children attend school only four days a week. The current state of the schools reminds me of Richard Shelton's enchanting book *Going Back to Bisbee,* the story of the author coming to Bisbee in the late 1950s and early 1960s to teach junior high school. He had quite the shock when he realized that because he was a first-year teacher in the poorest school district in Arizona, which at the time also had the lowest pay for teachers in the United States, he was, in fact, the lowest-paid teacher in the country! This story took place when the mine was still open, which meant there was money in the county coffers.

Since Freeport bought out Phelps Dodge, there has been a state of constant motion in and around Bisbee. Over the past several months, Freeport has quietly bought up the majority of Lowell. Within days, rumors began that the company was trying to buy up the old cemetery, a sure sign of the direction the pit would take. That rumor, like many, turned out to be false.

In the heyday of the mine, Lowell was a one-street bustling commercial area, with a theater, bar, and several stores located parallel to the mine offices. Today it is mostly abandoned buildings, many of which were either owned or leased for the long term by a few individuals. Freeport, which now owns most of the property, has begun leasing it back to the same occupants who owned it earlier, for almost nothing, on the condition that they can be kicked out at any time in the future. An art teacher I know pays $8 a month to rent a house in Lowell he sold to Freeport recently. He knows his time is limited, but for now he has a great deal.

The phone rings the next afternoon. It is Mike Jaworski, the Bisbee site manager. I ready my notepad.

"I always like to help local people," he says in a soothing and kind voice, "but there are new protocols at Freeport and there can be no contact with 'outside' sources without corporate office approval."

"I understand," I reply and hang up.

I walk outside to a perfect view of the mountain in front of me. A cardinal chirps in the almond tree, likely looking for a lost mate. I had ended the conversation with the site manager saying "I understand," when in truth it is becoming more and more clear that I don't, nor does anyone else in Bisbee, understand very much about the multinational company that owns the gigantic hole on the edge of town.

My wife and I have spent many nights talking about the local schools, the parks, and our uncomfortable feeling that the mine has become the sword of Damocles hanging over us, and this town, never knowing if, or when, it will drop. She talks of wanting to reach further than this town will allow. I can tell by listening to myself and to my wife that we have already made up our minds. We have decided it is time to begin the process of moving. We don't know exactly where to move, only that mentally and emotionally we are ready.

I go down the hall and look in on my daughters. My oldest daughter will take it hard, separating from her friends. Then I think of my infant daughter breathing in an invisible dust every day and night filled with radioactive waste, heavy metals, and not to mention a massive cloud of silica blowing in from Cananea, which as of 2011 is ramping up to be a world-class producer of copper. Either way, the air in Bisbee will only get worse. I am not an overly paranoid parent. I like it when my older daughter runs around dressed like a fairy eating dirt. I know pristine air and safety for our children are impossible to guarantee in today's world. Still, I don't want to subject my daughters to something I can avoid if I so choose.

As for the former site manager Tom Weiskopf, who was running the Tenke mine in the Congo, after a few years the company relocated him to Grasberg in Indonesia. My cynical view is that they pulled in Tom to give a better "face" to the company's social and environmental disaster of a mine in West Papua. And although my gut tells me he is someone who would want to mine efficiently and also correct misdeeds done to the local people and the environment, I suspect there is very little he can do at Grasberg except what has always been done. Meanwhile, the rest of the world, including me, will continue with our lives as the native population of West Papua fights every day to get Freeport-McMoRan out of their backyard.

16

Cyanide Cynthia

I will not go where people don't want us. I just won't.
—Cynthia Carroll, CEO of Anglo American

M ines. All of them, given time, tell a story. Mining executives, given time, will talk about how mines enhance our lives, our stories. But as I have said, these executives don't think like other people. Let me explain by telling a story.

On a scorching day in late May in downtown Tucson, I walk through a front yard covered in loose dirt and kid toys and knock on the door. Everett Thompson answers in shorts and flip-flops. Even though we've never met, he gives me a giant bear hug. Thirty-five years old, Everett has a ponytail that hangs to his shoulder blades and a large genuine smile across his face. He has the sturdy body of an Alaska fisherman, which he has been his entire life. An Alaskan native, Everett is more fair skinned than other natives from the Bristol Bay area, accounted for by the genetic mix of the Scandinavian and Russian fishermen marrying native women between the eighteenth and early twentieth centuries.

Ushering me inside, he introduces me to his daughter and offers me a beer, which I accept. I'm here to listen to his story. He knows exactly which one I am talking about.

Everett has spent the last two winters living in Tucson with his daughter and sister, Izetta, who is finishing law school so she can return to Alaska and work on native issues. The only reason I am in their house is that Everett and I have mutual fishermen friends, including Sharon Hart, the woman who was my fishing captain for four years. Also he is the grandson of Violet Wilson, the woman whose address in Naknek is found by following the sign that says KNIVES AND FURS.

But I am not here to swap fishing stories. Besides being a fisherman and a native of the Bristol Bay region, Everett is part of the gang of five: the five Alaskans who traveled to London to confront the shareholders of Anglo American about creating Pebble mine in their backyard. This is the story I want to hear.

Izetta walks out of the kitchen.

"What temperature again?" she asks Everett.

"Seventeen minutes at three hundred sixty-five degrees," he says and then returns his gaze to me. "I put lemon zest on the top of the fillet. Gives it a bit of a kick."

He gets up and goes down the hallway.

The salmon cooking in the oven was caught on his commercial fishing boat in Alaska. A horizontal freezer the size of a couch in the living room holds another hundred pounds of fillets, which he sells as a distributor under the name Naknek Family Fisheries.

Everett comes out of his bedroom with a whalebone necklace carved in the shape of a salmon. On one side is carved NO PEBBLE MINE. During the fishing season, he drapes a flag on the side of his boat with the same message. He hands me the necklace and tells me to keep it.

Izetta gives me a plate of salmon.

Everett asks me how the fish tastes.

"Amazing," I tell him and make a note to include lemon zest the next time I have sockeye salmon for dinner.

"Are you going fishing this season?" he asks.

I tell him I won't be able to and then ask what he will do if the mine is built and ruins the salmon run.

He looks at me with a painful smile and shakes his head at the thought of such a horrific act. I say nothing.

And then he begins to talk about his trip to London.

* * *

In April 2009, five Alaskan natives from the Bristol Bay region, including Everett, traveled to London to attend a shareholder meeting for Anglo American and to meet Cynthia Carroll, the American-born CEO of the second-largest mining company in the world and majority owner of Pebble mine, a position Anglo secured after investing $1.4 billion in the operation.

With its headquarters in London, Anglo has more than 150,000 employees spread out over forty-five countries, 90,000 of whom are located in South Africa, making Anglo the country's largest private-sector employer. Although Anglo has tried to distance itself from South Africa's apartheid past, it is impossible to separate the two. Using the backs and bodies of slavery under the apartheid system, Anglo became the largest company in South Africa.

It is the world's largest producer of platinum and owns 45 percent of De Beers, giving it significant control of the distribution of the world's rough-diamond production. It also mines zinc and copper and many other metals.

Nicknamed Cyanide Cynthia—a reference to the toxic chemical used to extract gold—Carroll's appointment represents a major shift in management from the day since Sir Ernest Oppenheimer and J.P. Morgan began the business in 1917 as a gold-mining operation. She is the first woman to run the company, and perhaps even more striking is that she is the first CEO not from South Africa. Her job prior to joining Anglo American was president and CEO of the Primary Metal Group of Alcan, one of the world's largest aluminum manufacturers. She must be doing something right in this boardroom of crusty old men because, according to *Forbes,* in 2008 she was the fifth most powerful woman in the world of business.

In London, the five travelers from Alaska were far from their comfort zone. They were entering a world of men and women accustomed to quietly collecting large dividend checks without ever needing, or possibly wanting, to know where or how that money was made. The five Alaskans were Thomas Tilden, chief of the Curyung Tribal Council; Bobby Andrew, board member of the Nunamta Aulukestai; Lydia Olympic, past president of the Igiugig Village Tribal Council; Peter Andrew, former president of New Stuyahok Village Ltd.; and Everett.

Anglo American officials knew they were coming to London and knew what they were going to say. They also knew how to respond. This was a well-rehearsed dance of diplomacy. To refuse a meeting with the five Bristol Bay Alaskan natives would be bad publicity. But there was little to no chance anything the five visitors said would fall on sympathetic ears. Since Anglo bought into Pebble, it has spent tens of millions advertising that it wants to be a good steward of the land and water. It maintains that there is a great future in the coexistence of commercial fishing and mining. It also states in many company releases that it "will not go where people don't want us." These five Alaskan natives were here to let Cynthia Carroll and the Anglo shareholders know that they don't want this company, or their mine, anywhere near their home.

There have been detailed polls taken in the Bristol Bay and surrounding areas regarding the mine, and overwhelmingly people are against it. When the mining executives hear this claim, they answer, "We haven't even submitted a plan yet. Wait to hear us out." This is true, to a degree. They have submitted various plans but not an official one. And that is part of their tactics. Because Alaska has long been so friendly to the oil and mining industries, almost everyone who has a stake in not allowing Pebble to be built knows that once the permitting process begins, it is almost a foregone conclusion the mine will be given a green light. There becomes too much money involved, too many political relationships invested, and eventually a contingent of the local people gets stuck on the money teat.

When the five Alaskans left the meeting with Carroll, they felt good about speaking their minds but also certain that nothing they said would stop this woman, this company, from moving forward. After all, the concept that mining and fish can live side by side is relative to who interprets it. To mining executives, if they kill fish, or ruin a major salmon creek, they will begin to talk of restocking fish in another creek, which, in their words, has a "zero net loss" on the fish. If you are a fisherman, a scientist, or a local native, that is double-talk. Everyone knows that salmon stocks from a particular creek are genetically geared to that specific water. Adding more fish elsewhere doesn't replace the native fish, it only introduces a new and foreign fish, one that is weaker and less able to replenish a vibrant salmon run.

Not to be discouraged, the gang of five left the CEO's office and went out and scored a major symbolic victory by getting several major jewelers, including Tiffany, to sign a petition stating that they would not buy any gold that came from the Pebble mine. The CEO of the Pebble Partnership, John Shively, reacted to the news of the Tiffany boycott by screwing up his eyes and shrugging his shoulders while saying, "Big deal." The boycott has grown since 2009, and as of February 2011, more than fifty jewelers, with more than $5 billion in annual sales, have said they will not source gold extracted from Pebble mine.

The boycott is a noble gesture, but its implications are most likely to have meaning primarily in the public relations arena. Enforcing this ban will be difficult because consumer gold is mined in many places and melted in only a few. Thus, like blended whiskey or mass-produced wine, no one really knows where any specific gold comes from once it gets included in the vast cauldron of melted gold. Still, for the Alaska five it was a victory.

The following day, the five rose early and went to the River Thames, which until 1883 had a small but regular salmon run that locals sold in the London fish markets. Today, a negligible number of salmon run the Thames, not enough to register as a sustainable or healthy run. Knowing they represented the largest sustainable salmon fishery in the world, the Alaskans made their way to the shareholder meeting with a singular focus.

They entered the large hall, crowded with interested investors. To make sure they were noticed, Everett Thompson, the youngest of the group, wore a necklace made of bear claws, attracting more than a few glances from the wealthy shareholders in suits and more suits. After various speakers and audience questions, the Alaskans were granted the floor. They had already decided that only Thomas Tilden would speak. In his short speech he spoke directly to the shareholders, the aggregate purse-string holders of Anglo. Thomas argued that "this mine will cost you money to build and we will not go away. Our resistance at the local level will also cost you. It is very simple. You are not welcome."

After he was finished, they were thanked for their input, and the room fell silent.

> As citizens of the world as well as the host communities in which we work, Anglo American recognizes the need for careful environmental stewardship. To that end we are fully committed to minimizing the impact of our operations and ensuring that they produce a legacy that will be welcomed by generations to come.

This comes from Anglo American, stressing its business principles. The statement was of course carefully crafted by lawyers and public relations officers. There may even have been testing of the wording with a focus group to see how they reacted. Finally, when everyone at the table agreed, the paragraph was set upon the world, one more statement lathered on with sincerity. One more lie dressed as an optimistic string of words that means little or nothing to anyone other than the shareholders, who are impressed with how these types of statements pop off the page in the annual report.

What they don't mention in that carefully worded statement is that in 2001 a study by the Association of Environmental & Engineering Geologists showed Anglo's mine Iron Duke, in Zimbabwe, had the highest levels of arsenic in the surface water of thirty-four mines tested around the world. The levels in the drinking water were the rough equivalent to battery acid.

Closer to home, Anglo owns Jerritt Canyon, a gold mine near Elko, Nevada. In 2000, the Environmental Protection Agency issued a database that showed Jerritt Canyon releasing ninety-four hundred pounds of mercury into the air, making it the largest single source of mercury pollution in the United States.

And in Colombia, Anglo is partial owner of the Cerrejón mine, the largest open-pit coal mine in the world. In 2001, the mine owners, which include Intercor, a subsidiary of ExxonMobil, bulldozed Tabaco, a small community of local farmers, in order to expand the mine. The village had a school, a health clinic, and a small population. This is not unusual in mining. The difference between Arizona and Colombia is that in Arizona there are laws that ensure compensation to the displaced residents. In Colombia, Anglo did not compensate the villagers. Instead they were told to leave and never come back. Period. The chairman of the board, Sir Mark Moody-Stuart, said in reaction to the outrage that the displacement of the locals was "not perfectly executed."

In 2002, the Colombia Supreme Court ruled in favor of the villagers of Tabaco against the mine owners. Seven years later, an agreement was reached between Cerrejón Coal owners and the Tabaco Relocation Committee on how to rebuild the village, along with other concessions by the mine operators.

After the shareholder meeting in London, Sir Mark, still the chairman of the board, and several others gathered around Everett, and his necklace, and began to tell big-game stories. Everyone was friendly. Everett was happy to speak with the men of Anglo American, perhaps hoping something he said might cause these carpetbaggers to leave his part of the world. The words spoken inside by Thomas Tilden were acknowledged by the Anglo gang, but when they gathered closer around Everett, these men, who controlled the lives of so many, seemed much more interested in talking about nature.

Everett, after traveling nearly eight thousand miles to deliver a message to the board, half expected they might have some intelligent and businesslike response to his plea. Instead all they wanted to know was how Everett got the grizzly bear claws that dangled from his neck.

"I told them I shot this bear one morning when it tried to enter my home." He smiles as we sit over two empty plates. Into our second beer, Everett shakes his head with a sense of bewilderment that the people who run these companies have no idea of the places they plunder.

"I didn't shoot the damn bear," admits Everett with a laugh. "There was a bear dead in the ditch on the side of the road and I pulled his claws out. I wouldn't kill a grizzly. Ever. But the sad thing is when I was telling the story to these guys in London, you could see the hunger in their eyes, to shoot a grizzly and pull his claws out. That crazy ignorant blood hunger is what we are up against."

I ask if he will profit from the mine, if it is built.

"I have a job. I make enough from commercial fish to feed my family all year. I have been doing it since I was a kid. And my father did it, and his father before him. My grandmother raised five kids, including my father, from fishing. The people in our region who want the mine are a small minority, and they don't fish. But they are naïve if they think this mine will help this region. The shareholders in that building will make money sitting in London telling that goddamn bear story to their friends while we have poison in our streams."

As I walk outside, I notice the train barreling down the middle of Tucson on an east–west track. More than fifty boxcars long, things going to and fro, moving all the gadgets we require, all of it coming either indirectly or directly from mining, including the train itself. I wonder how much copper is in those gadgets and in the train.

I get into my truck and head to the freeway, eager to get out of the city. At times I find there are just too many people, too many cars, too many lights, too many voices wanting to be heard. I pass Tombstone and the San Pedro River, flowing up from Cananea. I veer left and head up Banning Canyon, the homestretch.

I ponder the decision my wife and I have made. We will move by the end of summer. I will miss this drive. Bisbee has always been a refuge for me. I travel two to three months a year, and each time I leave the Tucson airport and drive the hundred miles to Bisbee, I feel as if I'm traveling backward in a time machine, not so much because Bisbee is a bit caught in the past century, but because this century hasn't found its way into every facet of Bisbee life. The miles traveled peel away. The stories, traffic jams, and jet lag fall to the side. I look forward to parking my car and not driving for a week, able to walk to anything I need. And even though I know that copper, iron, steel, zinc, cobalt, and who knows what other metals surround me every day of my life, the collective weight of this preponderance of metals feels less in Bisbee than in a city.

And then one day I will need something, like a new wrench, and I will get in my car and drive around the pit to the hardware store.

At that point I will remember Everett's story about his trip to England, reduced to what I remember most, that the majority of the Anglo shareholders will never go to the mine site in Alaska. They will never remember the letters of protest, the thousands who signed petitions. Instead they will be making more money than their grandfathers ever did, while sitting in London telling their friends about this young native kid who shot a bear and pulled the claws out to make a necklace.

I do not want to hear these kinds of stories. They make getting up in the morning a little bit more difficult. I know the wild still exists. I have seen it up close, and it has long teeth and sharp claws. Yet I'm positive it is not as dangerous as any gathering of elderly white-haired men sitting in large leather chairs plotting their next moneymaking scheme and telling secondhand stories as they sip their single-malt scotch.

17

The New Old World

China and India will, separately and together, unleash an explosion of demand.
— Mukesh Ambani, Indian businessman

Every night after I put my kids to sleep, I am reminded how wonderfully quiet it is in Bisbee. It is in these moments that I convince myself that mining is a thing of the past here, and the future will somehow magically shield this community from any destructive force. It can feel almost protected and untouchable by something as violent as a mining operation. Invariably I begin to wonder if moving is really necessary, if maybe we are overreacting.

Then I go back to my desk and reread an article on how China is investing heavily in a new technology to mine the world's *oceans* for copper. It turns out that magma-heated water occasionally breaks through the seafloor, and on its way from Earth's crust it collects all the minerals and metals that miners and geologists have to spend years studying rock formations to find. Gold, zinc, and copper shoot up from Earth's core and at the last moment mix with cold seawater, effectively mineralizing the elements, and presto, an instantaneous deposit of highly valuable metals. Since the beginning of Earth's formation, tall chimneys, called black smokers, have formed and then fallen. The first one recorded by a scientist was in 1977 near the Galápagos. Now an Australian geologist turned entrepreneur has invented a way to mine the chimneys, which often have 1.5 percent–grade copper, a quality rarely found on land anymore. The technology to mine the black smokers is still being perfected, but essentially a large vacuum sucks the seafloor minerals up to a processing boat on the surface. After the metals are extracted, the excess slurry is pumped overboard back into the ocean. No one is quite sure how to make this all work with a reasonable profit ratio, but the Chinese are intrigued.

The Chinese have a reason to be investing in this possible new pipeline of copper supply. In 2010, the world used seventeen million tons of copper. By 2015, worldwide demand for copper is expected to reach twenty-five million tons. China consumes almost 30 percent of the world's copper every year, a number that will increase to almost 40 percent by 2025. At the current rate of production, the world's supply of copper will catch up to China's demand around 2015. After that, most pro–copper industry talking heads argue that to meet the future demand, new large-capacity mines will have to come online. As the current large mines begin to produce less, mining companies are becoming more and more eager to begin digging new deposits, such as Pebble in Alaska, Resolution in Superior, and the Oyu Tolgoi in Mongolia.

The worldwide markets may rise and fall due to political decisions in Washington, D.C., and Berlin, but the continued expansion of countries like China, India, Brazil, and Indonesia is not going to stop. China is projected to keep growing at a rate of 9–10 percent a year for at least a decade. And although China is one of the top five producers of copper, year in and year out its domestic supply cannot keep up with its ravenous demand. As China builds more homes, buildings, phone lines, electrical lines, planes, ships, cars, and almost any electronic gadget the rest of the world consumes, its need for copper will grow. Likewise, India and Brazil are in the process of revamping their energy infrastructure, a sector that uses a tremendous amount of copper. The copper market's upward trend in price reflects this pressure to produce more, whether it is from old or new mines, scrap supply, or brownfields, sites such as Bisbee.

I have discussed this surging need for copper with friends in

Bisbee as a possible pressure that will one day mandate that Free-port reopen the mine. They shake their head as if to say they understand it is out of their hands, but at the same time they also believe that maybe, just maybe, there might be a way to influence that final decision. Maybe the town can convince Freeport that a mine is not wanted here. That is not going to happen. Bisbee is not Pebble, where the locals not only own some of the land that might be used but also are the guardians of the salmon run, which is a robust and viable economic model. In Bisbee we have no legitimate argument against reopening of the mine other than it would be unpleasant. Freeport may not have plans to reopen Bis-bee in the coming year, but it is difficult to say with certainty how the company will alter its plans under the pressure of the global market. It will feel like a vise being ratcheted tighter and tighter, which promises only to increase in the next ten years.

As mentioned earlier, China is in the middle of a major over-haul of its infrastructure and is in the process of building more and more cities. By 2020, China plans on creating even more megacities, with a few numbering between fifty and a hundred million people. All this building will put a large demand on the world copper markets. China also plans to build a high-speed rail-road, which uses large quantities of copper to conduct electricity, circling Beijing and Tianjin, creating a new region called the Bohai Economic Rim, with a population upward of 250 million.

An additional variable is that the Chinese are beginning to buy cars like westerners. The car fleet in China today stands at around 60 million. By 2035, it will grow to 135 million. With all this growth projected over the next few decades, China will become the world's largest polluter, passing the United States, but inter-estingly enough, at the same time it is, and most likely will con-tinue to be, the leader in developing and using green technology such as solar, wind, nuclear, and electric cars. The Chinese gov-ernment is acutely aware that its people are producing more pol-lution than is sustainable for a healthy population. China is in a race against itself to make green technology successful. And this means much more copper.

* * *

Because China has to import the vast majority of its copper, a metal the government considers fundamental to its economic health, the Chinese have long classified their stockpiles of copper as a strategic state secret. For years metal traders were forced to build into the market their best guess on the amount of physical copper they believed China had in stock. Then in September 2011, for the first time, Chinese officials announced they have almost two million tons of copper on hand. This announcement only adds to the influence China wields in the copper market. No one in the metal exchanges knows why the Chinese would make public their massive stockpile of copper, only that they must have done it for a reason. Some speculate it was done in order to drive the global market price down, which China needs to do from time to time after it has depleted its stock. It is a game of false perception. By stating it has large quantities of copper, China is broadcasting to the global market that it has enough copper for now, and that its demand will go down, which will inevitably push down the price of copper. As the price falls, the Chinese will slowly begin stockpiling again.

Besides wanting to influence the market, stockpiling copper on its own terms allows China to be free of the daily fluctuations of the LME spot pricing. In effect, China hordes copper as a way to create its own futures market on the metal, and by buying it in huge quantities during a low price cycle and then using the supply as needed during a period of high prices, it has effectively excused itself from the rigors of the LME.

In fact, China long ago decided not to buy copper from the LME. Instead, to meet the needs of its expanding economy, China pursued a more aggressive approach to acquiring copper. It began buying up mines all over the world. Not only copper but also iron ore, zinc, cobalt, and various other metals. It decided to own the source of the raw materials. Finding a country with vast amounts of copper with little or no foreign investment is rare, but China has made a strategic decision to invest heavily in countries that are often dangerous or politically unstable enough that most of the world has given up hope of extracting any metals from that source.

In Afghanistan, thirty miles south of Kabul, is a place the locals call Mes Aynak. In the local Dari language, Mes Aynak means "Little Copper Well." Even though the local people have known about the copper for centuries, the Russians were the first to try to mine the deposit on a large scale in 1979. That failed when the mujahideen fighters, supported by the United States, embroiled the Soviets in a decadelong war, which ended when the Russians retreated across the northern border. For the past decade, American troops have been fighting in this region, long known as the Taliban's transit highway in and out of Pakistan. This fact alone makes the reality of building a mine nearly impossible. Yet today, just off the only usable road in the area, there sits a housing development that resembles the one near the company town of Morenci, Arizona. I have no idea why these housing units look alike, other than the obvious, which is that they were all manufactured and built in China and exported to mines throughout the world. In any case, the housing units that dot the desert hills near Mes Aynak are filled with Chinese miners.

In 2007, while NATO forces fought against Al Qaeda and the Taliban, the Afghan government quietly sold a stake of Mes Aynak to China Metallurgical Group, better known as MCC, for $3 billion. This company is directly supported by the central Chinese government. The bidders that lost out to China were mining companies from Russia, Canada, and the United States. Most geological surveys estimate that the deposit has over two million tons of copper below the war-torn ground.

Included in that $3 billion are hefty infrastructure costs. MCC has promised to build an industrial-sized road—the first of its kind in Afghanistan. The company also plans to build a railroad from the northern border with Uzbekistan to its southeastern border with Pakistan, making it the first transnational railroad in Afghanistan's history. MCC will build an on-site copper smelter and a $500 million power station that will provide enough power for the mine with excess to supplement Kabul. It has also promised to build hospitals, homes, schools, and water treatment stations for the workers and surrounding villages. No one has explained how the company plans to do all this in a landscape of war. But seeing how the Chinese do robust business with some of the most brutal regimes in the world, I have a feeling they will find a way to make enough deals with all sides of this conflict to get what they came for, a steady supply of copper.

China owns mines in Pakistan, Indonesia, and several South American countries, but Africa has emerged as the priority in China's goal to grab as many sources of raw materials as it can over the next thirty years. For the past decade, as the United States and most of its Western allies sat on the sidelines, China answered the plea of African nations to invest in their continent. Much of the hesitation revolves around who is in charge in these nations. Corruption is rampant, with a small elite profiting while the average worker toils in poverty. Unlike most Western loans, which come with strings attached—liberalization, privatization, and democratization—China has a long-standing noninterference policy. This allows China to dance with the devil and profit from him at the same time. This has emboldened dictators like Robert Mugabe in Zimbabwe to rule his country like a tyrant while being buoyed up by the billions of dollars coming from the Chinese. In exchange, Chinese companies have been clear-cutting the forests of Zimbabwe to export the lumber to China.

By 2015, China will have invested nearly $50 billion in several African nations, and today bilateral trade between China and Africa exceeds $100 billion a year. All this will increase Africa's collective GDP by 6 percent. These investments are possible because the Chinese government offers interest-free loans to Chinese companies to travel to Africa and buy up either existing mines or new deposits. Then those companies, which are in effect the mouthpiece of the Chinese government, offer no-strings-attached loans to African nations to be repaid in raw materials, something China does not have enough of. By investing in such a resource-rich continent, with no real economic competition, China hopes to secure a long-term pipeline source of minerals and metals to supplement its plan to expand its economic dominance.

This relationship has been going on in some African countries for several years. In Nigeria, China loaned the government money to finance power plants. The money will be repaid in oil shipments. In Angola, the Chinese loaned money to build various infrastructure projects, also to be repaid in oil. In Gabon, China wants the timber. In Ghana, it financed a hydroelectric plant, which will be repaid in cocoa beans. In Zambia and Congo, copper is often the raw material the Chinese desire.

The investment model doesn't stop with an exchange of money for goods. In the next decade, the Chinese government will spend billions to establish five economic "free zones" throughout Africa. A nice term that translates to mean free-tax zones where China will provide huge amounts of start-up money for local business, but with one important caveat. Any infrastructure work being done using a Chinese loan will require the workforce to be at least 20 percent Chinese. In other words, Chinese companies will end up paying themselves the highest salaries while the locals work for pennies.

This loan process should sound familiar. America invented it. After World War II, the United States dumped cash into wherever it thought communism, real or imagined, was fighting for a foothold against democracy. Our history of economic exploitation is thick with dictators and strongmen ruling with brutal force. Marcos, Pinochet, Noriega, Mubarak, and Suharto all benefited from easy-to-get cheap loans that used American-based companies to build various projects in their countries.

Although the deals China makes with African nations tend to be slightly more favorable than competing foreign companies, there is an environmental price in allowing Chinese managers to operate a mine on their soil. At home, China cannot stem the prodigious emission of greenhouse gas. According to a 2010 *New York Times* report, industrial accidents in China that directly impact air and water quality average ten a month. A quarter of the country's rivers, lakes, and streams are too contaminated to use as drinking water. The negative impact of China's growing at such an accelerated rate struck an especially solemn note in 2007, when a report by the National Population and Family Planning Commission found birth defects had increased almost 40 percent from 2001 to 2006.

To think China will not continue its poor environmental behavior in Africa would be naïve. By building smelters in the Democratic Republic of Congo instead of new ones in Guangzhou, China hopes it can begin to at least mitigate its own pollution, and more important, export the nasty business of industrialization. By building tailing stacks in Zaire, it can both own the raw source of copper and then leave the toxic waste in Africa.

Further complicating this relationship is the fact that local Africans don't trust the Chinese. It is not a mystery why. They pay less, sometimes five times less, than other foreign companies. The working conditions are below all safety standards set by the mining industry in Africa. They build small Chinatowns to cater to their own needs and don't invest in personal relationships with the locals. The feeling on the ground is that they don't care about issues affecting the locals like the ballooning poverty or the relentless spread of HIV.

It may not help that more than one million Chinese have immigrated to African nations, a government-encouraged plan to move its labor to the source of supply. One place the Chinese have invested heavily is in Zambia, whose northern border straddles Africa's copper belt, a mineral-rich zone that stretches from northern Zambia into the DRC. In Lusaka, there are over a hundred Chinese-owned shops. There are hostels where Chinese workers reside for months at a time. The Chinese are building a new five-star hotel and recently opened a casino. In a region that suffers from 50 percent unemployment and where 85 percent of Zambians live below the poverty level, such infusions of capital may be welcome, and needed, but this importing of foreign workers making much more than the locals may be creating a combustible mix.

Add to this the fact that China's track record for mining safety is deplorable at best. If China is willing to let its own people die gathering specks of metal and slate, I doubt it cares what happens in Africa. In 2005, Chinese managers shot five Zambians during a riot over a wage dispute at a coal mine. In 2010, violence broke out again at the same mine. This time the Chinese managers shot another thirteen coal miners. Although charges were brought against the Chinese managers, the cases were eventually dismissed. China invested $1 billion in Zambia in 2010 and created fifteen thousand jobs, with $5 billion more to be invested in the next five years. That kind of money in a poverty-stricken country buys leeway. An even more cynical picture of this incident is how the coal from that mine is used. Once extracted, the coal is sent to a Chinese-owned copper mine in northern Zambia, in order to fuel the smelter. To complete the vicious circle, that copper is destined for Chinese ports.

China is not the only country in need of copper in the next ten to twenty years. The emerging markets are outpacing the established industrial centers such as Europe and the United States. India, Brazil, Indonesia, Turkey, and Taiwan are all economies primed to grow in the next ten years. Most economists, stock traders, and policy makers agree that China, India, Brazil, Indonesia, and a handful of emerging countries, all of which are beginning to build large infrastructure projects, and not the United States or Europe, will be the reason for any world economic growth between 2010 and 2020.

After China, India is the nation with the most growth potential. India has 1.2 billion people, second only to China, but by 2030, India is expected to have 1.5 billion people, becoming the most populated nation on Earth. In those twenty years, 270 million in India will enter the working-age population, an issue of particular concern to the Indian government. It realizes that to stave off unrest among this wave of young workers, it has to grow the economy to provide jobs. That means building larger cities, which will require more and more copper. Today there are forty-five cities with a population of a million or more. By 2030, there will be almost seventy. Thirty-two square miles of commercial and residential space need to be built, or a new Chicago every year. A typical eight-story building using state-of-the-art green technology with copper-based video and data installation uses between fifteen and twenty tons of copper. India hopes to build nearly forty-five hundred miles of new subway lines, all of which will use copper as a source of electricity. Then there are the cars, a major user of copper. Today there are forty million cars in India. By 2050 there are expected to be six hundred million cars and counting.

Unlike China, India currently exports more copper than it imports. This wasn't always the case, and is unusual since there isn't much of the metal in the ground. What the country does have is a robust refining industry. In 2007, India consumed 545,000 tons of copper but refined 710,000 tons. It imports raw copper concentrate from places such as Chile, Indonesia, and Australia, processes it, and then exports various forms of refined copper around the world. But with the economy expected to grow 7 percent a year for the next ten years, and with large infrastructure plans in the works, it may not be long before India returns to a country importing copper.

Although economists project economic growth to come from these emerging economies, and with countries like India, China, and Brazil announcing large plans for building "up" their societies, it doesn't mean any of it is going to happen. There is another theory of the future of the world economy, which is that it is in the beginning stages of an ultimate collapse, or at least a dramatic paradigm shift. This means that all this talk of supply and demand of metals and money will be dwarfed by the need for more basic items, such as food. If this is true, will copper really matter? I believe the answer is yes. The most perfect conductors of electricity are gold and platinum, but they are too expensive to use commercially and most likely always will be. If the markets collapse and the model of world economic expansion has reached its limits, I doubt there will be a lack of a need for copper, unless of course everything collapses to the point of complete anarchy. And at that point I suspect Bisbee will suffer from far worse threats than the reopening of the mine.

As I walk along the ridgeline of the mountain just outside my front door, I find it disheartening and disconcerting to think that the effects of a mine in Bisbee would be felt almost entirely locally, but the decision to expand the mine would be made entirely based on whether China decides to keep building twenty new cities a year, or if we need to produce another one billion cell phones. Demand is an invisible force that pulls at every facet of life. Sometimes I imagine the mine at the edge of town as a living creature, whose pulse quickens every time there is an uptick in the global demand, a demand that I, and everyone in this town, whether they realize it or not, are complicit in creating. I don't think installing an air-conditioning system in city hall is going to single-handedly cause the machines to begin digging in Bisbee, but in principle we are all part of the demand to get the copper out of the ground.

Of course it is completely understandable if a local resident walks the streets of Bisbee and has no idea that the future of the mine is not tied to local issues. By their nature, small towns can create narrow visions of reality. *If* Freeport announces that Bisbee will reopen, some people will protest in front of the town's post office. The town hall meetings will overflow with concerned citizens talking about the quality of life, both physical and mental. All those protests will be legitimate but will ultimately fall on deaf ears.

Then, when the final papers of the permitting process are done, Freeport will dig as fast as it can and continue around the clock for as long as it makes money. The increase in copper production will be a blip on the boards that hang above the ring in London. The voices of resistance in Bisbee will fade as those voices realize that the roar of the mining trucks will not be ending because of anything they say or do. And once this region is lost to the global yearning for copper, it will be lost forever. Nothing will be able to bring it back to what it looks like now.

It's June. Again. The decision is final. We move in one month. Our friends say they will miss us, that we are a vital part of the community. My wife and I are certain we are making the correct decision for our family, but we still struggle emotionally every day with the idea of moving.

But then again, the heat helps make me feel like leaving.

This is the worst month of the year, and the buildup to the monsoon feels like a frustrated sexual tension waiting to explode, but it won't, at least for a few more weeks. Sixty miles to the east, the Horseshoe 2 fire in the Chiricahua Mountains has burned more than 222,900 acres, almost 80 percent of the entire mountain range, home of Geronimo's people. Thirty miles to the west, the fire in the Huachuca Mountains has burned more than sixty homes, sending a plume of black smoke into Bisbee. People are calling 911 to report fires that don't exist. Others are talking of evacuation plans. I can hardly blame them. The town sits in a canyon lined with drought-starved oak trees, and with this kind of heat and wind, smoke makes the locals antsy.

That night, while reading a bedtime story to my three-year-old daughter, she quietly says, "Why do we have to move?"

"Mom and Dad want to show you a new town. It has big trees and in the winter there's lots of snow. But we will come back and visit our friends," I say.

"I know that, Dad," she says, with the swift confidence of a three-year-old. And then she gets sad. "But when are we going to come back to our house?"

A simple question, but one that Dad cannot answer in a simple way. Instead I kiss her on the forehead and tell her, "I'm not sure, honey, but let's keep reading."

We finish the book and I put her in bed next to my wife and our one-year-old. I turn out the lights, allowing the moonlight to shower our bedroom with a vanilla glow. I watch my wife and two daughters sleep, peacefully. I keep watching them, hoping to permanently imprint this image of our life here in my mind's eye.

I cannot answer the question. What is the future of Bisbee? No one knows for sure, but I am betting that as China and India continue to need more copper, it will have a ripple effect that will eventually trickle down to our town. I imagine it happening one quiet winter day when the memo is received at the Bisbee mine headquarters. The wording will be both vague and decisive, something along the lines of "The board has decided to pursue further exploration and development of the Bisbee site. The permitting process will begin in the second half of the year. There will be more announcements in the months to follow."

18

This Old Town

I really wonder what gives us the right to wreck this poor planet of ours.

—Kurt Vonnegut

I push plastic garbage bags of clothes into the last possible empty spaces of the moving truck, parked in front of our house. Today is the day. After ten very happy years of living in Bisbee, our family is leaving. We have rented a house in Flagstaff, six hours north of here. My wife will pursue her master's degree there. When the time comes, we will enroll the kids in the schools and take advantage of the city's plentiful parks and activities. I suspect we will enjoy being situated at seven thousand feet, smack-dab in the largest contiguous tract of ponderosa pine forest in the country. It will be difficult to leave our friends, our house, and in some ways our spiritual Shangri-la, but I suspect it will be a refreshing change.

By leaving Bisbee, I am conceding that my wife, kids, and I need more than what the town can offer, and what it can't offer, which is a promise the mine won't reopen.

To beat the heat, my wife and daughters left before noon, with plans to break up the drive by staying with friends in Tucson for the night. I have stayed behind so I can clean the house one final time. By sunset I have packed all our belongings—mostly books in boxes, bookshelves, a few beds, and some worn-out couches— into the twenty-foot moving truck. There are a few pieces of art,

245

tools, and a cat that will sit in the passenger seat of the truck in a small cage as I drive solo to Flagstaff. We had a garage sale a month ago, and what didn't sell we gave away. We'll be renting out our house in Bisbee. Selling in today's housing market feels like a burden we aren't equipped to deal with at the moment. Over the last few weeks, we said our good-byes, which amounted to little more than "See you soon." There were lots of promises between friends that both sides will visit, but six hours is a long way for most people, especially if they have kids. Many conversations end with something along the lines of, "See you in a few years, when you decide you have to come back to Bisbee."

Here is the problem. I have learned how copper functions in our society, how it is so entrenched in any economic growth, domestic or foreign. It is almost impossible for me to imagine mining companies walking away from known sources of copper. And I can't travel around the pit without thinking of the sulfuric plume leaking toward the town's aquifer. I can't think of Freeport without thinking of how it conducts itself in other parts of the world. I also know from traveling to several mining towns in the last few years that if the mine reopens, Bisbee's charm will suffer, to the point of losing that intangible asset that makes Bisbee such a great place to live: an abundance of interesting residents.

My dilemma is that I love where we live. I will miss my friends. I am deeply drawn to the location, the history, and the physical layout of the town. I find the inhabitants enchanting, even the crotchety hippies who forgot their liberal roots and moan and groan about any and all change, something they used to protest for. Strangely enough, I have come to see the pit on the edge of town as a sort of geological defense against the casual interloper. It attracts tourists for a day but discourages those looking for anything resembling "normal" in a community.

In the morning, after sleeping on the floor of the empty house, I decide to take one more drive down around the pit. As I do so, I find myself looking as deep as I can into the dark black holes that were once tunnels and imagine the work that was done here. I wonder how many thousands of immigrants' lives were started here. And ended here. I pass Lowell and head south toward the fire station, which is located on a stretch of highway that divides large quantities of waste rock.

I take notice of a traffic light Freeport installed on the outskirts of town so it can drive huge trucks and tractors across the highway, from one side of the mine to the other. Down the dirt road to the south, workers are busy putting a topsoil cap on the tailing piles in hopes of stopping the acid mine runoff that has been leaking off that mound for decades.

Leaving the mining district, I drive straight into a gusting headwind. It momentarily blows the truck slightly off the road. The monsoon storm heading up from Mexico should be here within the hour. I keep driving and pass a large swath of desert filled with ocotillo. Standing up to ten feet tall with multiple arms, the plant lives in clusters and for most of the year looks like a bunch of dead sticks. But when the rain begins, the branches will turn green and the tip blossoms red; its name means "little torch." In full bloom, ocotillo resembles an army of ghosts gently swaying in the wind. These sturdy plants, which have figured out how to survive in such an arid place, epitomize the natural beauty in the desert. I imagine these plants will survive a toxic aquifer, but I'm not sure the town will.

In some ways my entire journey through the world of copper has been a personal quest to answer a single question. Is it the work of each generation to protect what outside forces want to destroy? If so, then how do I go about saving Bisbee from a mine that already exists? I can't. No one can. It *is* a mining town. Perhaps a better question is, What *can* I save from outside forces?

If I was asked to choose between reopening the mine in Bisbee or seeing Pebble mine open up in Alaska, I would sacrifice Bisbee every time. I would stand in front of an angry town hall meeting in Bisbee and explain to my friends and my neighbors that Bisbee was always a copper town. We just lived here when it was shut down. Bisbee would not exist if it were not for copper mining. There would be no town dangling on the sides of these two canyons if George Warren had not found enough copper to supply the world with electricity. Bisbee is a copper mine that created a town—a lovely, interesting, and unique town that has evolved into a culture rarely found in America anymore. But it is a town living on borrowed time.

Of course this hypothetical choice of either opening Bisbee's mine or building Pebble mine will never be proffered up to the American public, but if it were, I would not only argue for the expansion of Bisbee, Ajo, Morenci, and Globe, I would say go ahead and develop the Resolution mine in Superior and the Rosemont mine in the Santa Rita Mountains. It would be worth it if it could stop Pebble from ever being built. This is not personal. This is not an armchair reaction of wanting to see nature preserved. The battle to stop Pebble mine is really a battle to define what we believe is the sensible stewardship of our resources. Although mining is imperative and critical to our way of life, not every mine is necessary, especially if located dangerously close to a vital natural resource. If this deposit were located a hundred miles inland, there would be very little push back on developing the mine. But being so close to Lake Iliamna and the headwaters of the largest sockeye run on Earth makes it nothing less than a desecration of holy ground. Such a resource, one that needs no help from us to keep thriving, is the prime example of when to stay out of nature's way. Thousands of Alaskan natives depend on the salmon as a food source and a vital part of their economic livelihood. Millions more around the world eat the salmon. Even the slightest chance of altering or destroying this resource is not worth anything we can pull up from the ground.

So, Bisbee, I love you and all your quirkiness, but you are a mining town and always were, and if I could I would sacrifice it a thousand times to save Bristol Bay from Pebble mine.

And now I must say good-bye.

It is August 22, 2011. Just after dawn, I head up the highway listening to NPR, with talking heads trying to make sense of the latest economic and political crisis in Washington. As I grow older, this endless crisis is beginning to feel increasingly tiresome, like an overbearing guest at the dinner table I want to kick out of the house. The markets are crashing again, but of course that is not new.

Cruising through Tucson and up Interstate 10, I am reminded that living in southern Arizona means constantly dealing with new copper mine projects. I read in the paper a few days ago that there is a copper mine planned for Florence that will not dig an open pit or a single tunnel. Instead it will send sulfuric acid deep into the earth through boreholes to interact with the copper ore. Then pumps will suck the copper slurry back up to the surface, to be extracted at a nearby plant. Basically copper mining's version of fracking. Curis Resources, the Canadian company that owns the site, states this is a safe procedure that will never threaten the groundwater. It's like a loop on a corporate answer machine, "All is well, just trust us." Well, I don't trust them. I don't hate them, either. In fact, I find it strange that I rarely had a bad encounter with anyone I met connected with the mining business, whether a miner, geologist, prospector, or executive. I just know they are trained to see the world in a different way, one where their notion of acceptable risk is far different from that of most people I know.

The cat and I get through Phoenix before noon and hit the mountains just north of Sedona by two o'clock. The rest of my family is a few hours behind, hurtling up the interstate in a mini-van full of hope and anxiety. Soon, the pine trees appear and I begin to dream of snowy winters and lakes with fish. I have lived in southern Arizona for ten years, longer than anywhere else in my life. I married my wife there. Two beautiful daughters were born there. We bought our first house there.

By late afternoon, I arrive at the house we have rented. There are large windows with views of the mountains and a yard big enough to keep the kids busy. I let the cat out of his cage and he walks around the house. Timid and scared, he will take days to make the place his own. I suspect my oldest daughter will behave in the same way. But the place will do. Soon I will able to take my kids out to the Navajo land, let them run around a place where time has a way of forgetting.

My family arrives and I unpack the truck, box after box. When I was younger and single I moved in a day, everything on the back of my motorcycle. Today it seems like the hardest task I can remember.

At bedtime, when my daughter asks when we are going back to our house in Bisbee, I tell her not to worry. I tuck her in, knowing in time this question will fade. My wife, exhausted from the trip, shrugs her shoulders and smiles, her way of saying she is okay with all this.

Later, I turn out the lights and stand in the living room thinking about how copper played a role in our moving here. We call it the eternal metal, and true to its name it is a metal I cannot escape. After what seems like half an hour of standing in the dark, I prick up my ears to hear a low dull hum, coming from somewhere in the house. I wander from room to room trying to pinpoint the noise. Maybe the hum is coming from a fan in the refrigerator? I look in the broom closet thinking maybe it is water filling up the water heater. I check my computer, but it silently blinks into the night, content to be sleeping. Maybe the hum is from a circuit breaker in the attic or from the printer, the dishwasher, or furnace in the basement.

As I wander the house, I return to my thoughts on copper, with my eyes alert for any clues of the hum. Perhaps what I have learned in all this is that there is no escaping the fact that we are all part of this large social experiment called modern civilization, where things magically work when they are plugged into the wall. Computers just turn on and do things we couldn't dream of fifteen years ago. Cars drive and then brake like an appendage to our bodies. There are many components that make these amenities of modern life possible—engineers, research and development, and countless failed attempts on the way to success—but metals, especially copper, are undeniably at the core of so much of what we use to exist each day.

After twenty minutes of searching all the rooms, the attic, and the circuit boards, I give up. I laugh a little at myself, realizing I was chasing a phantom hum, created by electronic pulse traveling along a thin copper wire, hidden deep in the walls. I may have left the copper belt of Arizona behind, but I will never escape the far reach of copper.

ACKNOWLEDGMENTS

Writing a book requires a great deal of support, and I am grateful to many people who assisted in the process. First, I thank my neighbors and friends in Bisbee, Arizona. They inspire me and reinforce the notion that having such a supportive community is a key component to a higher quality of life.

Thanks are in order for those who pointed me in the right direction. Shipherd Reed, the digital media producer at the Flandrau Science Center at the University of Arizona, oversaw the Miner's Story project and was a fountain of knowledge. Thanks also to Tom Zoellner for several key introductions.

One of the unspoken secrets of writing is that it is ultimately a collaborative process. At the top of the list of people who helped shape this story is Colin Harrison, my editor and a master craftsman. It is rare to have such a thoughtful editor, one who still puts pen to paper. Also a big thanks to my agent, Betsy Lerner, who helped give form to the original idea. Thanks to the vigilant copy editor Cynthia Merman and the gifted designer Oliver Munday.

I am grateful for the many people I met along the way, both those for and against mining, for their insights and opinions. I especially want to thank all the miners and their families for sharing their stories.

Thanks to John Tilton at the School of Mining at the University of Colorado for his analysis on the copper industry at large, and to Tony Davis at the *Arizona Daily Star* for his constant dedication to the story of mining in Arizona. Thanks to Alexandra Boneo for accompanying me on trips to Cananea, and to Greg Schreiber for assistance in New York City. Thanks to Everett

ACKNOWLEDGMENTS

Thompson, Izetta Chambers, Terry and Ginger Hoefferle, Bobby Andrew, Carl and Jannelle Adams, and Sharon Hart for all their assistance in Alaska. Thanks for the tireless efforts of Mike Phillips. And in Astoria, a big thanks to Clemente's and the Cannery Pier Hotel.

And a final bow to my family—to daughters, Josie and Poppy, and my wife, Leigh. They made this journey possible and, more important, joyous. Without them I am quite sure I would never find the will to sit so long at a desk.

BIBLIOGRAPHY

BOOKS

Bailey, Lynn. *Bisbee: Queen of the Copper Camps*. Tucson: Westernlore Press, 2010.

Byrkit, James. *Forging the Copper Collar*. Tucson: University of Arizona Press, 1982.

Cox, Annie. *History of Bisbee, 1877 to 1937*. Tucson: University of Arizona Press, 1938.

Glasscock, C. B. *The War of the Copper Kings: Greed, Power, and Politics: The Billion-Dollar Battle for Butte, Montana, the Richest Hill on Earth*. Helena, MT: Riverbend Publishing, 1935, reprinted 2002.

Hanson, Rob. *The Great Bisbee I.W.W. Deportation of July 12, 1917*. Berkeley, CA: Signature Press, 1989.

Hitchens, Christopher. *The Trial of Henry Kissinger*. New York: Verso, 2002.

Houston, Robert. *Bisbee '17*. Tucson: University of Arizona Press, 1999.

Hyde, Charles. *Copper for America: The United States Copper Industry from Colonial Times to the 1990s*. Tucson: University of Arizona Press, 1998.

Isaacson, Walter. *Steve Jobs*. New York: Simon & Schuster, 2011.

Janson, Lone. *The Copper Spike*. Anchorage: Todd Communications, 1975.

Kingsolver, Barbara. *Holding the Line: Women in the Great Arizona Mine Strike of 1983*. Ithaca, NY: Cornell University Press, 1996.

Klubock, Miller. *Contested Communities: Class, Gender, and Politics in Chile's el Teniente Copper Mine, 1904–1951*. Durham, NC: Duke University Press, 1998.

LeCain, Timothy. *Mass Destruction: The Men and Giant Mines That Wired America and Scarred the Planet*. Piscataway, NJ: Rutgers University Press, 2009.

Leith, Denise. *The Politics of Power: Freeport in Suharto's Indonesia*. Honolulu: University of Hawai'i Press, 2003.

Maquiladora Health & Safety Support Network. *Workplace Health and Safety Survey and Medical Screening of Miners at Grupo Mexico's Copper Mine, Cananea, Sonora, Mexico 2007*. Berkeley, CA, 2007.

Moody, Roger. *The Risks We Run: Mining, Communities and Political Risk Insurance*. Utrecht, Netherlands: International Books, 2005.

BIBLIOGRAPHY

Morris, Patrick. *Anaconda Montana: Copper Smelting Boom Town on the Western Frontier.* Bethesda, MD: Swann Publishing, 1997.

Nash, June. *We Eat the Mines and the Mines Eat Us: Dependency and Exploitation in Bolivian Tin Mines.* New York: Columbia University Press, 1993.

Nicholl, Boyd. *Bisbee, Arizona, Then and Now.* Phoenix: Cowboy Miner Productions, 2003.

Price, Ethel Jackson. *Images of America Series: Bisbee, Arizona.* Mount Pleasant, NC: Arcadia Publishing, 2004.

Rosenblum, Jonathan. *Copper Crucible: How the Arizona Miners' Strike of 1983 Recast Labor-Management Relations in America.* Ithaca, NY: Cornell University Press, 1998.

Shelton, Richard. *Going Back to Bisbee.* Tucson: University of Arizona Press, 1992.

Sheridan, Thomas. *Arizona: A History.* Tucson: University of Arizona Press, 1995.

Storms, Walter. *Mining Methods and Practices at the Mineral Hill Copper Mine, Banner Mining Co., Pima County, Arizona.* Washington, DC: U.S. Department of the Interior, 1957.

Tafoya, Onofre. *Mother Magma: A Memoir of Underground Life in the San Manuel Copper Mine.* Mesa, AZ: Hispanic Institute of Social Issues, 2006.

Weiner, Eric. *The Shadow Market: How a Group of Wealthy Nations and Powerful Investors Secretly Dominate the World.* New York: Scribner, 2010.

Wilson, Forbes. *Copper Mountain: A Vivid, Personal Account of the Discovery and Development of a Spectacular Outcrop of Ore in the Remote Peaks of Irian Jaya, Indonesia.* Saddle Brook, NJ: Stratford Press, 1981.

Workers for the Writers' Program of the Work Projects Administration in the State of Montana. *Copper Camp: The Lusty Story of Butte, Montana, the Richest Hill on Earth.* Helena, Montana: Riverbend Publishing, 1943, 1970, 2002.

PERIODICAL ARTICLES

Armistead, Louise. "As Copper Price Rises, Rumours Abound of Market Manipulators." *Telegraph* (UK), July 26, 2009, http://www.telegraph .co.uk/finance/newsbysector/industry/mining/5913224/As-copper -price-rises-rumours-abound-of-market-manipulators.html (accessed on August 24, 2009).

Barta, Patrick. "Small Firms in Position as Copper Prices Soar." *Washington Post,* August 17, 2006, http://www.washingtonpost.com/wp-dyn/content /article/2006/08/16/AR2006081601536_pf.html (accessed on November 3, 2010).

Callick, Rowan. "Miners Hope to Restart Bougainville Gold and Copper Mine." *Australian,* December 28, 2010, http://www.theaustralian.com.au /business/miners-hope-to-restart-bougainville-gold-and-copper-mine /story-e6frg8zx-1225976819323.

BIBLIOGRAPHY

"The Case for Mining Law Reform." *New York Times,* June 23, 2008, http://www.nytimes.com/2008/06/23/opinion/23mon2.html?_r=1 (accessed on May 14, 2009).

Chambers, Matt. "Norwegians Dump 'Unethical' Rio Tinto." *Australian,* September 11, 2008, http://www.theaustralian.com.au/business/norwegians-dump-unethical-rio/story-e6frg8zx-1111117447302 (accessed on December 14, 2009).

"Copper Bottomed?: The Afghan Government Has Grand Plans to Develop the Mining Industry." *Economist,* November 23, 2006.

Daly, Matthew. "House Approves Superior Mine Land Swap." *Arizona Daily Star,* October 27, 2011.

Davis, Tony. "UA Finds Tailings Have Troubling Tiny Particles." *Arizona Daily Star,* July 19, 2010, http://azstarnet.com/news/science/environment/article_3c5209e6-0e94-513e-8488-22867993fad8.html.

Harris, Elizabeth. "Unraveling Some Mystery Surrounding the Homes of a Reclusive Heiress." *New York Times,* March 19, 2012, http://www.nytimes.com/2012/03/20/nyregion/a-glimpse-into-huguette-clarks-manhattan-apartments.html?pagewanted=all.

Hitchens, Peter. "Around the World: How China Has Created a New Slave Empire in Africa." *Mail on Sunday* (UK), May 28, 2009, http://www.dailymail.co.uk/news/article-1063198/PETER-HITCHENS-How-China-created-new-slave-empire-Africa.html (accessed on June 5, 2009).

Hoffman, Andy. "Copper's Status: Like Gold, But Useful." *Globe and Mail* (UK), October 13, 2009, http://www.theglobeandmail.com/globe-investor/coppers-status-like-gold-but-useful/article1322274/ (accessed on November 2, 2009).

Hotter, Andrea. "China's Savvy Copper Call." *Wall Street Journal,* October 13, 2011.

Jarman, Max. "Bombings Near Freeport's Indonesia Mine." *Arizona Republic,* September 12, 2008.

———. "Slowing Superior Mine Plan." *Arizona Republic,* November 26, 2008.

Johnson, Andrew. "Fatalities Have Declined, Injury Rates Up." *Arizona Republic,* October 17, 2009.

———. "Funds Push for Environmental Expert on Freeport Board." *Arizona Republic,* May 10, 2009.

———. "Penalties vs. Mines Are Often Reduced." *Arizona Republic,* December 13, 2009.

Kaufman, Leslie. "Asarco Pays $1.79 Billion to Fix Sites." *New York Times,* December 11, 2009.

Kelly, Erin, and Dan Nowicki. "Swap for Copper Mine." *Arizona Republic,* May 21, 2009.

Kumar, Nikhil. "Kazakhmys Climbs on Copper Price Hopes." *Independent* (UK), August 6, 2009, http://www.independent.co.uk/news/business/sharewatch/market-report-kazakhmys-climbs-on-copper-price-hopes-1767882.html (accessed on September 2, 2009).

Leadbeater, Marie. "Super Fund Has a Way to Go When It Comes to Investing Ethically." *New Zealand Herald,* December 29, 2008, http://www.nzherald

BIBLIOGRAPHY

.co.nz/personal-finance/news/article.cfm?c_id=12&objectid=10549893 (accessed on April 30, 2009).

Levingston, Steven. "Seeing Growth in the Earth's Resources." *Washington Post,* October 19, 2008, http://www.washingtonpost.com/wp-dyn/content/article/2008/10/18/AR2008101800174.html (accessed on March 20, 2009).

Matthews, Guy. "Recession Erodes Resistance to Copper Mine." *Wall Street Journal,* April 13, 2009.

Montoto, Claudia, and Nadia Damouni. "Freeport-McMoRan Focused on Project Pipeline, CEO Says." *Financial Times,* October 8, 2009, http://www.ft.com/intl/cms/s/2/77f51fd4-953e-11dd-aedd-000077b07658,dwp_uuid=e8477cc4-c820-11db-b0dc-000b5df10621.html#axzz1usWd WFH6 (accessed on January 14, 2010).

Moore, Malcolm. "China to Create Largest Mega City in the World with 42 Million People." *Telegraph* (UK), January 24, 2011, http://www.telegraph.co.uk/news/worldnews/asia/china/8278315/China-to-create-largest-mega-city-in-the-world-with-42-million-people.html (accessed on October 10, 2011).

Murphy, Kim. "Alaska Natives Try to Halt Proposed Pebble Mine." *Los Angeles Times,* July 31, 2009, http://articles.latimes.com/2009/jul/31/nation/na-pebble-mine31 (accessed on September 23, 2009).

Pollack, Andrew. "Sumitomo's Huge Loss: The Trader: Global Copper Superstar or 'Ordinary Salaryman'?" *New York Times,* June 15, 1996, http://www.nytimes.com/1996/06/15/business/sumitomo-s-huge-loss-the-trader-global-copper-superstar-or-ordinary-salaryman.html (accessed on September 15, 2010).

Rudolf, John Collins. "Copper's Every Dip Is Felt in Arizona." *New York Times,* November 27, 2008.

Shumsky, Tatyana, and Carolyn Cui. "Trader Holds $3 Billion of Copper in London." *Wall Street Journal,* December 21, 2010, http://online.wsj.com/article/SB10001424052748704118504576034083436931412.html.

INTERNET SOURCES

Alfian. "Freeport Sues Workers for Refusing to Accept Layoffs." *Jakarta Post,* April 15, 2009, http://www.thejakartapost.com/news/2009/04/15/freeport-sues-workers-refusing-accept-layoffs.html (accessed on June 12, 2010).

"Analyzing China's Copper Industry." Report Buyer, January 2011, http://www.reportbuyer.com/industry_manufacturing/metals/copper/analyzing_chinas_copper_industry.html.

Anglo American Annual Report 2012, http://www.angloamerican.com/investors/reports/2012rep.

"Anglo American History." Funding Universe, March 5, 2009, http://www.fundinguniverse.com/company-histories/Anglo-American-PLC-Company-History.html.

BHP Billiton Annual Report 2011, http://www.bhpbilliton.com/home/investors/reports/Documents/2011/2011.

BIBLIOGRAPHY

Brundige, Elizabeth, Winter King, Priyneha Vahali, Stephen Vladeck, and Xiang Yuan. "Indonesian Human Rights Abuses in West Papua: Application of the Law of Genocide to the History of Indonesian Control." Allard K. Lowenstein International Human Rights Clinic, Yale Law School, April 2004, http://www.g-a-l.info/Yale%20Report%20on%20West%20 Papuah%20rights.pdf (accessed on April 19, 2010).

"City Air Harmful for Another 20–30 Years." *China Digital Times,* January 4, 2010, http://chinadigitaltimes.net/2012/01/city-air-harmful-for-another -20–30-years.

Clark, Simon, Michael Smith, and Franz Wild. "China Lets Child Workers Die Digging in Congo Mines for Copper." *Bloomberg,* July 22, 2008, http:// www.bloomberg.com/apps/news?pid=newsarchive&sid=aW8xVLQ4 Xhr8 (accessed on September 4, 2010).

"Congolese Children Still Dropping Out of School for Mining Due to Lack of Opportunities." *World News Journal,* July 17, 2010, http://africannews analysis.blogspot.com/search/label/Mining.

"Copper Insights." International Copper Promotion Council, India, September 23, 2011, http://www.copperindia.org/cu/wcms/en/home/about-copper /insights/index.html.

EPA Science Advisory Board. "Technologically Enhanced, Naturally Occuring Radioactive Materials." EPA, January 2, 2012, http://www.epa.gov/rpd web00/tenorm/.

FBI Criminal Intelligence Section. "Copper Theft Threatens U.S. Critical Infra-structure." FBI, September 15, 2008, http://www.fbi.gov/news/stories /2008/december/copper-theft-intel-report-unclass (accessed on October 30, 2011).

Ferguson, Niall. "Copper Is King." *Daily Beast,* April 24, 2011, http://www.the dailybeast.com/newsweek/2011/04/24/copper-is-king.print.html.

Firman, Carl, and Gary Meade. "Copper: On Fire or About to Crash and Burn?" Mineweb, August 3, 2009, http://www.mineweb.com/mineweb /view/mineweb/en/page36?oid=86993&sn=Detail (accessed on October 12, 2010).

Freeport McMoRan Annual Report 2010 and 2011, http://www.fcx.com/ir /ar.htm.

Fugate, Nelson. "Every American Born Will Need . . ." Mineral Informa-tion Institute, March 2007, http://www.kennecott.com/library/media /human%20consumption.pdf (accessed on June 3, 2009).

Gross, Daniel. "Obscure Economic Indicator: The Price of Copper." *Slate,* November 11, 2005, http://www.slate.com/articles/business/money box/2005/11/obscure_economic_indicator_the_price_of_copper.html (accessed on January 29, 2010).

Harper, Paul. "Copper Prices Leave Producers Feeling Wired." *Far Side Stocks,* December 16, 2008, http://mystockvoice.wordpress.com/2008/12/16 /copper-prices-leave-producers-feeling-wired/ (accessed on February 19, 2009).

Hongxiao, Tang, Wang Zijian, Liu Jingyi, German Mueller, and Alfred Yahya. "Ecological Effects of Heavy-Metal Pollution in the Dexing Copper

Mine Region (Jian Xi Province, China)." UNESCO, 1996, http://unesdoc
.unesco.org/images/0010/001036/103662m.pdf (accessed on May 19,
2010).

Hunt, Brian. "Copper Price: What It Is Saying About the Economy." Stockhouse,
September 8, 2010, http://www.stockhouse.com/Columnists/2010/Sept/8
/Copper-price—What-it-is-saying-about-the-economy.

"Indonesia May Change Mining Contracts." Mining-journal.com. December
24, 2008, http://www.intellasia.net/news/articles/resources/111254624
.shtml (accessed on April 16, 2009).

Ivanhoe Mines Annual Report 2011, http://www.ivanhoemines.com/s/Financials
_Tech_Reports.asp.

Kaste, Martin. "Planned Open-Pit Mine Stirs Environmental Fight."
NPR, October 8, 2007, http://www.npr.org/templates/story/story
.php?storyId=15053463 (accessed on May 15, 2010).

Kosich, Dorothy. "Papua Province Wants More Freeport-McMoRan Tax Revenue." Mineweb, October 8, 2008, http://www.mineweb.com/mineweb
/view/mineweb/en/page34?oid=70463&sn=Detail (accessed on March 6,
2010).

Krasnow, Jay. "Chile Copper Exports." Trade and Environmental Database:
Case Studies, November 1, 1997, http://www1.american.edu/ted/copper
.htm (accessed on January 15, 2010).

"Land Use and Resource Plan, Kijik Corporaton." 2011, http://www.kijikcorp
.com/pdf/LandUsePlan_Final.pdf.

"Letter to Securities and Exchange Commission: Proposed Acquisition of Phelps
Dodge by Freeport-McMoRan." Groundwater Awareness League, Inc.,
February 7, 2007, http://www.g-a-l.info/ComplaintTwo.htm (accessed on
July 17, 2009).

"London Calling Muses on the Latest Bout of Mining's Merger Mania." Mines
and Communities, January 25, 2008, http://www.minesandcommunities
.org/article.php?a=8416 (accessed on May 11, 2010).

Manson, Katrina. "Illegal Miners Overrun Freeport's Congo Mine." Reuters
Africa, August 10, 2010, http://af.reuters.com/article/investingNews
/idAFJOE6790PB20100810.

"Mine Plan of Operations." Rosemont Copper, January 1, 2010, http://www
.rosemontcopper.com/mpo.html.

Montlake, Simon. "Cave In: Freeport-McMoRan Digs a Heap of Trouble in
Indonesia." *Forbes*, January 26, 2012, http://www.forbes.com/sites
/simonmontlake/2012/01/26/cave-in-freeport-mcmoran/.

"'Mr. Copper' Marvels at High Prices." *Shakers Marketplace*, December 7, 2005,
http://www.redorbit.com/news/science/323719/mr_copper_marvels
_at_high_metal_prices_shakers_marketplace_by/ (accessed on July 10,
2010).

Nathalia, Telly. "Police Fire on Crowd in Indonesia's Papua, 3 Hurt." Reuters,
January 17, 2009, http://www.reuters.com/article/2009/01/27/indonesia
-papua-idUSJAK41014420090127.

NGO Taskforce on Business and Industry. "Scrapping Bottom: Freeport McMo-

Ran in Irian Jaya." January 1997, http://isforum.org/tobi/reports/minding /freeportmcmoran.aspx (accessed on December 12, 2010).

Patel, Simit. "What Does the Price of Copper Tell Us About the Economy?" Seeking Alpha, February 5, 2009, http://seekingalpha.com/article/118660 -what-does-the-price-of-copper-tell-us-about-the-economy.

"Pebble Mine Would Be a Deadly Disease of the Earth." Channel 2-KTUU, *10 P.M. News,* July 4, 1985, http://www.youtube.com/watch?v=nXvdq6DKQF4.

"The Pebble Project: The Future of US Mining and Metals." International Mining, July 17, 2009, http://www.im-mining.com/2009/07/17/the-pebble-project -the-future-of-us-mining-and-metals/ (accessed on December 20, 2009).

Resolution Copper Mining, http://www.resolutioncopper.com/.

Rickstad, Eric. "Alaska's Bristol Bay World-Famous Salmon Rivers Threatened by Pebble Mine. Help Save Them." Orvis, http://www.orvis.com/intro .aspx?subject=4571&csc=true.

Rio Tinto Annual Report 2011, http://www.riotinto.com/documents/Investors /Rio_Tinto_2011_Annual_report.pdf.

"Robert Friedland." *New Internationalist Magazine,* no. 392 (August 1, 2006), http://www.newint.org/columns/worldbeaters/2006/08/01/ (accessed on September 19, 2010).

Rosenberg, Mica. "Mexican Govt. Decides Striking Cananea Miners Can Be Fired." Mineweb, April 16, 2009, http://www.mineweb.com/mineweb /view/mineweb/en/page59?oid=81938&sn=Detail (accessed on November 12, 2010).

Sergeant, Barry. "Is the Congo Returning to Dark Days?" Mineweb, April 18, 2009, http://www.mineweb.net/mineweb/view/mineweb/en/page72068 ?oid=82036&sn=Detail.

Solly, Richard. "Reflection on the December 2008 Agreement Between Cerrejon Coal and Tabaco Relocation Committee." Colombia Solidarity Campaign, January 1, 2009, http://www.colombiasolidarity.org.uk/mining/446 -reflection-on-the-december-2008-agreement-between-cerrejon-coal-and -the-tabaco-relocation-committee (accessed on May 16, 2010).

"Spotlight: Carol Ann Woody." Trout Unlimited, June 2010, http://www.tu.org /conservation/alaska/spotlight-carol-ann-woody.

Stempel, Jonathan. "U.S. Court Revives Human Rights Case vs. Rio Tinto." Reuters, October 25, 2011, http://af.reuters.com/article/metalsNews /idAFN1E79O15M20111025?sp=true.

Thompkin, Gwen. "Can the Mining Industry Brighten Congo's Economy?" NPR, April 24, 2008, http://www.npr.org/templates/story/story .php?storyId=89905058 (accessed on July 17, 2009).

"What Is Happening in Copper?" *Mining News,* February 17, 2009, http:// miningbeat.blogspot.com/2009/02/what-is-happening-in-copper.html (accessed on May 5, 2009).

"World Record for Copper Mines." BBC News, May 27, 2004, http://news.bbc .co.uk/2/hi/uk_news/wales/south_east/3753447.stm (accessed on July 20, 2010).

Xiong Tong. "Zambian Mine to Invest $500 Million in Expansion Drive."

BIBLIOGRAPHY

English.news.cn, January 20, 2012, http://news.xinhuanet.com/english /business/2012-01/20/c_131371197.htm (accessed on January 21, 2012).

Zhang Ming'ai. "3 Chinese Firms to Develop Afghan Copper Mine." China .org.cn, November 23, 2007, http://www.china.org.cn/english/business /232927.htm (accessed on September 26, 2011).

INDEX

ABOUT THE AUTHOR

Bill Carter is the author of *Red Summer: The Danger, Madness, and Exaltation of Salmon Fishing in a Remote Alaskan Village* and *Fools Rush In: A True Story of Love, War, and Redemption* and the director of *Miss Sarajevo,* an award-winning documentary executive produced by Bono. He has written for *Rolling Stone, Outside, Men's Journal,* and other publications on topics such as drug trafficking in Mexico, crime in Algiers, and trekking across southern Utah with no more than a cup, a knife, a compass, and an extra pair of socks. He lives with his family in Flagstaff, Arizona. Visit his website at www.billcarter.cc.